lonely planet

Latin American Spanish

PHRASEBOOK & DICTIONARY

Acknowledgments
Associate Publisher Tali Budlender
Managing Editor Annelies Mertens
Editors Jodie Martire, Kristin Odijk, Branislava Vladisavljevic
Series Designer Mark Adams
Managing Layout Designer Chris Girdler
Layout Designers Carol Jackson, Joseph Spanti
Production Support Ruth Cosgrove, Yvonne Kirk
Language Writer Roberto Esposto

Thanks
Jane Atkin, Sasha Baskett, Yvonne Bischofberger, Laura Crawford, Frank Deim, Brendan Dempsey, Paul Iacono, Indra Kilfoyle, Nic Lehman, Naomi Parker, Trent Paton, Piers Pickard, Averil Robertson, Kirsten Rawlings, Jacqui Saunders, John Taufa, Gerard Walker, Juan Winata

Published by Lonely Planet Publications Pty Ltd
ABN 36 005 607 983

6th Edition – May 2012
ISBN 978 1 74220 187 0

Cover Image Two traditionally dressed women on floating islands, Lake Titicaca, Peru, Sean Caffrey / Lonely Planet Images ©

Printed in China 10 9 8 7 6 5 4 3 2 1

Contact lonelyplanet.com/contact

HOW TO USE THIS BOOK

Look out for the following icons throughout the book:

'Shortcut' Phrase
Easy to remember alternative to the full phrase

Q&A Pair
'Question-and-answer' pair – we suggest a response to the question asked

Look For
Phrases you may see on signs, menus etc

Listen For
Phrases you may hear from officials, locals etc

LANGUAGE TIP **Language Tip**
An insight into the foreign language

CULTURE TIP **Culture Tip**
An insight into the local culture

How to read the phrases:

- Coloured words and phrases throughout the book are phonetic guides to help you pronounce the foreign language.
- Lists of phrases with tinted background are options you can choose to complete the phrase above them.

These abbreviations will help you choose the right words and phrases in this book:

f	feminine	m	masculine	pol	polite
inf	informal	pl	plural	sg	singular
lit	literal				

See also p7 for the abbreviations of country-specific terms.

ABOUT THIS BOOK

Contents

PAGE 6

About Latin American Spanish

Learn about Latin American Spanish, build your own sentences and pronounce words correctly.

PAGE 29

Travel Phrases

Ready-made phrases for every situation – buy a ticket, book a hotel and much more.

INTRO

Latin American Spanish

español latinoamericano
es·pa·*nyol* la·tee·no·a·me·ree·*ka*·no

Who speaks Latin American Spanish?

Why Bother

With an entire continent of gregarious Spanish-speaking locals to chat with, you don't want to be limited to 'gringo lingo' – and you'll find that revving up your *eres* *e*·res (*r*'s) and grunting out your *jotas* *kho*·tas (*j*'s) is fun.

Distinctive Sounds

The strong and rolled r, and kh (pronounced as in the Scottish *loch*).

Spanish in the World

Over the last 500 years, Spanish in Latin America has evolved differently to the

300 MILLION speak Latin American Spanish as their first language

100 MILLION speak Latin American Spanish as their second language

Spanish spoken in Europe. You'll recognise Spaniards by the 'lisp' in their speech – eg *cerveza* (beer) is ser·*ve*·sa across Latin America but ther·*ve*·tha in Spain.

Spanish in Latin America

There's no doubting the richness of the language that has lent itself to the 'magic realism' of world-famous authors such as Gabriel García Márquez. Influenced by indigenous languages, Latin American Spanish varies slightly from country to country, especially when it comes to vocabulary. In this book country-specific terms are indicated with abbreviations (see below).

Language Family

Romance (developed from Vulgar Latin spoken by Romans during the conquest of the Iberian Peninsula from the 3rd to the 1st century BC). Close relatives include Portuguese, Italian, French and Romanian.

Must-Know Grammar

Spanish has a formal and informal word for 'you' (*Usted* oo·*ste* and *tú* too respectively). The verbs have a different ending for each person, like the English 'I do' vs 'he/she does'.

Abbreviations of country-specific terms used in this book

Arg	Argentina	**Cub**	Cuba	**Par**	Paraguay
Bol	Bolivia	**Ecu**	Ecuador	**Per**	Peru
CAm	Central America	**Gua**	Guatemala	**Pue**	Puerto Rico
		Hon	Honduras	**Sal**	El Salvador
Chi	Chile	**Mex**	Mexico	**SAm**	South America
Cos	Costa Rica	**Nic**	Nicaragua	**Uru**	Uruguay
Col	Colombia	**Pan**	Panama	**Ven**	Venezuela

5 Phrases to Learn Before You Go

1 Can you recommend private lodgings?

¿Puede recomendar una casa particular?

pwe·de re·ko·men·*dar* *oo*·na *ka*·sa par·tee·koo·*lar*

Staying with locals will give you a true Cuban experience and an opportunity to sample hearty home-cooked dishes.

2 I'd like the fixed-price menu, please.

Quisiera el menú del día, por favor.

kee·*sye*·ra el me·*noo* del *dee*·a por fa·*vor*

Eateries in Guatemala and Mexico usually offer a fixed-price meal which may include up to four courses and is great value.

3 Where can I get a shared taxi/minibus?

¿Dónde se puede tomar un colectivo?

don·de se *pwe*·de to·*mar* oon ko·lek·*tee*·vo

Cheap transport options in Peru and other countries are shared taxis or minibuses – ask locally as there are no obvious stops.

4 Where can we go salsa/tango dancing?

¿Dónde podemos ir a bailar salsa/tango?

don·de po·*de*·mos eer a bai·*lar* *sal*·sa/*tan*·go

In dance-crazy Colombia and Argentina you won't be lacking in dance-hall options, but you may want a local recommendation.

5 How do you say ... in your language?

¿Cómo se dice ... en su lengua?

ko·mo se *dee*·se ... en su *len*·gwa

Among hundreds of indigenous languages in Latin America are Quechua, Aymara, Mayan languages, Náhuatl and Guaraní.

10 Phrases to Sound Like a Local

What's up?	**¿Qué más?** (Col)	ke mas
What's up?	**¿Qué bolá asere?** (Cub)	ke bo·*la* a·se·re
Cool!	**¡Chévere!** (Col/Ven)	*che*·ve·re
How cool!	**¡Qué chido!** (Mex)	ke *chee*·do
No problem.	**No hay drama.**	no ai *dra*·ma
Get on with it!	**¡Ponte las pilas!** (Arg)	*pon*·te las *pee*·las
It's messed up.	**Está en llama.** (Cub)	es·*ta* en *ya*·ma
Come off it!	**¡No manches!** (Mex)	no *man*·ches
No way!	**¡Ni hablar!** (Arg)	nee a·*blar*
Of course!	**¡Claro!**	*kla*·ro

ABOUT LATIN AMERICAN SPANISH

Pronunciation

Latin American Spanish pronunciation differs from the Castilian Spanish spoken in Spain. The most obvious difference is the lack of the lisping 'th' sound which is found in Castilian Spanish. Pronunciation in Latin America also varies to an extent from country to country and from region to region (see p12). In this book we've used pronunciation guides which will allow you to be understood in all parts of Latin America. If you read them as if they were English, you should get your meaning across.

Vowel Sounds

Vowels are pronounced crisply. There are four vowel sounds that roughly correspond to diphthongs (vowel-sound combinations) in English.

SYMBOL	ENGLISH EQUIVALENT	SPANISH EXAMPLE	TRANSLITERATION
a	father	agua	*a*·gwa
ai	aisle	bailar	bai·*lar*
ay	say	seis	says
e	red	bebé	be·*be*
ee	bee	día	*dee*·a
o	hot	ojo	*o*·kho
oo	moon	gusto	*goo*·sto
ow	cow	autobús	ow·to·*boos*
oy	boy	hoy	oy

Consonant Sounds

SYMBOL	ENGLISH EQUIVALENT	SPANISH EXAMPLE	TRANSLITERATION
b	big	barco	*bar*·ko
ch	chili	chica	*chee*·ka
d	dog	dinero	dee·*ne*·ro
f	fun	fiesta	*fye*·sta
g	go	gato	*ga*·to
k	kick	cabeza, queso	ka·*be*·sa, *ke*·so
kh	as in the Scottish 'loch'	jardín, gente	khar·*deen*, *khen*·te
l	loud	lago	*la*·go
m	man	mañana	ma·*nya*·na
n	no	nuevo	*nwe*·vo
ny	canyon	señora	se·*nyo*·ra
p	pig	padre	*pa*·dre
r	run (strongly rolled, especially at the start of a word and as *rr*)	mariposa, ritmo, burro	ma·ree·*po*·sa, *reet*·mo, *boo*·ro
s	so	semana, zarzuela, cinco	se·*ma*·na, sar·*swe*·la, *seen*·ko
t	tin	tienda	*tyen*·da
v	very soft 'v' (between 'v' and 'b')	severo	se·*ve*·ro
w	win	guardia	*gwar*·dya
y	yes	viaje, llamada	*vya*·khe, ya·*ma*·da

Regional Variations

As mentioned previously, pronunciation varies across Latin America so you may expect to hear some of these variations as part of local accents:

The letters *ll* are pronounced as the 'y' in 'yes' in much of Latin America. Where this is the case, the y sound drops out altogether before the vowel sounds e and ee. Be alert, though: in Argentina and Uruguay you'll hear it pronounced as 'sh', in Colombia and Venezuela as the 'dg' in 'judge', and elsewhere you may hear it pronounced like the 'lli' in 'million' or the 's' in 'measure'. You'll hear the same range of sounds for the letter *y*.

In some parts of Latin America s is reduced to just a slight 'h' sound when at the end of a syllable or a word, so *tos* tos (cough) may sound like to followed by a barely audible 'h'.

Throughout Latin America there's confusion between the sounds r and l and you may hear one substituted for the other in a random way.

Word Stress

Latin American Spanish has stress. This means you emphasise one syllable in a word over another. Rule of thumb: when a word ends in *n*, *s* or a vowel, the stress falls on the second-last syllable. Otherwise, the last syllable is stressed. If you see an accent mark over a syllable, it cancels out these rules and you just stress that syllable instead. You needn't worry about these rules though, as the stressed syllables are always italicised in our pronunciation guides.

Reading & Writing

The relationship between Spanish sounds and their spelling is quite straightforward and consistent. The rules in the table opposite will help you read any written Spanish you may come across.

~ SPELLBOUND ~

c	before *e* or *i* pronounced as the 's' in 'so'; before *a*, *o* and *u* pronounced as the 'k' in 'kick'	cerveza, cita carro, corto, cubo	ser·*ve*·sa, *see*·ta *ka*·ro, *kor*·to, *koo*·bo
g	before *e* or *i* pronounced as the 'ch' in the Scottish *loch*; before *a*, *o* and *u* pronounced as the 'g' in 'go'	gente, gitano gato, gordo, guante	*khen*·te, khee·*ta*·no *ga*·to, *gor*·do, *gwan*·te
gue, gui, güi	as the 'g' in 'go' (the *u* is not pronounced unless there are two dots over the *u*)	guerra, guinda güiski	*ge*·ra, *geen*·da *gwees*·kee
h	never pronounced	haber	a·*ber*
j	as the 'ch' in the Scottish *loch*	jardín	khar·*deen*
ll	generally as the 'y' in 'yes'	llave	*ya*·ve
ñ	as the 'ny' in 'canyon'	niño	*nee*·nyo
qu	as the 'k' in 'kick' (the *u* is not pronounced)	quince	*keen*·se
z	as the 's' in 'soup'	zorro	*so*·ro

~ SPANISH ALPHABET ~

A a	a	**J j**	*kho*·ta	**R r**	e·re
B b	be *lar*·ga	**K k**	ka	**S s**	e·se
C c	se	**L l**	e·le	**T t**	te
D d	de	**M m**	e·me	**U u**	oo
E e	e	**N n**	e·ne	**V v**	be kor·*ta*
F f	e·fe	**Ñ ñ**	e·nye	**W w**	*do*·ble be
G g	khe	**O o**	o	**X x**	e·kees
H h	*a*·che	**P p**	pe	**Y y**	ee *grye*·ga
I i	ee la·*tee*·na	**Q q**	koo	**Z z**	*se*·ta

ABOUT LATIN AMERICAN SPANISH

Grammar

This chapter is designed to explain the main grammatical structures you need in order to make your own sentences. Look under each heading – listed in alphabetical order – for information on functions which these grammatical categories express in a sentence. For example, demonstratives are used for giving instructions, so you'll need them to tell the taxi driver where your hotel is, etc. A glossary of grammatical terms is included at the end of the chapter to help you.

Adjectives & Adverbs

Describing People/Things • Doing Things

Adjectives in Spanish have different endings depending on whether the noun they describe is masculine or feminine, and singular or plural (see **gender** and **plurals**).

~ ADJECTIVES ~

m sg	**fantastic hotel**	hotel fantástico	o·*tel* fan·*tas*·tee·ko
f sg	**fantastic meal**	comida fantástica	ko·*mee*·da fan·*tas*·tee·ka
m pl	**fantastic books**	libros fantásticos	*lee*·bros fan·*tas*·tee·kos
f pl	**fantastic cakes**	tortas fantásticas	*tor*·tas fan·*tas*·tee·kas

As the examples show, adjectives generally come after the noun in Spanish. However, adjectives of quantity (such as 'much', 'a lot', 'little/few'), and possessive adjectives ('my' and 'your') and demonstratives ('this' and 'that') always precede the noun. See also **demonstratives** and **possessives**.

many tourists	muchos turistas (lit: many-**m-pl** tourists) *moo*·chos too·*rees*·tas
my car	mi carro (lit: my-**sg** car) mee *ka*·ro

Most adverbs in Spanish are derived from adjectives by adding the ending *-mente ·men·*te to the singular feminine form of the adjective (ie the form ending in *-a*), just like you add the ending '-ly' to the adjective in English. In Spanish, adverbs are generally placed after the verb they refer to.

a slow train	un tren lento (lit: a-**m-sg** train slow-**m-sg**) oon tren *len*·to
to speak slowly	hablar lentamente (lit: to-speak slowly) ab·*lar* len·ta·*men*·te

Articles

Naming People/Things

Spanish has two words for 'a/an': *un* oon and *una oo*·na. The gender of the noun determines which one you use. *Un* and *una* also have plural forms: *unos oo*·nos and *unas oo*·nas (some).

~ **INDEFINITE ARTICLES** ~

m sg	**an egg**	un huevo	oon *we*·vo
m pl	**some eggs**	unos huevos	oo·nos *we*·vos
f sg	**a llama**	una llama	oo·na *ya*·ma
f pl	**some llamas**	unas llamas	oo·nas *ya*·mas

The articles *el* el and *la* la both mean 'the'. Whether you use *el* or *la* also depends on the gender of the noun. For the plural, use *los* los and *las* las for masculine and feminine respectively. See also **gender** and **plurals**.

~ DEFINITE ARTICLES ~

m sg	**the car**	el carro	el *ka*·ro
m pl	**the cars**	los carros	los *ka*·ros
f sg	**the shop**	la tienda	la *tyen*·da
f pl	**the shops**	las tiendas	las *tyen*·das

Be

Describing People/Things • Making Statements

Spanish has two words for the English verb 'be': *ser* ser and *estar* es·*tar*, which are used depending on the context.

~ USE OF *SER* (TO BE) ~

permanent characteristics of persons/things	Ángel is very nice.	Ángel es muy amable. *an*·khel es mooy a·*ma*·ble
occupation or nationality	Sarita is from Puerto Rico.	Sarita es de Puerto Rico. sa *ree*·ta es de *pwer*·to *ree*·ko
time and location of events	It's 3 o'clock.	Son las tres. son las tres
possession	Whose backpack is this?	¿De quién es esta mochila? de kyen es *es*·ta mo·*chee*·la

~ USE OF *ESTAR* (TO BE) ~

temporary characteristics of persons/things	The meal is cold.	La comida está fría. la ko·*mee*·da es·*ta free*·a
time and location of persons/things	We are in Buenos Aires.	Estamos en Buenos Aires. es·*ta*·mos en *bwe*·nos *ai*·res
a person's mood	I'm happy.	Estoy contento/a. **m/f** es·*toy* kon·*ten*·to/a

~ *SER* (TO BE) – PRESENT TENSE ~

I	**am**	yo	soy	yo	soy
you sg inf	**are**	tú*	eres*	too	e·res
you sg pol	**are**	Usted	es	oos·*te*	es
he/she	**is**	él/ella	es	el/*e*·ya	es
we	**are**	nosotros m nosotras f	somos	no·*so*·tros no·*so*·tras	*so*·mos
you pl	**are**	Ustedes	son	oos·*te*·des	son
they	**are**	ellos m ellas f	son	*e*·yos *e*·yas	son

* Note that *vos sos* is used instead of *tú eres* in Argentina, Uruguay and Central America (see **personal pronouns**).

~ *ESTAR* (TO BE) – PRESENT TENSE ~

I	**am**	yo	estoy	yo	es·*toy*
you sg inf	**are**	tú	estás	too	es·*tas*
you sg pol	**are**	Usted	está	oos·*te*	es·*ta*
he/she	**is**	él/ella	está	el/*e*·ya	es·*ta*
we	**are**	nosotros m nosotras f	estamos	no·*so*·tros no·*so*·tras	es·*ta*·mos
you pl	**are**	Ustedes	están	oos·*te*·des	es·*tan*
they	**are**	ellos m ellas f	están	*e*·yos *e*·yas	es·*tan*

Demonstratives

Giving Instructions • Indicating Location • Pointing Things Out

To point something out, the easiest phrases to use are *es* es (it is) or *eso es* *e*·so es (that is).

Eso es mi pasaporte.	e·so es mee pa·sa·*por*·te That is my passport. (lit: that is my-sg passport)

The Spanish words for 'this' and 'that' vary, depending on whether something or someone is close (this), away from you (that) or even further away in time or distance (that over there). They also take the gender and number of the noun they refer to. See also **gender** and **plurals**.

~ DEMONSTRATIVES ~

	m sg		m pl	
this (close)	éste	*es*·te	éstos	*es*·tos
that (away)	ése	*e*·se	ésos	*e*·sos
that (further away)	aquél	a·*kel*	aquéllos	a·*ke*·yos
	f sg		**f pl**	
this (close)	ésta	*es*·ta	éstas	*es*·tas
that (away)	ésa	*e*·sa	ésas	*e*·sas
that (further away)	aquélla	a·*ke*·ya	aquéllas	a·*ke*·yas

Diminutives

Naming People/Things

A fun feature of Latin American Spanish is the use of diminutives. These are formed by adding word endings such as *-ito/a* ·*ee*·to/a, *-cito/a* ·*see*·to/a, *-ico/a* ·*ee*·ko/a and *-cillo/a* ·*see*·yo/a.

They're often used to indicate the smallness of something – eg *gato* *ga*·to (cat) becomes *gatito* ga·*tee*·to (kitten) – but they're also a way of expressing how a speaker feels about something. They may indicate that a speaker finds something charming, eg saying *perrito* pe·*ree*·to instead of *perro* *pe*·ro (dog) is akin to saying 'doggy' instead of 'dog' in English. Many Spanish terms of endearment end in *-ito/a* or *-illo/a*, eg *palomita* pa·lo·*mee*·ta (darling) is a diminutive of *paloma* pa·*lo*·ma (dove). Diminutives are used a lot in talking to children too.

These endings can give a friendly tone to a conversation. For instance, *un momentito* oon mo·men·*tee*·to (just a moment) sounds more light-hearted than *un momento* oon mo·*men*·to.

Gender

Naming People/Things

In Spanish, all nouns – words which denote a thing, person or concept – are either masculine or feminine. The dictionary will tell you what gender a noun is, but here are some handy tips to help you determine gender:

- gender is masculine when talking about a man and feminine when talking about a woman
- words ending in *-o* or *-or* are often masculine
- words ending in *-a*, *-d*, *-z* or *-ión* are often feminine

In this book, masculine forms appear before the feminine forms. If you see a word ending in *-o/a*, it means the masculine form ends in *-o*, and the feminine form ends in *-a* (that is, you replace the *-o* ending with the *-a* ending to make it feminine). The same goes for the plural endings *-os/as*. If you see a word ending in (*a*) between brackets, eg *escritor(a)* es·kree·*tor*/es·kree·*to*·ra, it means you have to add the 'a' in order to make that word feminine. In other cases we spell out the whole word. In this book, masculine and feminine forms are indicated with m and f respectively where needed.

See also **adjectives**, **articles** and **possessives**.

Have

Possessing

Possession can be indicated in various ways in Spanish (see also **possessives**). The easiest way is by using the verb *tener* te·*ner* (have). For negative forms with 'have', see **negatives**.

I have two brothers.	Tengo dos hermanos. (lit: I-have two brothers) *ten*·go dos er·*man*·os

~ *TENER* (TO HAVE) – PRESENT TENSE ~

I	**have**	yo	tengo	yo	*ten*·go
you sg inf	**have**	tú*	tienes*	too	*tye*·nes
you sg pol	**have**	Usted	tiene	oos·*te*	*tye*·ne
he/she	**has**	él/ella	tiene	el/*e*·ya	*tye*·ne
we	**have**	nosotros m nosotras f	tenemos	no·*so*·tros no·*so*·tras	te·*ne*·mos
you pl	**have**	Ustedes	tienen	oos·*te*·des	*tye*·nen
they	**have**	ellos m ellas f	tienen	*e*·yos *e*·yas	*tye*·nen

* Note that *vos tenés* is used instead of *tú tienes* in Argentina, Uruguay and Central America (see **personal pronouns**).

Negatives

Negating

To make a negative statement, just add the word *no* no (not) before the main verb of the sentence:

I don't live with my family.	No vivo con mi familia. (lit: not I-live with my family) no *vee*·vo kon mee fa·*mee*·lya

Contrary to English, Spanish uses double negatives:

I have nothing to declare.	No tengo nada que declarar. (lit: not I-have nothing that to-declare) no *ten*·go *na*·da ke dek·la·*rar*

Personal Pronouns

Making Statements • Naming People/Things

Personal pronouns ('I', 'you' etc) change form in Spanish depending on whether they're the subject or the object of a sentence. It's the same in English, which has 'I' and 'me' as the subject and object pronouns (eg 'I see her' and 'She sees me'). The subject pronoun is usually omitted in Spanish because the subject is obvious from the corresponding verb form (see **verbs**).

I'm a student. — Soy estudiante.
(lit: I-am student)
soy es·too·*dyan*·te

~ SUBJECT PRONOUNS ~

I	yo	yo	**we**	nosotros m nosotras f	no·so·tros no·so·tras
you sg inf	tú/ vos	too/ vos	**you** pl	Ustedes	oos·*te*·des
you sg pol	Usted	oos·*te*			
he **she**	él ella	el e·ya	**they**	ellos m ellas f	e·yos e·yas

As the table shows, Latin American Spanish has two forms for the singular 'you'. When talking to someone familiar to you or younger than you, use the informal form *tú* too, rather than the polite form *Usted* oos·*te*. The polite form should be used when you're meeting someone for the first time, talking to someone much older than you or when you're in a formal situation (eg when talking to the police, customs officers etc). In this phrasebook we have chosen the appropriate form for the situation. Where both forms are used, they are indicated by pol and inf. Note that in Latin American Spanish there's no polite/informal distinction for the plural 'you' – you always use *Ustedes* oos·*te*·des.

In many Latin American countries (particularly in Argentina, Chile, Paraguay, Uruguay and some Central American countries), you'll hear *vos* vos instead of *tú*. The form of the verb that goes with *vos* may differ slightly from the form of the verb that goes with *tú*. The *vos* verb form that you're likely to hear most is *sos* sos, from the verb *ser* ser (be): instead of *¿Eres de Australia?* *e*·res de ow·*stra*·lya (Are you from Australia?), you may hear *¿Sos de Australia?* sos de ow·*stra*·lya. In this book we've only used *tú* (and the verb form that goes with it). You'll be perfectly well understood if you use *tú*, just be aware that locals may use *vos* forms instead.

Plurals

Naming People/Things

In general, if the word ends in a vowel, you add *-s* for plural. If the noun ends in a consonant (or *y*), you add *-es*. In this book, singular and plural forms are shown with sg and pl respectively where needed.

~ SINGULAR ~			~ PLURAL ~		
bed	cama	*ka*·ma	**beds**	camas	*ka*·mas
woman	mujer	moo·*kher*	**women**	mujeres	moo·*khe*·res

Possessives

Possessing

A common way of indicating possession is by using a possessive adjective before the noun it describes. As with any other adjectives, possessive adjectives always agree with the noun in number (singular or plural) and gender (masculine or feminine). See also **gender** and **plurals**.

This is our daughter.	Ésta es nuestra hija. (lit: this-f-sg is our-f-sg daughter) *es*·ta es *nwes*·tra *ee*·kha

~ POSSESSIVE ADJECTIVES ~

my	mi/ mis	mee/ mees	**our**	nuestro/ nuestros m nuestra/ nuestras f	*nwes*·tro/ *nwes*·tros *nwes*·tra/ *nwes*·tras
your sg inf	tu/ tus	too/ toos	**your** pl inf	vuestro/ vuestros m vuestra/ vuestras f	*vwes*·tro/ *vwes*·tros *vwes*·tra/ *vwes*·tras
your sg pol	su/ sus	soo/ soos	**your** pl pol	su/ sus	soo/ soos
his her its	su/ sus	soo/ soos	**their**	su/ sus	soo/ soos

In the table above, the forms separated by a slash are used with a singular/plural noun.

In Spanish, ownership can also be expressed by using the word *de* de (of).

This is my friend's tent.	Esta es la carpa de mi amiga. (lit: this-f-sg is the-f-sg tent of my-sg friend-f) *es*·ta es la *kar*·pa de mee a·*mee*·ga

Another way to express possession is by using the verb *tener* te·*ner* (to have). For more information, see **have**.

Prepositions

Giving Instructions • Indicating Location • Pointing Things Out

Like English, Spanish uses prepositions to explain where things are in time or space. Common prepositions are listed in the table overleaf. For more prepositions, see the **dictionary**.

~ PREPOSITIONS ~

after	después de	des·*pwes* de	**from**	de	de
at (time)	a	a	**in (place)**	en	en
before	antes de	*an*·tes de	**to**	a	a

Questions

Asking Questions • Negating

To ask a 'yes/no' question, simply make a statement, but raise your intonation towards the end of the sentence, as you would in English. The inverted question mark in written Spanish prompts you to do so.

Do you have a car? ¿Tienes un carro?
(lit: you-have-**sg-inf** a-**m-sg** car)
tye·nes oon *ka*·ro

It's not impolite to answer questions with a simple *sí* see (yes) or *no* no (no) in Spanish, even when you'd like to say 'Yes, it is/does', or 'No, it isn't/doesn't'.

~ QUESTION WORDS ~

How?	¿Cómo?	*ko*·mo
How many?	¿Cuántos? **m pl** ¿Cuántas? **f pl**	*kwan*·tos *kwan*·tas
How much?	¿Cuánto?	*kwan*·to
What?	¿Qué?	ke
When?	¿Cuándo?	*kwan*·do
Where?	¿Dónde?	*don*·de
Which?	¿Cuál? **sg** ¿Cuáles? **pl**	kwal *kwa*·les
Who?	¿Quién? **sg** ¿Quiénes? **pl**	kyen *kye*·nes
Why?	¿Por qué?	por ke

Verbs

Doing Things • Making Statements

There are three verb categories in Spanish – verbs whose infinitive (dictionary form) ends in *-ar*, *-er* or *-ir*, eg *hablar* ab·*lar* (talk), *comer* ko·*mer* (eat), *vivir* vee·*veer* (live). Tenses are formed by adding various endings for each person to the verb stem (the part that remains after removing *-ar*, *-er* or *-ir* from the infinitive) or simply to the infinitive, and for most verbs these endings follow regular patterns. The verb endings for the present, past and future tenses are presented in the tables on the following pages. For negative forms of verbs, see **negatives**.

~ PRESENT TENSE ~

		hablar	comer	vivir
I	yo	hablo	como	vivo
you sg inf	tú	hablas	comes	vives
you sg pol	Usted	habla	come	vive
he **she**	él ella	habla	come	vive
we	nosotros m nosotras f	hablamos	comemos	vivimos
you pl	Ustedes	hablan	comen	viven
they	ellos m ellas f	hablan	comen	viven

See also **be** and **have** for present-tense forms of these two verbs, and **personal pronouns** for more information about the 'you' forms.

~ PAST TENSE ~

		hablar	comer	vivir
I	yo	hablé	comí	viví
you sg inf	tú	hablaste	comiste	viviste
you sg pol	Usted	habló	comió	vivió
he/she	él/ella	habló	comió	vivió
we	nosotros m nosotras f	hablamos	comimos	vivimos
you pl	Ustedes	hablaron	comieron	vivieron
they	ellos m ellas f	hablaron	comieron	vivieron

In the future tense, all three verb categories have the same endings added to the infinitive:

~ FUTURE TENSE ~

		hablar	comer	vivir
I	yo	hablaré	comeré	viviré
you sg inf	tú	hablarás	comerás	vivirás
you sg pol	Usted	hablará	comerá	vivirá
he/she	él/ella	hablará	comerá	vivirá
we	nosotros m nosotras f	hablaremos	comeremos	viviremos
you pl	Ustedes	hablarán	comerán	vivirán
they	ellos m ellas f	hablarán	comerán	vivirán

Word Order

Making Statements

Sentences in Spanish have a basic word order of subject–verb–object. The subject pronoun can be omitted because the subject is understood from the corresponding verb form (see **verbs**).

I study business.	Yo estudio comercio. (lit: I I-study business) yo es·*too*·dyo ko·*mer*·syo Estudio comercio. (lit: I-study business) es·*too*·dyo ko·*mer*·syo

CULTURE TIP

Latin American Currencies

Argentina, Chile, Colombia and Uruguay use *peso* *pe*·so (lit: weight). Cuba has two currencies: *peso convertible* *pe*·so kon·ver·*tee*·ble and Cuban *peso* (the latter is also called *moneda nacional* mo·*ne*·da na·syo·*nal*).

Bolivia	*boliviano*	bo·lee·*vya*·no
Costa Rica	*colón* (named after Christopher Columbus)	ko·*lon*
Ecuador	*dólar*	*do*·lar
Guatemala	*quetzal* (a native bird)	ke·*tsal*
Honduras	*lempira* (the name of an indigenous chief)	lem·*pee*·ra
Nicaragua	*córdoba* (in honour of a Spanish explorer)	*kor*·do·ba
Panama	*balboa* (named after a Spanish explorer); *dólar*	bal·*bo*·a; *do*·lar
Paraguay	*guaraní* (an Amerindian people)	gwa·ra·*nee*
Peru	*nuevo sol* (lit: new sun)	*nwe*·vo sol
Venezuela	*bolívar* (named after Simón Bolívar)	bo·*lee*·var

~ GLOSSARY ~

adjective	a word that describes something – 'he was the **greatest** mariachi of his time'
adverb	a word that explains how an action is done – 'he sang **beautifully**'
article	the words 'a', 'an' and 'the'
demonstrative	a word that means 'this' or 'that'
direct object	the thing or person in the sentence that has the action directed to it – 'and the crowd loved **him**'
gender	classification of *nouns* into classes (like masculine and feminine), requiring other words (eg *adjectives*) to belong to the same class
indirect object	the person or thing in the sentence that is the recipient of the action – 'the public yelled to **him**'
infinitive	dictionary form of a *verb* – 'to **play** more'
noun	a thing, person or idea – 'the **ensemble** was excited'
number	whether a word is singular or plural – 'and they performed more **songs**'
personal pronoun	a word that means 'I', 'you' etc
possessive adjective	a word that means 'my', 'your' etc
possessive pronoun	a word that means 'mine', 'yours' etc
preposition	a word like 'for' or 'before' in English
subject	the thing or person in the sentence that does the action – 'the **musicians** played for hours'
tense	form of a *verb* that tells you whether the action is in the present, past or future – eg 'run' (present), 'ran' (past), 'will run' (future)
verb	a word that tells you what action happened – 'and **went** home late'
verb stem	part of a *verb* that doesn't change – eg '**play**' in '**play**ing' and '**play**ed'

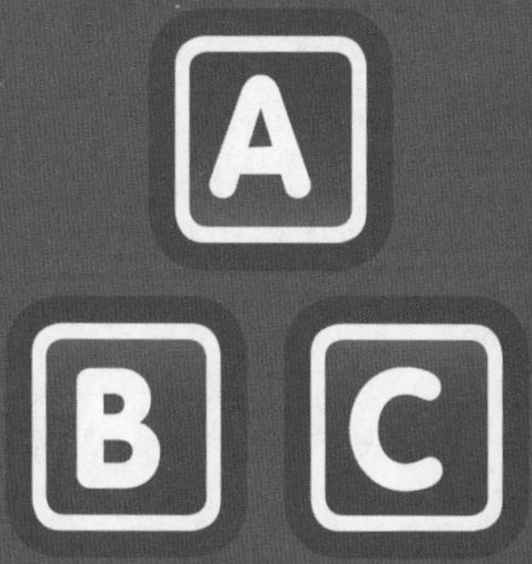

Basics

Understanding

KEY PHRASES

Do you speak English?	¿Habla/Hablas inglés? pol/inf	*a*·bla/*a*·blas een·*gles*
I don't understand.	No entiendo.	no en·*tyen*·do
What does ... mean?	¿Qué significa ...?	ke seeg·nee·*fee*·ka ...

Q **Do you speak (English)?**	¿Habla/Hablas (inglés)? pol/inf *a*·bla/*a*·blas (een·*gles*)
Q **Does anyone speak (English)?**	¿Hay alguien que hable (inglés)? ai *al*·gyen ke *a*·ble (een·*gles*)
A **I speak Spanish/ English.**	Hablo castellano/inglés. *a*·blo kas·te·*ya*·no/een·*gles*
A **I speak a little.**	Hablo un poco. *a*·blo oon *po*·ko
Q **Do you understand?**	¿Me entiende/entiendes? pol/inf me en·*tyen*·de/en·*tyen*·des
A **I (don't) understand.**	(No) Entiendo. (no) en·*tyen*·do
What does ... mean?	¿Qué significa ...? ke seeg·nee·*fee*·ka ...
How do you write ...?	¿Cómo se escribe ...? *ko*·mo se es·*kree*·be ...
How do you pronounce this?	¿Cómo se pronuncia esto? *ko*·mo se pro·*noon*·sya *es*·to

LANGUAGE TIP

False Friends

Beware of 'false friends' – words which look and/or sound like an English word but have a different meaning altogether.

embarazada f em·ba·ra·*sa*·da pregnant
(not 'embarrassed', which is *avergonzado/a* m/f a·ver·gon·*sa*·do/a)

injuria f een·*khoo*·rya insult
(not 'injury', which is *herida* e·*ree*·da)

parientes m pl pa·*ryen*·tes relatives
(not 'parents', which is *padres* *pa*·dres)

I'd like to learn some of your (indigenous) language.	Me gustaría aprender un poco de su lengua (indígena). me goos·ta·*ree*·a a·pren·*der* oon *po*·ko de soo *len*·gwa (een·*dee*·khe·na)
Would you like me to teach you some English?	¿Le/te gustaría que le/te enseñe un poco de inglés? pol/inf le/te goos·ta·*ree*·a ke le/te en·*se*·nye oon *po*·ko de een·*gles*
Could you please repeat that?	¿Puede repetirlo, por favor? *pwe*·de re·pe·*teer*·lo por fa·*vor*
Could you please write it down?	¿Puede escribirlo, por favor? *pwe*·de es·kree·*beer*·lo por fa·*vor*
Could you please speak more slowly?	¿Puede hablar más despacio, por favor? *pwe*·de a·*blar* mas des·*pa*·syo por fa·*vor*

Slowly, please! ¡Despacio, por favor! des·*pa*·syo por fa·*vor*

Numbers & Amounts

KEY PHRASES

How much?	¿Cuánto?	*kwan*·to
a little	un poco	oon *po*·ko
a lot	mucho	*moo*·cho

Cardinal Numbers

1	uno	*oo*·no
2	dos	dos
3	tres	tres
4	cuatro	*kwa*·tro
5	cinco	*seen*·ko
6	seis	says
7	siete	*sye*·te
8	ocho	*o*·cho
9	nueve	*nwe*·ve
10	diez	dyes
11	once	*on*·se
12	doce	*do*·se
13	trece	*tre*·se
14	catorce	ka·*tor*·se
15	quince	*keen*·se
16	dieciséis	dye·see·*says*
17	diecisiete	dye·see·*sye*·te
18	dieciocho	dye·see·*o*·cho

19	diecinueve	dye·see·*nwe*·ve
20	veinte	*vayn*·te
21	veintiuno	vayn·tee·*oo*·no
30	treinta	*trayn*·ta
40	cuarenta	kwa·*ren*·ta
50	cincuenta	seen·*kwen*·ta
60	sesenta	se·*sen*·ta
70	setenta	se·*ten*·ta
80	ochenta	o·*chen*·ta
90	noventa	no·*ven*·ta
100	cien	syen
200	doscientos	do·*syen*·tos
1000	mil	meel
1,000,000	un millón	oon mee·*yon*

Ordinal Numbers

1st	primero/a **m/f**	pree·*me*·ro/a
2nd	segundo/a **m/f**	se·*goon*·do/a
3rd	tercero/a **m/f**	ter·*se*·ro/a

Amounts

How much?	¿Cuánto/a? **m/f**	*kwan*·to/a
How many?	¿Cuántos? **m pl** ¿Cuántas? **f pl**	*kwan*·tos *kwan*·tas
a little	un poco	oon *po*·ko
a lot/much	mucho/a **m/f**	*moo*·cho/a
many	muchos/as **m/f pl**	*moo*·chos/as
some	algunos/as **m/f pl**	al·*goo*·nos/as

For other useful amounts, see **self-catering** (p182).

Time & Dates

KEY PHRASES

What time is it?	¿Qué hora es?	ke *o*·ra es
At what time ...?	¿A qué hora ...?	a ke *o*·ra ...
What date?	¿Qué fecha?	ke *fe*·cha

Telling the Time

When telling the time in Spanish, 'It's ...' is expressed by *Son las ...* son las ... followed by a number. However, 'It's one o'clock' is *Es la una* es la *oo*·na, and 'It's midnight' and 'It's midday' are *Es el medio-día* es el me·dyo·*dee*·a and *Es la medianoche* es la me·dya·*no*·che respectively. Both the 12-hour and the 24-hour clocks are commonly used.

Q **What time is it?**	¿Qué hora es? ke *o*·ra es
A **It's one o'clock.**	Es la una. es la *oo*·na
A **It's (10) o'clock.**	Son las (diez). son las (dyes)
A **Quarter past (two).**	(Las dos) y cuarto. (las dos) ee *kwar*·to
A **Twenty past (two).**	(Las dos) y veinte. (las dos) ee *vayn*·te
A **Half past (two).**	(Las dos) y media. (las dos) ee *me*·dya
A **Twenty to (three).**	(Las tres) menos veinte. (las tres) *me*·nos *vayn*·te
A **Quarter to (three).**	(Las tres) menos cuarto. (las tres) *me*·nos *kwar*·to

It's early.	Es temprano.	es tem·*pra*·no
It's late.	Es tarde.	es *tar*·de
am	de la mañana	de la ma·*nya*·na
pm	de la tarde	de la *tar*·de
in the morning	por la mañana	por la ma·*nya*·na
in the afternoon	por la tarde	por la *tar*·de
in the evening	por la noche	por la *no*·che
at night	por la noche	por la *no*·che
midday	mediodía **m**	me·dyo·*dee*·a
midnight	medianoche **f**	me·dya·*no*·che
sunrise	amanecer **m**	a·ma·ne·*ser*
sunset	atardecer **m**	a·tar·de·*ser*
Q **At what time ...?**	¿A qué hora ...?	a ke *o*·ra ...
A **At one o'clock.**	A la una.	a la *oo*·na
A **At (six) o'clock.**	A las (seis).	a las (says)

The Calendar

Monday	lunes **m**	*loo*·nes
Tuesday	martes **m**	*mar*·tes
Wednesday	miércoles **m**	*myer*·ko·les
Thursday	jueves **m**	*khwe*·ves
Friday	viernes **m**	*vyer*·nes
Saturday	sábado **m**	*sa*·ba·do
Sunday	domingo **m**	do·*meen*·go

January	enero **m**	e·*ne*·ro
February	febrero **m**	fe·*bre*·ro
March	marzo **m**	*mar*·so
April	abril **m**	a·*breel*
May	mayo **m**	*ma*·yo
June	junio **m**	*khoo*·nyo
July	julio **m**	*khoo*·lyo
August	agosto **m**	a·*gos*·to
September	septiembre **m**	sep·*tyem*·bre
October	octubre **m**	ok·*too*·bre
November	noviembre **m**	no·*vyem*·bre
December	diciembre **m**	dee·*syem*·bre
What date?	¿Qué fecha?	ke *fe*·cha
Q **What's today's date?**	¿Qué día es hoy?	ke *dee*·a es oy
A **It's (18 October).**	Es (el dieciocho de octubre).	es (el dye·see·*o*·cho de ok·*too*·bre)
summer	verano **m**	ve·*ra*·no
autumn	otoño **m**	o·*to*·nyo
winter	invierno **m**	een·*vyer*·no
spring	primavera **f**	pree·ma·*ve*·ra

Present

now	ahora	a·*o*·ra
today	hoy	oy
this morning	esta mañana	es·ta ma·*nya*·na
this afternoon	esta tarde	es·ta *tar*·de
tonight	esta noche	es·ta *no*·che
this week	esta semana	es·ta se·*ma*·na

LANGUAGE TIP

Tongue Twisters

Tongue twisters are known as *trabalenguas* tra·ba·*len*·gwas in Spanish. Try exercising your tongue with these two:

Comí chirimoyas, me enchirimoyé.
Ahora, para desenchirimoyarme,
¿cómo me desenchirimoyaré?
ko·*mee* chee·ree·*mo*·yas me en·chee·ree·mo·*ye*
a·*o*·ra *pa*·ra des·en·chee·ree·mo·*yar*·me
ko·mo me des·en·chee·ree·mo·ya·*re*
I ate custard apples, I ate too many custard apples.
Now, to get un-custard-appled,
how shall I un-custard-apple myself?

Poquito a poquito Paquito empaca poquitas copitas en pocos paquetes.
po·*kee*·to a po·*kee*·to pa·*kee*·to em·*pa*·ka po·*kee*·tas ko·*pee*·tas en *po*·kos pa·*ke*·tes
Little by little Paquito is packing a few small wineglasses in few boxes.

this month	este mes	*es*·te mes
this year	este año	*es*·te *a*·nyo

Past

yesterday	ayer	a·*yer*
day before yesterday	anteayer	an·te·a·*yer*
(three days) ago	hace (tres días)	*a*·se (tres *dee*·as)
since (May)	desde (mayo)	*des*·de (*ma*·yo)
last night	anoche	a·*no*·che
last week	la semana pasada	la se·*ma*·na pa·*sa*·da
last month	el mes pasado	el mes pa·*sa*·do

last year	el año pasado	el *a*·nyo pa·*sa*·do
yesterday morning	ayer por la mañana	a·*yer* por la ma·*nya*·na
yesterday afternoon	ayer por la tarde	a·*yer* por la *tar*·de
yesterday evening	ayer por la noche	a·*yer* por la *no*·che

Future

tomorrow	mañana	ma·*nya*·na
day after tomorrow	pasado mañana	pa·*sa*·do ma·*nya*·na
in (six days)	dentro de (seis días)	*den*·tro de (says *dee*·as)
until (June)	hasta (junio)	*as*·ta (*khoo*·nyo)
next week	la semana que viene	la se·*ma*·na ke *vye*·ne
next month	el mes que viene	el mes ke *vye*·ne
next year	el año que viene	el *a*·nyo ke *vye*·ne
tomorrow morning	mañana por la mañana	ma·*nya*·na por la ma·*nya*·na
tomorrow afternoon	mañana por la tarde	ma·*nya*·na por la *tar*·de
tomorrow evening	mañana por la noche	ma·*nya*·na por la *no*·che

CULTURE TIP

Donations to English

Thanks to Columbus' discovery of the New World in 1492, a large corpus of words from indigenous American languages has entered English via Latin American Spanish, eg *barbecue, canoe, hammock, potato, tobacco, chocolate* ...

Practical

Transport

KEY PHRASES

When's the next bus?	¿A qué hora es el próximo autobús?	a ke *o*·ra es el *prok*·see·mo ow·to·*boos*
A ticket to ..., please.	Un boleto a ..., por favor.	oon bo·*le*·to a ... por fa·*vor*
Can you tell me when we get to ...?	¿Me puede decir cuándo lleguemos a ...?	me *pwe*·de de·*seer kwan*·do ye·*ge*·mos a ...
Please take me to this address.	Por favor, lléveme a esta dirección.	por fa·*vor* *ye*·ve·me a *es*·ta dee·rek·*syon*
I'd like to hire a car.	Quisiera alquilar un carro.	kee·*sye*·ra al·kee·*lar* oon *ka*·ro

Getting Around

Can we get there by public transport?	¿Podemos llegar allí en transporte público? po·*de*·mos ye·*gar* a·*yee* en trans·*por*·te *poo*·blee·ko
I'd prefer to walk there.	Prefiero caminar para ir allí. pre·*fye*·ro ka·mee·*nar* *pa*·ra eer a·*yee*
What time's the first/last bus?	¿A qué hora es el primer/último autobús? a ke *o*·ra es el pree·*mer*/*ool*·tee·mo ow·to·*boos*

What time's the next bus?	¿A qué hora es el próximo autobús? a ke *o*·ra es el *prok*·see·mo ow·to·*boos*
What time does the ... leave?	¿A qué hora sale ...? a ke *o*·ra *sa*·le ...

boat	el barco	el *bar*·ko
bus (city)	el autobús; la chiva **(Col)**; el colectivo **(Arg)**; la guagua **(Cub)**; el micro **(Bol, Chi)**	el ow·to·*boos*; la *chee*·va; el ko·lek·*tee*·vo; la *gwa*·gwa; el *mee*·kro
bus (intercity)	el ómnibus; el micro **(Arg)**	el *om*·nee·boos; el *mee*·kro
metro	el subterráneo; el subte **(Arg)**	el soob·te·*ra*·ne·o; el *soob*·te
plane	el avión	el a·*vyon*
train	el tren	el tren
tram	el tranvía	el tran·*vee*·a

Could you give me a ride in your (pick-up)?	¿Me podría llevar en su (pick-up)? me po·*dree*·a ye·*var* en soo (*peek*·oop)
Are you waiting for more people?	¿Está esperando a más gente? es·*ta* es·pe·*ran*·do a mas *khen*·te
How much do I owe you?	¿Cuánto le debo? *kwan*·to le *de*·bo
Can you tell me when we get to (San Miguel)?	¿Me puede decir cuándo lleguemos a (San Miguel)? me *pwe*·de de·*seer* *kwan*·do ye·*ge*·mos a (san mee·*gel*)

LISTEN FOR

Está cancelado.	es·*ta* kan·se·*la*·do	It's cancelled.
Está completo.	es·*ta* kom·*ple*·to	It's full.
Está retrasado.	es·*ta* re·tra·*sa*·do	It's delayed.

I want to get off here.	Quiero bajarme aquí. *kye*·ro ba·*khar*·me a·*kee*
That's my seat.	Ése es mi asiento. *e*·se es mee a·*syen*·to
Is this seat free?	¿Está libre este asiento? es·*ta lee*·bre *es*·te a·*syen*·to

Is it free? ¿Está libre? es·*ta lee*·bre

For phrases about getting through customs and immigration, see **border crossing** (p54).

Buying Tickets

Where can I buy a ticket?	¿Dónde puedo comprar un boleto? *don*·de *pwe*·do kom·*prar* oon bo·*le*·to
Do I need to book?	¿Tengo que reservar? *ten*·go ke re·ser·*var*
Can I get a stand-by ticket?	¿Puede ponerme en la lista de espera? *pwe*·de po·*ner*·me en la *lees*·ta de es·*pe*·ra
How long does the trip take?	¿Cuánto se tarda? *kwan*·to se *tar*·da
Is it a direct route?	¿Es un viaje directo? es oon *vya*·khe dee·*rek*·to

Buying a Ticket

What time is the next ...?

¿A qué hora sale el próximo ...?

a ke o·ra sa·le el prok·see·mo ...

boat barco *bar·ko*

bus autobús *ow·to·boos*

train tren *tren*

One ... ticket, please.

Un boleto ..., por favor.

oon bo·le·to ... por fa·vor

one-way de ida *de ee·da*

return de ida y vuelta *de ee·da ee vwel·ta*

I'd like a/an ... seat.

Quisiera un asiento ...

kee·sye·ra oon a·syen·to ...

aisle de pasillo *de pa·see·yo*

window junto a la ventana *khoon·to a la ven·ta·na*

Which platform does it depart from?

¿De cuál plataforma sale?

de kwal pla·ta·for·ma sa·le

What time do I have to check in?	¿A qué hora tengo que facturar mi equipaje? a ke o·ra *ten*·go ke fak·too·*rar* mee e·kee·*pa*·khe
I'd like to cancel my ticket, please.	Quisiera cancelar mi boleto, por favor. kee·*sye*·ra kan·se·*lar* mee bo·*le*·to por fa·*vor*
I'd like to change my ticket, please.	Quisiera cambiar mi boleto, por favor. kee·*sye*·ra kam·*byar* mee bo·*le*·to por fa·*vor*
I'd like to confirm my ticket, please.	Quisiera confirmar mi boleto, por favor. kee·*sye*·ra kon·feer·*mar* mee bo·*le*·to por fa·*vor*
A ... ticket to (Lima), please.	Un boleto ... a (Lima), por favor. oon bo·*le*·to ... a (*lee*·ma) por fa·*vor*

1st-class	de primera clase	de pree·*me*·ra *kla*·se
2nd-class	de segunda clase	de se·*goon*·da *kla*·se
child's	infantil	een·fan·*teel*
one-way	de ida	de ee·da
return	de ida y vuelta	de ee·da ee *vwel*·ta
student's	de estudiante	de es·too·*dyan*·te

I'd like an aisle seat.	Quisiera un asiento de pasillo. kee·*sye*·ra oon a·*syen*·to de pa·*see*·yo

I'd like a window seat.	Quisiera un asiento junto a la ventana. kee·*sye*·ra oon a·*syen*·to *khoon*·to a la ven·*ta*·na
I'd like a (non)smoking seat.	Quisiera un asiento de (no) fumadores. kee·*sye*·ra oon a·*syen*·to de (no) foo·ma·*do*·res
Is there (a) ...?	¿Hay ... ? ai ...

air-conditioning	aire acondicionado	*ai*·re a·kon·dee·syo·*na*·do
blanket	una frazada	*oo*·na fra·*sa*·da
toilet	baños	*ba*·nyos
video	vídeo	*vee*·de·o

Luggage

My luggage has been damaged.	Mi equipaje ha sido dañado. mee e·kee·*pa*·khe a *see*·do da·*nya*·do
My luggage has been lost/stolen.	Mi equipaje ha sido perdido/robado. mee e·kee·*pa*·khe a *see*·do per·*dee*·do/ro·*ba*·do
I'd like a luggage locker.	Quisiera un casillero de consigna. kee·*sye*·ra oon ka·see·*ye*·ro de kon·*seeg*·na
I'd like some coins/tokens.	Quisiera unas monedas/fichas. kee·*sye*·ra *oo*·nas mo·*ne*·das/*fee*·chas

Bus, Tram & Metro

Which bus goes to (the centre of town)?	¿Qué autobús va al (centro de la cuidad)? ke ow·to·*boos* va al (*sen*·tro de la syoo·*da*)
Which bus goes to (Cochabamba)?	¿Qué ómnibus va a (Cochabamba)? ke *om*·nee·boos va a (ko·cha·*bam*·ba)
Tram number (three).	El tranvía número (tres). el tran·*vee*·a *noo*·me·ro (tres)
How many stops to (the museum)?	¿Cuántas paradas hay hasta (el museo)? *kwan*·tas pa·*ra*·das ai *as*·ta (el moo·*se*·o)
Do you stop at (the market)?	¿Tiene parada en (el mercado)? *tye*·ne pa·*ra*·da en (el mer·*ka*·do)

Train

What station is this?	¿Cuál es esta estación? kwal es *es*·ta es·ta·*syon*

LANGUAGE TIP

Regionalisms

Throughout Latin America the general name for a bus station is *una estación de autobuses* *oo*·na es·ta·*syon* de ow·to·*boo*·ses, although in Argentina it's known as *una terminal de ómnibuses* *oo*·na ter·mee·*nal* de *om*·nee·boo·ses. In Venezuela and Colombia you'll hear the term *una terminal terrestre* *oo*·na ter·mee·*nal* te·*re*·stre (lit: land terminal) or *una terminal de pasajeros* *oo*·na ter·mee·*nal* de pa·sa·*khe*·ros (lit: passenger terminal).

What's the next station?	¿Cuál es la próxima estación? kwal es la *prok*·see·ma es·ta·*syon*
Does this train stop at (Veracruz)?	¿Para el tren en (Veracruz)? *pa*·ra el tren en (ve·ra·*kroos*)
Do I need to change trains?	¿Tengo que cambiar de tren? *ten*·go ke kam·*byar* de tren
Which carriage is 1st class?	¿Cuál es el coche de primera clase? kwal es el *ko*·che de pree·*me*·ra *kla*·se
Which carriage is for (Buenos Aires)?	¿Cuál es el coche para (Buenos Aires)? kwal es el *ko*·che *pa*·ra (*bwe*·nos *ai*·res)
Which carriage is for dining?	¿Cuál es el coche comedor? kwal es el *ko*·che ko·me·*dor*
This/That one.	Éste./Ése. *es*·te/*es*·e

Boat

Where do we get on the boat?	¿Dónde subimos al barco? *don*·de soo·*bee*·mos al *bar*·ko
Are there life jackets?	¿Hay chalecos salvavidas? ai cha·*le*·kos sal·va·*vee*·das
What's the sea like today?	¿Cómo está el mar hoy? *ko*·mo es·*ta* el mar oy
I feel seasick.	Estoy mareado/a. **m/f** es·*toy* ma·re·*a*·do/a
wharf	embarcadero **m** em·bar·ka·*de*·ro malecón **m (CAm, Per)** ma·le·*kon*

Taxi

I'd like a taxi at (9am).	Quisiera un taxi a las (nueve de la mañana). kee·*sye*·ra oon *tak*·see a las (*nwe*·ve de la ma·*nya*·na)
I'd like a taxi now/ tomorrow.	Quisiera un taxi ahora/ mañana. kee·*sye*·ra oon *tak*·see a·*o*·ra/ ma·*nya*·na
Is this taxi free?	¿Está libre este taxi? es·*ta* *lee*·bre *es*·te *tak*·see

Is it free?	¿Está libre?	es·*ta* *lee*·bre

How much is it (to the airport)?	¿Cuánto cuesta ir (al aeropuerto)? *kwan*·to *kwes*·ta eer (al a·e·ro·*pwer*·to)

LOOK FOR

Acceso	ak·*se*·so	Entrance
Aparcamiento	a·par·ka·*myen*·to	Parking
Ceda el Paso	*se*·da el *pa*·so	Give Way
Dirección Única	dee·rek·*syon* *oo*·nee·ka	One Way
Pare	*pa*·re	Stop
Peaje	pe·*a*·khe	Toll
Peligro	pe·*lee*·gro	Danger
Prohibido Aparcar	pro·ee·*bee*·do a·par·*kar*	No Parking
Prohibido el Paso	pro·ee·*bee*·do el *pa*·so	No Entry
Salida de Autopista	sa·*lee*·da de ow·to·*pees*·ta	Exit Freeway

Quiero bajarme aquí.
kye·ro ba·khar·me a·kee
I want to get off here.
el turismo
netizen

Please put the meter on.	Por favor, ponga el taxímetro. por fa·*vor pon*·ga el tak·*see*·me·tro
Please take me to (this address).	Por favor, lléveme a (esta dirección). por fa·*vor ye*·ve·me a (*es*·ta dee·rek·*syon*)
✂ **To ...**	A ... a ...
Please slow down.	Por favor vaya más despacio. por fa·*vor va*·ya mas des·*pa*·syo
Please wait here.	Por favor espere aquí. por fa·*vor* es·*pe*·re a·*kee*

Stop at the corner.	Pare en la esquina. *pa*·re en la es·*kee*·na
Stop here.	Pare aquí. *pa*·re a·*kee*

Car & Motorbike

I'd like to hire a/an ...	Quisiera alquilar ... kee·*sye*·ra al·kee·*lar* ...

4WD	un todo terreno	oon *to*·do te·*re*·no
automatic	un carro automático	oon *ka*·ro ow·to·*ma*·tee·ko
car	un carro; un auto (SAm)	oon *ka*·ro; oon *ow*·to
manual	un carro manual	oon *ka*·ro man·*wal*
motorbike	una moto	*oo*·na *mo*·to

LANGUAGE TIP

Regionalisms

The word *gasolinera* ga·so·lee·*ne*·ra is the standard term for 'petrol/gas station', and will be understood throughout Latin America. You may also come across these country-specific terms:

Argentina	estación f de servicio	es·ta·*syon* de ser·*vee*·syo
Bolivia	surtidor m	soor·tee·*dor*
Central America, Colombia, Mexico	bomba f	*bom*·ba
Chile	bencinera f	ben·see·*ne*·ra
Peru	grifo m	*gree*·fo

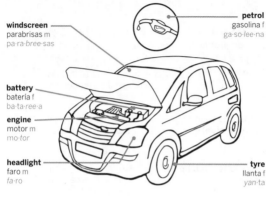

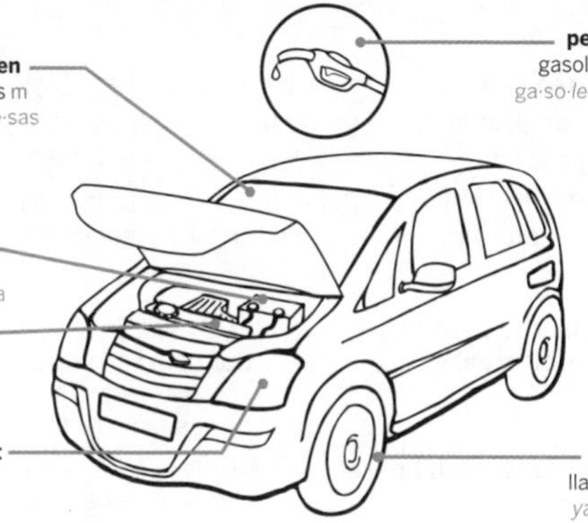

with air-conditioning	con aire acondicionado kon *ai*·re a·kon·dee·syo·*na*·do
with a driver	con un chofer kon oon cho·*fer*
How much for daily/ weekly hire?	¿Cuánto cuesta alquilar por día/semana? *kwan*·to *kwes*·ta al·kee·*lar* por *dee*·a/se·*ma*·na
What's the city speed limit?	¿Cuál es el límite de velocidad en la ciudad? kwal es el *lee*·mee·te de ve·lo·see·*da* en la syoo·*da*
What's the country speed limit?	¿Cuál es el límite de velocidad en el campo? kwal es el *lee*·mee·te de ve·lo·see·*da* en el *kam*·po

LOOK FOR

bencina (Chi)	ben·*see*·na	petrol/gas
con plomo	kon *plo*·mo	leaded (regular)
gasolina	ga·so·*lee*·na	petrol/gas
nafta (Arg)	*naf*·ta	petrol/gas
sin plomo	seen *plo*·mo	unleaded

Is this the road to (Tegucigalpa)?	¿Se va a (Tegucigalpa) por esta carretera? se va a (te·goo·see·*gal*·pa) por es·ta ka·re·*te*·ra
(How long) Can I park here?	¿(Por cuánto tiempo) Puedo aparcar aquí? (por *kwan*·to *tyem*·po) *pwe*·do a·par·*kar* a·*kee*
Where's a petrol/gas station?	¿Dónde hay una gasolinera? *don*·de ai *oo*·na ga·so·lee·*ne*·ra
Please fill it up.	Lleno, por favor. *ye*·no por fa·*vor*
I'd like (20) litres.	Quiero (veinte) litros. *kye*·ro (*vayn*·te) *lee*·tros
Where do I pay?	¿Dónde se paga? *don*·de se *pa*·ga
I need a mechanic.	Necesito un mecánico. ne·se·*see*·to oon me·*ka*·nee·ko
I had an accident.	Tuve un accidente. *too*·ve oon ak·see·*den*·te
The car has broken down (in Granada).	El carro se ha averiado (en Granada). el *ka*·ro se a a·ve·*rya*·do (en gra·*na*·da)

Bicycle

Can we get there by bike?	¿Podemos llegar allí en bicicleta? *po·de·mos lye·gar a·yee en bee·see·kle·ta*
I have a puncture.	Se me pinchó una rueda. *se me peen·cho oo·na rwe·da*
Where can I hire a bicycle?	¿Dónde se puede alquilar una bicicleta? *don·de se pwe·de al·kee·lar oo·na bee·see·kle·ta*
Where can I buy a second-hand bike?	¿Dónde se puede comprar una bicicleta de segunda mano? *don·de se pwe·de kom·prar oo·na bee·see·kle·ta de se·goon·da ma·no*
How much is it per day?	¿Cuánto cuesta por un día? *kwan·to kwes·ta por oon dee·a*
How much is it per hour?	¿Cuánto cuesta por hora? *kwan·to kwes·ta por o·ra*

LISTEN FOR

¿De qué marca es?	*de ke mar·ka es* What make/model is it?
Tengo que pedir ese repuesto.	*ten·go ke pe·deer e·se re·pwes·to* I have to order that part.

Border Crossing

KEY PHRASES

I'm here for ... days.	Estoy aquí por ... días.	es·*toy* a·*kee* por ... *dee*·as
I'm staying at ...	Me estoy alojando en ...	me es·*toy* a·lo·*khan*·do en ...
I have nothing to declare.	No tengo nada que declarar.	No *ten*·go *na*·da ke de·kla·*rar*

Border Crossing

I'm here in transit.	Estoy aquí en tránsito. es·*toy* a·*kee* en *tran*·see·to
I'm here on business/ holiday.	Estoy aquí de negocios/ vacaciones. es·*toy* a·*kee* de ne·*go*·syos/ va·ka·*syo*·nes
I'm here for (four) days.	Estoy aquí por (cuatro) días. es·*toy* a·*kee* por (*kwa*·tro) *dee*·as
I'm here for (two) weeks.	Estoy aquí por (dos) semanas. es·*toy* a·*kee* por (dos) se·*ma*·nas

LISTEN FOR

Su pasaporte, por favor.	soo pa·sa·*por*·te por fa·*vor* Your passport, please.
¿Está viajando solo/a? m/f	es·*ta* vya·*khan*·do *so*·lo/a Are you travelling on your own?

LOOK FOR

Aduana	a·*dwa*·na Customs
Artículos Libres de Impuestos	ar·*tee*·koo·los *lee*·bres de eem·*pwes*·tos Duty-Free Goods
Control de Pasaportes	kon·*trol* de pa·sa·*por*·tes Passport Control

I'm here for (three) months.	Estoy aquí por (tres) meses. es·*toy* a·*kee* por (tres) *me*·ses
I'm staying at ...	Me estoy alojando en ... me es·*toy* a·lo·*khan*·do en ...
I have a visa.	Tengo un visado. *ten*·go oon vee·*sa*·do
I have a study/work permit.	Tengo un permiso de estudios/trabajo. *ten*·go oon per·*mee*·so de es·*too*·dyos/tra·*ba*·kho

At Customs

I have nothing to declare.	No tengo nada que declarar. no *ten*·go *na*·da ke de·kla·*rar*
I have something to declare.	Tengo algo que declarar. *ten*·go *al*·go ke de·kla·*rar*
I didn't know I had to declare it.	No sabía que tenía que declararlo. no sa·*bee*·a ke te·*nee*·a ke de·kla·*rar*·lo
Do you have this form in (English)?	¿Tiene ese formulario en (inglés)? *tye*·ne e·se for·moo·*la*·ryo en (een·*gles*)

Directions

KEY PHRASES

Where's ...?	¿Dónde está ...?	*don*·de es·*ta* ...
What's the address?	¿Cuál es la dirección?	kwal es la dee·rek·*syon*
How far is it?	¿A cuánta distancia está?	a *kwan*·ta dees·*tan*·sya es·*ta*

Q	**Where's (the bank)?**	¿Dónde está (el banco)? *don*·de es·*ta* (el *ban*·ko)
A	**It's ...**	Está ... es·*ta* ...
	I'm looking for (the public toilets).	Busco (los baños). *boos*·ko (los *ba*·nyos)
	Which way's (the post office)?	¿Por dónde se va (a correos)? por *don*·de se va (a ko·*re*·os)
	How can I get there?	¿Cómo puedo ir? *ko*·mo *pwe*·do eer
	How far is it?	¿A cuánta distancia está? a *kwan*·ta dees·*tan*·sya es·*ta*
	Can you show me (on the map)?	¿Me lo podría indicar (en el mapa)? me lo po·*dree*·a een·dee·*kar* (en el *ma*·pa)
	What's the address?	¿Cuál es la dirección? kwal es la dee·rek·*syon*
	It's (100) metres.	Está a (cien) metros. es·*ta* a (syen) *me*·tros
	It's (two) kilometres.	Está a (dos) kilómetros. es·*ta* a (dos) kee·*lo*·me·tros
	It's (five) minutes.	Está a (cinco) minutos. es·*ta* a (*seen*·ko) mee·*noo*·tos

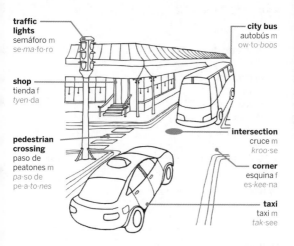

LOOK FOR

Abierto	*a·byer·to*	Open
Caliente	*ka·lyen·te*	Hot
Cerrado	*se·ra·do*	Closed
Entrada	*en·tra·da*	Entry
Frío	*free·o*	Cold
Información	*een·for·ma·syon*	Information
No Tocar	*no to·kar*	Don't Touch
Prohibido Tomar Fotos	*pro·ee·bee·do to·mar fo·tos*	No Photography
Reservado	*re·ser·va·do*	Reserved
Salida	*sa·lee·da*	Exit

LISTEN FOR

acá (Arg)	a·*ka*	there
adelante de ...	a·de·*lan*·te de ...	in front of ...
ahí	a·*ee*	there
al lado de ...	al *la*·do de ...	next to ...
aquí	a·*kee*	here
cerca	*ser*·ka	near
detrás de ...	de·*tras* de ...	behind ...
frente a ...	*fren*·te a ...	opposite ...
lejos	*le*·khos	far away
todo derecho	*to*·do de·*re*·cho	straight ahead

by bus	en autobús en ow·to·*boos*
by taxi	en taxi en *tak*·see
by train	en tren en tren
on foot	a pie a pye
Turn left.	Doble a la izquierda. *do*·ble a la ees·*kyer*·da
Turn right.	Doble a la derecha. *do*·ble a la de·*re*·cha
Turn at the corner.	Doble en la esquina. *do*·ble en la es·*kee*·na
Turn at the traffic lights.	Doble en el semáforo. *do*·ble en el se·*ma*·fo·ro

Accommodation

KEY PHRASES

Where's a hotel?	¿Dónde hay un hotel?	*don*·de ai oon o·*tel*
Do you have a double room?	¿Tiene una habitación doble?	*tye*·ne *oo*·na a·bee·ta·*syon do*·ble
How much is it per night?	¿Cuánto cuesta por noche?	*kwan*·to *kwes*·ta por *no*·che
Is breakfast included?	¿El desayuno está incluído?	el de·sa·*yoo*·no es·*ta* een·kloo·ee·do
What time is checkout?	¿A qué hora hay que dejar libre la habitación?	a ke *o*·ra ai ke de·*khar lee*·bre la a·bee·ta·*syon*

Finding Accommodation

Can you recommend somewhere ...?
¿Puede recomendar algún sitio ...?
pwe·de re·ko·men·*dar* al·*goon see*·tyo ...

cheap	barato	ba·*ra*·to
good	bueno	*bwe*·no
luxurious	de lujo	de *loo*·kho
nearby	cercano	ser·*ka*·no
romantic	romántico	ro·*man*·tee·ko

What's the address?
¿Cuál es la dirección?
kwal es la dee·rek·*syon*

Where's a ...?	¿Dónde hay ...? *don*·de ai ...

bed and breakfast	una pensión con desayuno	*oo*·na pen·*syon* kon de·sa·*yoo*·no
cabin	una cabaña	*oo*·na ka·*ba*·nya
campsite	un terreno de cámping	oon te·*re*·no de *kam*·peen
guesthouse	una pensión; una casa de huéspedes; una hostería **(Arg, Chi)**	*oo*·na pen·*syon;* *oo*·na *ka*·sa de *wes*·pe·des; *oo*·na os·te·*ree*·a
hotel	un hotel	oon o·*tel*
youth hostel	un albergue juvenil	oon al·*ber*·ge khoo·ve·*neel*

For getting there, see **directions** (p56).

Booking Ahead & Checking In

Do you have a double room?	¿Tiene una habitación doble? *tye*·ne *oo*·na a·bee·ta·*syon* *do*·ble
Do you have a single room?	¿Tiene una habitación individual? *tye*·ne *oo*·na a·bee·ta·*syon* een·dee·vee·*dwal*
Do you have a twin room?	¿Tiene una habitación con dos camas? *tye*·ne *oo*·na a·bee·ta·*syon* kon dos *ka*·mas
How much is it per night?	¿Cuánto cuesta por noche? *kwan*·to *kwes*·ta por *no*·che

Finding a Room

Do you have a ... room?

¿Tiene una habitación ...?
tye·ne *oo*·na a·bee·ta·*syon* ...

double
doble
do·ble

single
individual
een·dee·vee·*dwal*

How much is it per ...?

¿Cuánto cuesta por ...?
kwan·to *kwes*·ta por ...

night
noche
no·che

person
persona
per·*so*·na

Is breakfast included?

¿El desayuno está incluído?
el de·sa·*yoo*·no es·*ta* een·kloo·*ee*·do

Can I see the room?

¿Puedo verla?
pwe·do *ver*·la

I'll take it.

La alquilo.
la al·*kee*·lo

I won't take it.

No la alquilo.
no la al·*kee*·lo

How much is it per person?	¿Cuánto cuesta por persona? *kwan*·to *kwes*·ta por per·*so*·na
How much is it per week?	¿Cuánto cuesta por semana? *kwan*·to *kwes*·ta por se·*ma*·na
Is breakfast included?	¿El desayuno está incluído? el de·sa·*yoo*·no es·*ta* een·kloo·*ee*·do
I'd like to book a room, please.	Quisiera reservar una habitación. kee·*sye*·ra re·ser·*var* *oo*·na a·bee·ta·*syon*

Are there rooms?	¿Hay cuartos disponibles?	ai *kwar*·tos dis·po·*nee*·bles

I have a reservation.	Tengo una reserva. *ten*·go *oo*·na re·*ser*·va
For (three) nights/weeks.	Para (tres) noches/semanas. *pa*·ra (tres) *no*·ches/ se·*ma*·nas
From (July 2) to (July 6).	Desde (el dos de julio) hasta (el seis de julio). *des* de (el dos de *khoo*·lyo) *as*·ta (el says de *khoo*·lyo)
Can I see it?	¿Puedo verla? *pwe*·do *ver*·la

LISTEN FOR

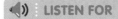

¿Por cuántas noches?	por *kwan*·tas *no*·ches For how many nights?
Lo siento, está completo.	lo *syen*·to es·*ta* kom·*ple*·to I'm sorry, we're full.
La llave está en recepción.	la *ya*·ve es·*ta* en re·sep·*syon* The key is at reception.

I'll take it.	La alquilo. la al·*kee*·lo

For methods of payment, see **money & banking** (p88).

Requests & Queries

When/Where is breakfast served?	¿Cuándo/Dónde se sirve el desayuno? *kwan*·do/*don*·de se *seer*·ve el de·sa·*yoo*·no
Please wake me at (seven).	Por favor, despiérteme a (las siete). por fa·*vor* des·*pyer*·te·me a (las *sye*·te)
Can I get another ...?	¿Puede darme otro/a ...? **m/f** *pwe*·de *dar*·me *o*·tro/a ...
Can I use the ...?	¿Puedo usar el/la ...? **m/f** *pwe*·do oo·*sar* el/la ...
Do you have a/an ...?	¿Hay ...? ai ...

elevator	ascensor **m**	a·sen·*sor*
kitchen	cocina **f**	ko·*see*·na
laundry	lavandería **f**	la·van·de·*ree*·a
message board	tablón **m** de anuncios; pizarra **f** de anuncios **(CAm)**; diario **m** mural **(Chi)**	ta·*blon* de a·*noon*·syos; pee·*sa*·ra de a·*noon*·syos; *dya*·ryo moo·*ral*
safe	caja **f** fuerte	*ka*·kha *fwer*·te
swimming pool	piscina **f (SAm)**; pileta **f (Arg)**	pee·*see*·na; pee·*le*·ta
telephone	teléfono **m**	te·*le*·fo·no

Do you arrange tours here?	¿Aquí organizan paseos guiados? *a·kee or·ga·nee·san pa·se·os gee·a·dos*
Do you change money here?	¿Aquí cambian dinero? *a·kee kam·byan dee·ne·ro*
Can I leave a message for someone?	¿Puedo dejar un mensaje para alguien? *pwe·do de·khar oon men·sa·khe pa·ra al·gyen*
Is there a message for me?	¿Hay algún mensaje para mí? *ai al·goon men·sa·khe pa·ra mee*
There's no need to change my sheets.	No hace falta cambiar mis sábanas. *no a·se fal·ta kam·byar mees sa·ba·nas*
The (bathroom) door is locked.	La puerta (del baño) está cerrada con llave. *la pwer·ta (del ba·nyo) es·ta se·ra·da kon ya·ve*

Complaints

The room is too ...	La habitación es demasiado ... *la a·bee·ta·syon es de·ma·sya·do ...*

cold	fría	*free·a*
dark	oscura	*os·koo·ra*
dirty	sucia	*soo·sya*
light/bright	luminosa	*loo·mee·no·sa*
noisy	ruidosa	*rwee·do·sa*
small	pequeña	*pe·ke·nya*

The ... doesn't work.	No funciona ... no foon·*syo*·na ...

air-conditioning	el aire acondicionado	el *ai*·re a·kon·dee·syo·*na*·do
fan	el ventilador	el ven·tee·la·*dor*
heater	la estufa	la es·*too*·fa
toilet	el baño	el *ba*·nyo
window	la ventana	la ven·*ta*·na

The toilet smells.	El baño huele mal. el *ba*·nyo *we*·le mal
The room smells.	La habitación huele mal. la a·bee·ta·*syon we*·le mal
There's no hot water.	No hay agua caliente. no ai *a*·gwa ka·*lyen*·te
his ... isn't clean.	Este/a ... no está limpio/a. m/f *es*·te/a ... no es·*ta leem*·pyo/a
e's a mistake in the	Hay un error en la cuenta. ai oon e·*ror* en la *kwen*·ta

ering the Door

	¿Quién es? kyen es
nt.	Un momento. oon mo·*men*·to
	Adelante. a·de·*lan*·te
lease.	¿Puede volver más tarde, por favor? *pwe*·de vol·*ver* mas *tar*·de por fa·*vor*

Checking Out

What time is checkout?	¿A qué hora hay que dejar libre la habitación? a ke *o*·ra ai ke de·*khar* *lee*·bre la a·bee·ta·*syon*
Can I have a late checkout?	¿Puedo dejar libre la habitación más tarde? *pwe*·do de·*khar* *lee*·bre la a·bee·ta·*syon* mas *tar*·de
How much extra to stay until (six o'clock)?	¿Cuánto más cuesta quedarse hasta (las seis)? *kwan*·to mas *kwes*·ta ke·*dar*·se *as*·ta (las says)
Can I leave my luggage here?	¿Puedo dejar el equipaje aquí? *pwe*·do de·*khar* el e·kee·*pa*·khe a·*kee*
I'm leaving now.	Me voy ahora. me voy a·*o*·ra
Can you call a taxi for me (for 11 o'clock)?	¿Me puede pedir un taxi (para las once)? me *pwe*·de pe·*deer* oon *tak*·see (*pa*·ra las *on*·se)
Could I have my deposit, please?	¿Me puede dar mi depósito, por favor? me *pwe*·de dar mee de·*po*·see·to por fa·*vor*
Could I have my passport, please?	¿Me puede dar mi pasaporte, por favor? me *pwe*·de dar mee pa·sa·*por*·te por fa·*vo*
Could I have my valuables, please?	¿Me puede dar mis objetos de valor, por me *pwe*·de dar mee ob·*khe*·tos de va·*lor*

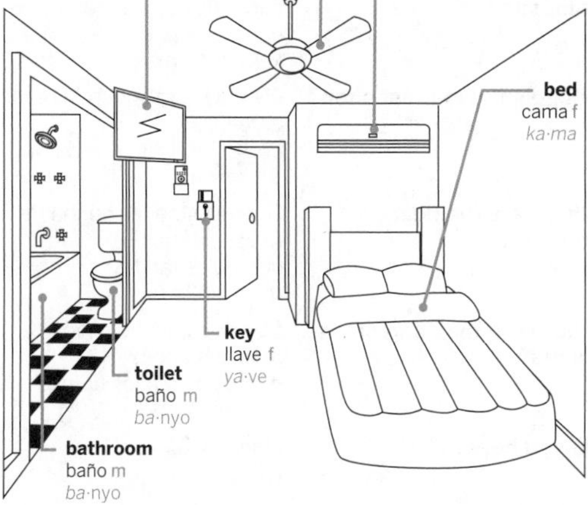

I'll be back in (three) days.	Volveré en (tres) días. vol·ve·*re* en (tres) *dee*·as
I'll be back on (Tuesday).	Volveré el (martes). vol·ve·*re* el (*mar*·tes)
I had a great stay, thank you.	Tuve una estancia muy agradable, gracias. *too*·ve *oo*·na es·*tan*·sya mooy a·gra·*da*·ble *gra*·syas
You've been terrific.	Fueron muy amables. *fwe*·ron mooy a·*ma*·bles
I'll recommend it to my friends.	Se lo recomendaré a mis amigos. se lo re·ko·men·da·*re* a mees a·*mee*·gos

Camping

Where's the nearest campsite?	¿Dónde está el terreno de cámping más cercano? *don*·de es·*ta* el te·*re*·no de *kam*·peen mas ser·*ka*·no
Where's the nearest shop?	¿Dónde está la tienda más cercana? *don*·de es·*ta* la *tyen*·da mas ser·*ka*·na
Where are the nearest showers?	Donde están las duchas más cercanas? *don*·de es·*tan* las *doo*·chas mas ser·*ka*·nas
Where are the nearest toilets?	Donde están los baños más cercanos? *don*·de es·*tan* los *ba*·nyos mas ser·*ka*·nos
Do you have ...?	¿Tiene ...? *tye*·ne ...

a site	lugar	loo·*gar*
electricity	electricidad	e·lek·tree·see·*da*
shower facilities	duchas	*doo*·chas
tents for hire	carpas para alquilar	*kar*·pas *pa*·ra al·kee·*lar*

How much is it per ...?	¿Cuánto vale por ...? *kwan*·to *va*·le por ...

caravan	caravana	ka·ra·*va*·na
person	persona	per·*so*·na
tent	carpa	*kar*·pa
vehicle	vehículo	ve·*ee*·koo·lo

¿Dónde hay un hotel?
don·de ai oon o·*tel*
Where's a hotel?

Who do I ask to stay here?	¿Con quién tengo que hablar para quedarme aquí? kon kyen *ten*·go ke a·*blar* *pa*·ra ke·*dar*·me a·*kee*
Can I camp here?	¿Se puede acampar aquí? se *pwe*·de a·kam·*par* a·*kee*
Can I park next to my tent?	¿Se puede estacionar al lado de mi carpa? se *pwe*·de es·ta·syo·*nar* al *la*·do de mee *kar*·pa
Is it coin-operated?	¿Funciona con monedas? foon·*syo*·na kon mo·*ne*·das
Is the water drinkable?	¿Se puede beber el agua? se *pwe*·de be·*ber* el *a*·gwa

Could I borrow (a mallet)?	¿Me podría prestar (un mazo)? me po·*dree*·a pres·*tar* (oon *ma*·so)

For more words related to camping, see the **dictionary**.

Renting

I'm here about (the room) for rent.	Vengo por (la habitación) que anuncian para alquilar. *ven*·go por (la a·bee·ta·*syon*) ke a·*noon*·syan *pa*·ra al·kee·*lar*
Do you have a/an ... for rent?	¿Tiene ... para alquilar? *tye*·ne ... *pa*·ra al·kee·*lar*

apartment	un departamento	oon de·par·ta·*men*·to
cabin	una cabaña	*oo*·na ka·*ba*·nya
house	una casa	*oo*·na *ka*·sa
room	una habitación	*oo*·na a·bee·ta·*syon*
villa	un chalet	oon cha·*le*

Do I need to pay upfront?	¿Necesito pagar por adelantado? ne·se·*see*·to pa·*gar* por a·de·lan·*ta*·do
furnished	amueblado/a **m/f** a·mwe·*bla*·do/a
partly furnished	parcialmente amueblado/a **m/f** par·syal·*men*·te a·mwe·*bla*·do/a
unfurnished	sin amueblar seen a·mwe·*blar*

Staying with Locals

Can I stay at your place?	¿Me podría quedar en su/tu casa? **pol/inf** me po·*dree*·a ke·*dar* en soo/too *ka*·sa
Is there anything I can do to help?	¿Puedo ayudar en algo? *pwe*·do a·yoo·*dar* en *al*·go
I have my own mattress.	Tengo mi propio colchón. *ten*·go mee *pro*·pyo kol·*chon*
I have my own sleeping bag.	Tengo mi propia bolsa de dormir. *ten*·go mee *pro*·pya *bol*·sa de dor·*meer*
Can I ...?	¿Puedo ...? *pwe*·do ...

bring anything for the meal	traer algo para la comida	tra·*er* *al*·go *pa*·ra la ko·*mee*·da
do the dishes	lavar los platos	la·*var* los *pla*·tos
set/clear the table	poner/quitar la mesa	po·*ner*/kee·*tar* la *me*·sa
take out the rubbish	sacar la basura	sa·*kar* la ba·*soo*·ra

Thanks for your hospitality.	Gracias por su/tu hospitalidad. **pol/inf** *gra*·syas por soo/too os·pee·ta·lee·*da*

If you're dining with your hosts, see **eating out** (p166) for more phrases.

Shopping

KEY PHRASES

I'd like to buy ...	Quisiera comprar ...	kee·*sye*·ra kom·*prar* ...
Can I look at it?	¿Puedo verlo?	*pwe*·do *ver*·lo
Can I try it on?	¿Me lo puedo probar?	me lo *pwe*·do pro·*bar*
How much is it?	¿Cuánto cuesta esto?	*kwan*·to *kwes*·ta *es*·to
That's too expensive.	Es muy caro.	es mooy *ka*·ro

Looking For ...

Where's (a supermarket)?	¿Dónde hay (un supermercado)? *don*·de ai (oon soo·per·mer·*ka*·do)
Where can I buy (locally produced goods/souvenirs)?	¿Dónde puedo comprar (productos/recuerdos locales)? *don*·de *pwe*·do kom·*prar* (pro·*dook*·tos/re·*kwer*·dos lo·*ka*·les)

For asking and giving directions, see **directions** (p56), and for types of shops, see the **dictionary**.

Making a Purchase

I'd like to buy ...	Quisiera comprar ... kee·*sye*·ra kom·*prar* ...

I'm just looking.	Sólo estoy mirando. *so*·lo es·*toy* mee·*ran*·do
Can I look at it?	¿Puedo verlo? *pwe*·do *ver*·lo
How much is it?	¿Cuánto cuesta esto? *kwan*·to *kwes*·ta *es*·to

How much?	¿Cuánto cuesta?	*kwan*·to *kwes*·ta

Can you write down the price?	¿Puede escribir el precio? *pwe*·de es·kree·*beer* el *pre*·syo
Do you have any others?	¿Tiene otros? *tye*·ne *o*·tros
Does it have a guarantee?	¿Tiene garantía? *tye*·ne ga·ran·*tee*·a
It's faulty.	Es defectuoso. es de·fek·*two*·so
I don't like it.	No me gusta. no me *goos*·ta
Could I have a bag, please?	¿Podría darme una bolsa, por favor? po·*dree*·a *dar*·me *oo*·na *bol*·sa por fa·*vor*
Could I have it wrapped?	¿Me lo podría envolver? me lo po·*dree*·a en·vol·*ver*
Could I have a receipt, please?	¿Podría darme un recibo, por favor? po·*dree*·a *dar*·me oon re·*see*·bo por fa·*vor*

Receipt, please.	Un recibo, por favor.	oon re·*see*·bo por fa·*vor*

PRACTICAL SHOPPING

LISTEN FOR

¿En qué le puedo servir?	en ke le *pwe*·do ser·*veer*	Can I help you?
¿Qué quisiera?	ke kee·*sye*·ra	What would you like?
No tenemos ninguno.	no te·*ne*·mos neen·*goo*·no	We don't have any.

I'd like my change, please.	Quisiera mi cambio, por favor.	kee·*sye*·ra mee *kam*·byo por fa·*vor*
I'd like my money back, please.	Quisiera que me devuelva el dinero, por favor.	kee·*sye*·ra ke me de·*vwel*·va el dee·*ne*·ro por fa·*vor*
I'd like to return this, please.	Quisiera devolver esto, por favor.	kee·*sye*·ra de·vol·*ver* *es*·to por fa·*vor*

Bargaining

That's too expensive.	Es muy caro.	es mooy *ka*·ro
Can you lower the price (a little)?	¿Podría bajar (un poco) el precio?	po·*dree*·a ba·*khar* (oon *po*·ko) el *pre*·syo
Do you have something cheaper?	¿Tiene algo más barato?	*tye*·ne *al*·go mas ba·*ra*·to
I'll give you ...	Le daré ...	le da·*re* ...

Making a Purchase

I'd like to buy ...

Quisiera comprar ...
kee·*sye*·ra kom·*prar* ...

How much is it?

¿Cuánto cuesta esto?
kwan·to *kwes*·ta *es*·to

OR

Can you write down the price?

¿Puede escribir el precio?
pwe·de es·kree·*beer* el *pre*·syo

Do you accept credit cards?

¿Aceptan tarjetas de crédito?
a·*sep*·tan tar·*khe*·tas de *kre*·dee·to

Could I have a ..., please?

¿Podría darme ..., por favor?
po·*dree*·a *dar*·me ... por fa·*vor*

receipt
un recibo
oon re·*see*·bo

bag
una bolsa
oo·na *bol*·sa

LISTEN FOR

cazador m **de ofertas**	ka·sa·*dor* de o·*fer*·tas	bargain hunter
estafa f	es·*ta*·fa	rip-off
ganga f	*gan*·ga	bargain
saldos m pl	*sal*·dos	specials
venta f	*ven*·ta	sale

What's your final price?	¿Cuál es su precio final? kwal es soo *pre*·syo fee·*nal*

Books & Reading

Is there an English-language bookshop/ section?	¿Hay alguna librería/ sección en inglés? ai al·*goo*·na lee·bre·*ree*·a/ sek·*syon* en een·*gles*
Is there a/an (English-language) entertainment guide?	¿Hay alguna guía de espectáculos (en inglés)? ai al·*goo*·na *gee*·a de es·pek·*ta*·koo·los (en een·*gles*)
Do you have a book by ...?	¿Tiene un libro de ...? *tye*·ne oon *lee*·bro de ...

Clothes

Can I try it on?	¿Me lo puedo probar? me lo *pwe*·do pro·*bar*
My size is (medium).	Uso la talla (mediana). *oo*·so la *ta*·ya (me·*dya*·na)
It doesn't fit.	No me queda bien. no me *ke*·da byen

For different types of clothing, see the **dictionary**, and for sizes, see **numbers & amounts** (p32).

¿Tiene otros?
tye·ne o·tros
Do you have any others?

Music & DVD

I'd like a CD/DVD.	Quisiera un cómpact/DVD. kee·*sye*·ra oon *kom*·pak/de·ve·*de*
I'd like some headphones.	Quisiera unos auriculares. kee·*sye*·ra *oo*·nos ow·ree·koo·*la*·res
I heard a singer called ...	Escuché un/una cantante que se llama ... m/f es·koo·*che* oon/*oo*·na kan·*tan*·te ke se *ya*·ma ...
I heard a band called ...	Escuché un grupo que se llama ... es·koo·*che* oon *groo*·po ke se *ya*·ma ...

LANGUAGE TIP

Regionalisms

In Latin America the common term for 'general store' is *una tienda* *oo*·na *tyen*·da. Look out for some of these regional variations:

Argentina	un almacén	oon al·ma·*sen*
Bolivia, Central America, Colombia, Ecuador, Mexico, Peru	una tienda de abarrrotes	*oo*·na *tyen*·da de a·ba·*ro*·tes
Central America	una bodega	*oo*·na bo·*de*·ga
Chile, Costa Rica	una pulpería	*oo*·na pool·pe·*ree*·a
Venezuela	un abasto	oon a·*bas*·to

What's his/her best recording?	¿Cuál es su mejor disco? kwal es soo me·*khor dees*·ko
Can I listen to this?	¿Puedo escuchar éste? *pwe*·do es·koo·*char es*·te
What region is this DVD for?	¿Para qué región es este DVD? *pa*·ra ke re·*khyon* es *es*·te de·ve·*de*

Photography

Can you print digital photos?	¿Se puede imprimir fotos digitales? se *pwe*·de eem·pree·*meer fo*·tos dee·khee·*ta*·les
Can you recharge the battery?	¿Se puede recargar la pila? se *pwe*·de re·kar·*gar* la *pee*·la
Can you transfer my photos to CD?	¿Se puede pasar las fotos a un CD? se *pwe*·de pa·*sar* las *fo*·tos a oon se·*de*

Do you have batteries for this camera?	¿Tiene pilas para esta cámara? *tye*·ne *pee*·las *pa*·ra *es*·ta *ka*·ma·ra
Do you have a memory card for this camera?	¿Tiene tarjeta de memoria para esta cámara? *tye*·ne tar·*khe*·ta de me·*mo*·rya *pa*·ra *es*·ta *ka*·ma·ra
Can you load my film?	¿Puede cargar el carrete? *pwe*·de kar·*gar* el ka·*re*·te
Can you develop this film?	¿Puede revelar este carrete? *pwe*·de re·ve·*lar* *es*·te ka·*re*·te
When will it be ready?	¿Cuándo estará listo? *kwan*·do es·ta·*ra* *lees*·to
I need ... film for this camera.	Necesito un carrete de película ... para esta cámara. ne·se·*see*·to oon ka·*re*·te de pe·*lee*·koo·la ... *pa*·ra *es*·ta *ka*·ma·ra

(400) speed	de sensibilidad (cuatrocientos)	de sen·see·bee·lee·*da* (*kwa*·tro·*syen*·tos)
B&W	en blanco y negro	en *blan*·ko ee *ne*·gro
colour	en color	en ko·*lor*
slide	para diapositivas	*pa*·ra dya·po·see·*tee*·vas

I'm not happy with these photos.	No estoy contento/a con estas fotos. m/f no es·*toy* kon·*ten*·to/a kon *es*·tas *fo*·tos

For more photographic equipment, see the **dictionary**.

CULTURE TIP

Market-Hopping

Mercados mer·*ka*·dos (markets) are a colourful feature of Latin American life. Smaller, open-air street markets are known as *ferias* *fe*·ryas. If it's vibrant folk art you're after, the place to visit is a *mercado de artesanía* mer·*ka*·do de ar·te·sa·*nee*·ya (craft market). Here are some souvenirs you can look for:

alpaca jumper	chompa f de alpaca	*chom*·pa de al·*pa*·ka
cigars	cigarros m pl	see·*ga*·ros
hammock	hamaca f	a·*ma*·ka
jewellery	joyería f	kho·ye·*ree*·a
leather bag	cartera f de cuero	kar·*te*·ra de *kwe*·ro
panpipes	zampoña f	sam·*po*·nya
Peruvian hat	chullo m	*choo*·yo
pottery	alfarería f	al·fa·re·*ree*·a
silverware	plata f	*pla*·ta
weaving	tejido m	te·*khee*·do
woodcarving	talla f de madera	*ta*·ya de ma·*de*·ra

Repairs

Can I have my backpack/ camera repaired here?	¿Puede reparar mi mochila/cámara aquí? *pwe*·de re·pa·*rar* mee mo·*chee*·la/*ka*·ma·ra a·*kee*
Can I pick it up later?	¿Puedo recogerlo más tarde? *pwe*·do re·ko·*kher*·lo mas *tar*·de
When will my glasses/ shoes be ready?	¿Cuándo estarán listos mis anteojos/zapatos? *kwan*·do es·ta·*ran lees*·tos mees an·te·*o*·khos/sa·*pa*·tos

Communications

KEY PHRASES

Where's the local internet cafe?	¿Dónde hay un cibercafé cercano?	*don*·de ai oon see·ber·ka·*fe* ser·*ka*·no
I'd like to check my email.	Quisiera revisar mi correo electrónico.	kee·*sye*·ra re·vee·*sar* mee ko·*re*·o e·lek·*tro*·nee·ko
I'd like to send a parcel.	Quisiera enviar un paquete.	kee·*sye*·ra en·*vyar* oon pa·*ke*·te
I want to make a call to ...	Quiero hacer una llamada a ...	*kye*·ro a·*ser* *oo*·na ya·*ma*·da a ...
I'd like a SIM card.	Quisiera comprar una tarjeta SIM.	kee·*sye*·ra kom·*prar* *oo*·na tar·*khe*·ta seem

The Internet

Where's the local internet cafe?	¿Dónde hay un cibercafé cercano? *don*·de ai oon see·ber·ka·*fe* ser·*ka*·no
Is there (wireless) internet access here?	¿Hay acceso al internet (inalámbrico) aquí? ai ak·*se*·so al een·ter·*net* (ee·na·*lam*·bree·ko) a·*kee*
Can I connect my laptop here?	¿Se puede enchufar mi portátil aquí? se *pwe*·de en·choo·*far* mee por·*ta*·teel a·*kee*

I'd like to ...	Quisiera ... *kee·sye·ra* ...

check my email	revisar mi correo electrónico	re·vee·*sar* mee ko·*re*·o e·lek·*tro*·nee·ko
download my photos	descargar mis fotos	des·kar·*gar* mees *fo*·tos
use a printer	usar una impresora	oo·*sar oo*·na eem·pre·*so*·ra
use a scanner	usar un escáner	oo·*sar* oon es·*ka*·ner
use Skype	usar el Skype	oo·*sar* el es·*kai*·pe

How much per ...?	¿Cuánto cuesta por ...? *kwan*·to *kwes*·ta por ...

(10) minutes	(diez) minutos	(dyes) mee·*noo*·tos
CD	cómpact	*kom*·pak
hour	hora	*o*·ra
page	página	*pa*·khee·na

Do you have headphones (with a microphone)?	¿Tiene audífonos (con micrófono)? *tye*·ne ow·*dee*·fo·nos (kon mee·*kro*·fo·no)
Do you have PCs/Macs?	¿Tiene PC/MacIntosh? *tye*·ne *pe*·se/ma·*keen*·tosh
Do you have a Zip drive?	¿Tiene unidad de Zip? *tye*·ne oo·nee·*da* de seep
How do I log on?	¿Cómo me conecto al sistema? *ko*·mo me ko·*nek*·to al sees·*te*·ma

I need help with the computer.	Necesito ayuda con la computadora. ne·se·*see*·to a·*yoo*·da kon la kom·poo·ta·*do*·ra
It's crashed.	Se ha quedado colgado. se a ke·*da*·do kol·*ga*·do
I've finished.	He terminado. e ter·mee·*na*·do

Mobile/Cell Phone

I'd like a/an ...	Quisiera ... kee·*sye*·ra ...

adaptor plug	un adaptador	oon a·dap·ta·*dor*
charger for my phone	un cargador para mi teléfono	oon kar·ga·*dor* *pa*·ra mee te·*le*·fo·no
mobile/cell phone for hire	un móvil para alquilar	oon *mo*·veel *pa*·ra al·kee·*lar*
prepaid mobile/ cell phone	un móvil pagado por adelantado	oon *mo*·veel pa·*ga*·do por a·de·lan·*ta*·do
SIM card for your network	una tarjeta SIM para su red	*oo*·na tar·*khe*·ta seem *pa*·ra soo re

What are the rates?	¿Cuáles son las tarifas? *kwa*·les son las ta·*ree*·fas

LISTEN FOR

(Treinta centavos) por (treinta) segundos.	(*trayn*·ta sen·*ta*·vos) por (*trayn*·ta) se·*goon*·dos (30c) per (30) seconds.

Phone

Where's the nearest public phone?	¿Dónde está la cabina telefónica más cercana? *don*·de es·*ta* la ka·*bee*·na te·le·*fo*·nee·ka mas ser·*ka*·na
I want to make a (reverse-charge/collect) call to ...	Quiero hacer una llamada (a cobro revertido) a ... *kye*·ro a·*ser oo*·na ya·*ma*·da (a *ko*·bro re·ver·*tee*·do) a ...
I want to buy a phone card.	Quiero comprar una tarjeta telefónica. *kye*·ro kom·*prar oo*·na tar·*khe*·ta te·le·*fo*·nee·ka
I want to speak for (three) minutes.	Quiero hablar por (tres) minutos. *kye*·ro a·*blar* por (tres) mee·*noo*·tos
How much does a (three)-minute call cost?	¿Cuánto cuesta una llamada de (tres) minutos? *kwan*·to *kwes*·ta *oo*·na ya·*ma*·da de (tres) mee·*noo*·tos
How much does each extra minute cost?	¿Cuánto cuesta cada minuto extra? *kwan*·to *kwes*·ta *ka*·da mee·*noo*·to *eks*·tra
Q **What's your phone number?**	¿Cuál es su número de teléfono? kwal es soo *noo*·me·ro de te·*le*·fo·no
A **The number is ...**	El número es ... el *noo*·me·ro es ...
What's the area/country code for ...?	¿Cuál es el prefijo de ...? kwal es el pre·*fee*·kho de ...

It's engaged.	Está ocupada. es·*ta* o·koo·*pa*·da
The connection's bad.	Es mala conexión. es *ma*·la ko·nek·*syon*
I've been cut off.	Me han cortado (la comunicación). me an kor·*ta*·do (la ko·moo·nee·ka·*syon*)
Hello. (making a call)	¡Hola! *o*·la
Hello. (answering a call)	¿Diga? *dee*·ga
It's ... (identifying yourself)	Habla ... *a*·bla ...
Can I speak to ...?	¿Está ...? es·*ta* ...
Can I leave a message?	¿Puedo dejar un mensaje? *pwe*·do de·*khar* oon men·*sa*·khe

LISTEN FOR

¿De parte de quién?	de *par*·te de kyen Who's calling?
¿Con quién quiere hablar?	kon kyen *kye*·re a·*blar* Who do you want to speak to?
Lo siento, pero ahora no está.	lo *syen*·to *pe*·ro a·*o*·ra no es·*ta* I'm sorry he's/she's not here.
Lo siento, tiene el número equivocado.	lo *syen*·to *tye*·ne el *noo*·me·ro e·kee·vo·*ka*·do Sorry, wrong number.
Sí, aquí está.	see a·*kee* es·*ta* Yes, he/she is here.

Please tell him/her I called.	Dile/Dila que llamé, por favor. m/f *dee*·le/*dee*·la ke ya·*me* por fa·*vor*
I'll call back later.	Ya llamaré más tarde. ya ya·ma·*re* mas *tar*·de
I don't have a contact number.	No tengo número de contacto. no *ten*·go *noo*·me·ro de kon·*tak*·to

Post Office

I want to send a letter.	Quisiera enviar una carta. kee·*sye*·ra en·*vyar oo*·na *kar*·ta
I want to send a postcard.	Quisiera enviar una postal. kee·*sye*·ra en·*vyar oo*·na pos·*tal*

LOOK FOR

In Latin America dwellings may not be numbered and addresses are sometimes short descriptive passages. Be prepared to decipher an address such as this one:

Marirosa Ferrer Botero	Marirosa Ferrer Botero
la casa azul en	the blue house on
la esquina de	the corner of
Avenida de la Paz y	Avenida de la Paz and
Calle 12	12th Street
cerca de la farmacia	near the pharmacy
una manzana al norte	one block north
de la catedral	of the cathedral
Tegucigalpa	Tegucigalpa
Honduras	Honduras

LISTEN FOR

¿Adónde lo manda?	a·*don*·de lo *man*·da	Where are you sending it?
¿Por correo urgente o normal?	por ko·*re*·o oor·*khen*·te o nor·*mal*	By express or regular post?
correo m **aéreo**	ko·*re*·o a·e·re·o	airmail
correo m **certificado**	ko·*re*·o ser·tee·fee·*ka*·do	registered mail
declaración f **de aduana**	de·kla·ra·*syon* de a·*dwa*·na	customs declaration
por vía terrestre	por *vee*·a te·*res*·tre	by surface mail

I want to buy an envelope.	Quisiera comprar un sobre.	kee·*sye*·ra kom·*prar* oon *so*·bre
I want to buy stamps.	Quisiera comprar unos sellos.	kee·*sye*·ra kom·*prar* *oo*·nos *se*·yos
Please send it by airmail/ surface mail (to ...).	Por favor, mándelo por vía aérea/terrestre (a ...).	por fa·*vor* *man*·de·lo por *vee*·a a·e·re·a/te·*res*·tre (a ...)
It contains ...	Contiene ...	kon·*tye*·ne ...
Where's the poste restante section?	¿Dónde está la lista de correos?	*don*·de es·*ta* la *lees*·ta de ko·*re*·os
Is there any mail for me?	¿Hay alguna carta para mí?	ai al·*goo*·na *kar*·ta *pa*·ra mee

Money & Banking

KEY PHRASES

How much is it?	¿Cuánto cuesta?	*kwan*·to *kwes*·ta
What's the exchange rate?	¿Cuál es la tasa de cambio?	kwal es la *ta*·sa de *kam*·byo
Where's the nearest ATM?	¿Dónde está el cajero automático más cercano?	*don*·de es·*ta* el ka·*khe*·ro ow·to·*ma*·tee·ko mas ser·*ka*·no
I'd like to change money.	Me gustaría cambiar dinero.	me goos·ta·*ree*·ya kam·*byar* dee·*ne*·ro
Can I have smaller notes?	¿Me lo puede dar en billetes más pequeños?	me lo *pwe*·de dar en bee·*ye*·tes mas pe·*ke*·nyos

Paying the Bill

Q **How much is it?**	¿Cuánto cuesta? *kwan*·to *kwes*·ta
A **It's free.**	Es gratis. es *gra*·tees
A **It's ... (pesos).**	Cuesta ... (pesos). *kwes*·ta ... (*pe*·sos)
Can you write down the price?	¿Puede escribir el precio? *pwe*·de es·kree·*beer* el *pre*·syo

Do I need to pay upfront?	¿Hay que pagar por adelantado? ai ke pa·*gar* por a·de·lan·*ta*·do
Do you accept credit/debit cards?	¿Aceptan tarjetas de crédito/débito? a·*sep*·tan tar·*khe*·tas de *kre*·dee·to/*de*·bee·to
Do you accept travellers cheques?	¿Aceptan cheques de viajero? a·*sep*·tan *che*·kes de vya·*khe*·ro
I'd like a receipt, please.	Quisiera un recibo, por favor. kee·*sye*·ra oon re·*see*·bo por fa·*vor*
I'd like my change, please.	Quisiera mi cambio, por favor. kee·*sye*·ra mee *kam*·byo por fa·*vor*

LISTEN FOR

Su identificación, por favor.	soo ee·den·tee·fee·ka·*syon* por fa·*vor* Your ID, please.
Hay un problema con su cuenta.	ai oon pro·*ble*·ma kon soo *kwen*·ta There's a problem with your account.
No podemos hacer eso.	no po·*de*·mos a·*ser* *e*·so We can't do that.
¿Puede escribirlo?	*pwe*·de es·kree·*beer*·lo Could you write it down?
Por favor firme aquí.	por fa·*vor* *feer*·me a·*kee* Please sign here.

There's a mistake in the bill.	Hay un error en la cuenta. ai oon e·*ror* en la *kwen*·ta
I don't want to pay the full price.	No quiero pagar el precio íntegro. no *kye*·ro pa·*gar* el *pre*·syo *een*·te·gro

Banking

What time does the bank open?	¿A qué hora abre el banco? a ke *o*·ra *a*·bre el *ban*·ko
Where's the nearest ATM?	¿Dónde está el cajero automático más cercano? *don*·de es·*ta* el ka·*khe*·ro ow·to·*ma*·tee·ko mas ser·*ka*·no
Where's the nearest foreign exchange office?	¿Dónde está la oficina de cambio más cercana? *don*·de es·*ta* la o·fee·*see*·na de *kam*·byo mas ser·*ka*·na
Do you change money here?	¿Se cambia dinero aqui? se *kam*·bya dee·*ne*·ro a·*kee*
What's the exchange rate?	¿Cuál es la tasa de cambio? kwal es la *ta*·sa de *kam*·byo
What's the commission?	¿Cuál es la comisión? kwal es la ko·mee·*syon*
What's the charge for that?	¿Cuánto hay que pagar por eso? *kwan*·to ai ke pa·*gar* por e·so
The ATM took my card.	El cajero automático se ha tragado mi tarjeta. el ka·*khe*·ro ow·to·*ma*·tee·ko se a tra·*ga*·do mee tar·*khe*·ta
I've forgotten my PIN.	Me he olvidado del NPI. me e ol·vee·*da*·do del e·ne·pe·ee

Where can I ...?	¿Dónde puedo ...? *don*·de *pwe*·do ...
I'd like to ...	Me gustaría ... me goos·ta·*ree*·a ...

arrange a transfer	organizar una transferencia	or·ga·nee·*sar* *oo*·na trans·fe·*ren*·sya
cash a cheque	cobrar un cheque	ko·*brar* oon *che*·ke
change a travellers cheque	cambiar un cheque de viajero	kam·*byar* oon *che*·ke de vya·*khe*·ro
change money	cambiar dinero	kam·*byar* dee·*ne*·ro
get a cash advance	obtener un adelanto	ob·te·*ner* oon a·de·*lan*·to
use internet banking	usar la banca por internet	oo·*sar* la *ban*·ka por een·ter·*net*
withdraw money	sacar dinero	sa·*kar* dee·*ne*·ro

Can I use my credit card to withdraw money?	¿Puedo usar mi tarjeta de crédito para sacar dinero? *pwe*·do oo·*sar* mee tar·*khe*·ta de *kre*·dee·to *pa*·ra sa·*kar* dee·*ne*·ro
Can I have smaller notes?	¿Me lo puede dar en billetes más pequeños? me lo *pwe*·de dar en bee·*ye*·tes mas pe·*ke*·nyos
Has my money arrived yet?	¿Ya ha llegado mi dinero? ya a ye·*ga*·do mee dee·*ne*·ro
How long will it take to arrive?	¿Cuánto tiempo tardará en llegar? *kwan*·to *tyem*·po tar·da·*ra* en ye·*gar*

Business

KEY PHRASES

I'm attending a conference.	Asisto a un congreso.	a·*sees*·to a oon kon·*gre*·so
I have an appointment with ...	Tengo una cita con ...	*ten*·go *oo*·na *see*·ta kon ...
Can I have your business card?	¿Me dará su tarjeta de visita?	me da·*ra* soo tar·*khe*·ta de vee·*see*·ta

Where's the business centre?	¿Dónde está el servicio secretarial? *don*·de es·*ta* el ser·*vee*·syo se·kre·ta·*ryal*
Where's the conference?	¿Dónde está el congreso? *don*·de es·*ta* el kon·*gre*·so
Where's the meeting?	¿Dónde está la reunión? *don*·de es·*ta* la re·oo·*nyon*
I have an appointment with ...	Tengo una cita con ... *ten*·go *oo*·na *see*·ta kon ...
I'm attending a ...	Asisto a ... a·*sees*·to a ...

conference	un congreso	oon kon·*gre*·so
course	un curso	oon *koor*·so
meeting	una reunión	*oo*·na re·oo·*nyon*
trade fair	una feria de muestras	*oo*·na *fe*·rya de *mwes*·tras

I'm here with my colleagues.	Estoy aquí con mis colegas. es·*toy* a·*kee* kon mees ko·*le*·gas	
I'm alone.	Estoy solo/a. m/f es·*toy* *so*·lo/a	
I'm expecting a call.	Estoy esperando una llamada. es·*toy* es·pe·*ran*·do *oo*·na ya·*ma*·da	
I need ...	Necesito ... ne·se·*see*·to ...	

a computer	una computadora	*oo*·na kom·poo·ta·*do*·ra
a connection to the internet	una conexión al internet	*oo*·na ko·nek·*syon* al een·ter·*net*
an interpreter	un/una intérprete m/f	oon/*oo*·na een·*ter*·pre·te
more business cards	más tarjetas de visita	mas tar·*khe*·tas de vee·*see*·ta

Q **Can I have your business card?**	¿Me dará su tarjeta de visita? me da·*ra* soo tar·*khe*·ta de vee·*see*·ta
A **Here's my business card.**	Aquí tiene mi tarjeta de visita. a·*kee* *tye*·ne mee tar·*khe*·ta de vee·*see*·ta
Let me introduce you to my colleague.	¿Puedo presentarle a mi colega? *pwe*·do pre·sen·*tar*·le a mee ko·*le*·ga
That went very well.	Eso salió muy bien. e·so sa·*lyo* mooy byen
Shall we go for a drink/meal?	¿Vamos a tomar/comer algo? *va*·mos a to·*mar*/ko·*mer* *al*·go

Sightseeing

KEY PHRASES

I'd like a guide.	Quisiera un/ una guía. m/f	kee·*sye*·ra oon/ *oo*·na *gee*·a
Can I take photos?	¿Puedo sacar fotos?	*pwe*·do sa·*kar* *fo*·tos
When's the museum open?	¿A qué hora abre el museo?	a ke *o*·ra *a*·bre el moo·*se*·o
I'm interested in ...	Me interesa ...	me een·te·*re*·sa ...
When is the next tour?	¿A qué hora sale el próximo recorrido?	a ke *o*·ra *sa*·le el *prok*·see·mo re·ko·*ree*·do

I'd like to see ...	Me gustaría ver ... me goos·ta·*ree*·a ver ...
I'd like a/an ...	Quisiera ... kee·*sye*·ra ...

audio set	un equipo audio	oon e·*kee*·po *ow*·dyo
catalogue	un catálogo	oon ka·*ta*·lo·go
guide	un/una guía m/f	oon/*oo*·na *gee*·a
guidebook (in English)	una guía turística (en inglés)	*oo*·na *gee*·a too·*rees*·tee·ka (en een·*gles*)
(local) map	un mapa (de la zona)	oon *ma*·pa (de la *so*·na)

Do you have information on ... sights?	¿Tiene información sobre los lugares ... de interés? *tye*·ne een·for·ma·*syon so*·bre los loo·*ga*·res ... de een·te·*res*	

cultural	culturales	kool·too·*ra*·les
local	locales	lo·*ka*·les
religious	religiosos	re·lee·*khyo*·sos
unique	únicos	*oo*·nee·kos

What's that?	¿Qué es eso? ke es *e*·so
Who made it?	¿Quién lo hizo? kyen lo *ee*·so
How old is it?	¿De cuándo es? de *kwan*·do es
Could you take a photograph of me?	¿Me puede sacar una foto? me *pwe*·de sa·*kar oo*·na *fo*·to
Can I take photographs (of you)?	¿(Le/Te) Puedo sacar fotos? **pol/inf** (le/te) *pwe*·do sa·*kar fo*·tos
I'll send you the photograph.	Le/Te mandaré la foto. **pol/inf** le/te man·da·*re* la *fo*·to

Getting In

What time does it open/close?	¿A qué hora abre/cierra? a ke *o*·ra *a*·bre/*sye*·ra
What's the admission charge?	¿Cuánto cuesta la entrada? *kwan*·to *kwes*·ta la en·*tra*·da

Is there a discount for ...?	¿Hay descuentos para ...? ai des·*kwen*·tos *pa*·ra ...

children	niños	*nee*·nyos
groups	grupos	*groo*·pos
pensioners	pensionados; jubilados **(Arg)**	pen·syo·*na*·dos; khoo·bee·*la*·dos
students	estudiantes	es·too·*dyan*·tes

Galleries & Museums

When's the gallery open?	¿A qué hora abre la galería? a ke *o*·ra *a*·bre la ga·le·*ree*·a
When's the museum open?	¿A qué hora abre el museo? a ke *o*·ra *a*·bre el moo·*se*·o
Q **What kind of art are you interested in?**	¿Qué tipo de arte le/te interesa? **pol/inf** ke *tee*·po de *ar*·te le/te een·te·*re*·sa
A **I'm interested in ... art.**	Me interesa el arte ... me een·te·*re*·sa el *ar*·te ...
A **I like the works of ...**	Me gusta la obra de ... me *goos*·ta la *o*·bra de ...
Q **What's in the collection?**	¿Qué hay en la colección? ke ai en la ko·lek·*syon*
A **It's an exhibition of (pottery).**	Hay una exposición de (alfarería). ai *oo*·na ek·spo·see·*syon* de (al·fa·re·*ree*·a)
Q **What do you think of ...?**	¿Qué piensa/piensas de ...? **pol/inf** ke *pyen*·sa/*pyen*·sas de ...
A **It reminds me of ...**	Me recuerda ... me re·*kwer*·da ...

¿Qué es eso?
ke es *e*·so
What's that?

... art — arte ... — *ar*·te ...

Aztec	azteca	as·*te*·ka
graphic	gráfico	*gra*·fee·ko
Inca	inca	*een*·ka
Mayan	maya	*ma*·ya
pre-Columbian	precolombino	pre·ko·lom·*bee*·no

Tours

Can you recommend a tour?
¿Puede recomendar algún recorrido?
pwe·de re·ko·men·*dar* al·*goon* re·ko·*ree*·do

Can you recommend a boat trip?	¿Puede recomendar algún paseo en barca? *pwe*·de re·ko·men·*dar* al·*goon* pa·*se*·o en *bar*·ka
When's the next day trip?	¿Cuándo es la próxima excursión de un día? *kwan*·do es la *prok*·see·ma eks·koor·*syon* de oon *dee*·a
When's the next tour?	¿Cuándo es el próximo recorrido? *kwan*·do es el *prok*·see·mo re·ko·*ree*·do
Is ... included?	¿Incluye ...? een·*kloo*·ye ...

accommodation	alojamiento	a·lo·kha·*myen*·to
equipment	equipo	e·*kee*·po
food	comida	ko·*mee*·da
transport	transporte	trans·*por*·te

Can we hire a (local) guide?	¿Podemos alquilar un guía (local)? po·*de*·mos al·kee·*lar* oon *gee*·a (lo·*kal*)
How long is the tour?	¿Cuánto dura el recorrido? *kwan*·to *doo*·ra el re·ko·*ree*·do
What time should I be back?	¿A qué hora tengo que volver? a ke *o*·ra *ten*·go ke vol·*ver*
The guide will pay.	El guía va a pagar. el *gee*·a va a pa·*gar*
I'm with them.	Voy con ellos. voy kon *e*·yos
I've lost my group.	He perdido mi grupo. e per·*dee*·do mee *groo*·po

Senior & Disabled Travellers

KEY PHRASES

I need assistance.	Necesito asistencia.	ne·se·*see*·to a·sees·*ten*·sya
Is there wheelchair access?	¿Hay acceso para silla de ruedas?	ai ak·*se*·so *pa*·ra *see*·ya de *rwe*·das
Are there toilets for people with a disablity?	¿Hay baños para discapacitados?	ai *ba*·nyos *pa*·ra dees·ka·pa·see·*ta*·dos

I have a disability.	Soy discapacitado/a. m/f soy dees·ka·pa·see·*ta*·do/a
I need assistance.	Necesito asistencia. ne·se·*see*·to a·sees·*ten*·sya
What services do you have for people with a disability?	¿Qué servicios tienen para discapacitados? ke ser·*vee*·syos *tye*·nen *pa*·ra dees·ka·pa·see·*ta*·dos
Is there wheelchair access?	¿Hay acceso para silla de ruedas? ai ak·*se*·so *pa*·ra *see*·ya de *rwe*·das
Is there a lift?	¿Hay ascensor? ai a·sen·*sor*
How many steps are there?	¿Cuántos escalones hay? *kwan*·tos es·ka·*lo*·nes ai

How wide is the entrance?	¿Cuánto es de ancha la entrada? *kwan*·to es de *an*·cha la en·*tra*·da
Are guide dogs permitted?	¿Se permite la entrada a los perros guía? se per·*mee*·te la en·*tra*·da a los *pe*·ros *gee*·a
Are there toilets for people with a disablity?	¿Hay baños para discapacitados? ai *ba*·nyos *pa*·ra dees·ka·pa·see·*ta*·dos
Is there somewhere I can sit down?	¿Hay algún sitio dónde me pueda sentar? ai al·*goon see*·tyo *don*·de me *pwe*·da sen·*tar*
Could you call me a taxi for the disabled, please?	¿Me podría llamar a un taxi para discapacitados? me po·*dree*·a ya·*mar* a oon *tak*·see *pa*·ra dees·ka·pa·see·*ta*·dos
Could you help me cross this street?	¿Me puede ayudar a cruzar la calle? me *pwe*·de a·yoo·*dar* a kroo·*sar* la *ka*·ye
disabled person	persona **f** discapacitada per·*so*·na dees·ka·pa·see·*ta*·da
guide dog	perro **m** guía *pe*·ro *gee*·a
ramp	rampa **f** *ram*·pa
space (to move around)	espacio **m** (para moverse) es·*pa*·syo (*pa*·ra mo·*ver*·se)
wheelchair	silla **f** de ruedas *see*·ya de *rwe*·das

Travel with Children

KEY PHRASES

Are children allowed?	¿Se admiten niños?	se ad·*mee*·ten *nee*·nyos
Is there a family discount?	¿Hay un descuento familiar?	ai oon des·*kwen*·to fa·mee·*lyar*
Is there a baby change room?	¿Hay una sala en la que pueda cambiarle el pañal al bebé?	ai *oo*·na *sa*·la en la ke *pwe*·da kam·*byar*·le el pa·*nyal* al be·*be*

Are children allowed?	¿Se admiten niños? se ad·*mee*·ten *nee*·nyos
Is this suitable for (two)-year-old children?	¿Es apto para niños de (dos) años? es *ap*·to *pa*·ra *nee*·nyos de (dos) *a*·nyos
I need a ...	Necesito ... ne·se·*see*·to ...

baby seat	un asiento de seguridad para bebés	oon a·*syen*·to de se·goo·ree·*da* *pa*·ra be·*bes*
booster seat	un asiento de seguridad para niños	oon a·*syen*·to de se·goo·ree·*da* pa·ra *nee*·nyos
potty	una bacinica; una pelela **(SAm)**	*oo*·na ba·see·*nee*·ka; *oo*·na pe·*le*·la
stroller	un cochecito	oon ko·che·*see*·to

Do you mind if I breastfeed here?	¿Le molesta que dé de pecho aquí?	le mo·*les*·ta ke de de *pe*·cho a·*kee*
Is there a/an ...?	¿Hay ...?	ai ...

baby change room	una sala en la que pueda cambiarle el pañal al bebé	*oo*·na *sa*·la en la ke *pwe*·da kam·*byar*·le el pa·*nyal* al be·*be*
(English-speaking) babysitter	niñera (de habla inglesa)	nee·*nye*·ra (de *a*·bla een·*gle*·sa)
child-minding service	servicio de cuidado de niños	ser·*vee*·syo de kwee·*da*·do de *nee*·nyos
children's menu	menú infantil	me·*noo* een·fan·*teel*
creche	guardería	gwar·de·*ree*·a
family discount	descuento familiar	des·*kwen*·to fa·mee·*lyar*
highchair	trona	*tro*·na
park	un parque	oon *par*·ke
playground nearby	un parque infantil cercano	oon *par*·ke een·fan·*teel* ser·*ka*·no
theme park	un parque de atracciones	oon *par*·ke de a·trak·*syo*·nes
toyshop	una juguetería	*oo*·na khoo·ge·te·*ree*·a

If your child is sick, see **health** (p156). For talking with children, see **meeting people** (p112).

Social

Meeting People

KEY PHRASES

My name is ...	Me llamo ...	me *ya*·mo ...
I'm from ...	Soy de ...	soy de ...
I work in ...	Trabajo en ...	tra·*ba*·kho en ...
I'm ... years old.	Tengo ... años.	*ten*·go ... *a*·nyos
And you?	¿Y Usted/tú? **pol/inf**	ee oos·*te*/too

Basics

Yes.	Sí. see
No.	No. no
Please.	Por favor. por fa·*vor*
Thank you (very much).	(Muchas) Gracias. (*moo*·chas) *gra*·syas
You're welcome.	De nada. de *na*·da Con mucho gusto. **(CAm)** kon *moo*·cho *goo*·sto
Sorry. (condolence)	Lo siento. lo *syen*·to
Sorry. (apology)	Perdón. per·*don*
Excuse me. (regret)	Perdón. per·*don*

Excuse me. (attention/apology)	Disculpe. dees·*kool*·pe Con permiso. **(CAm)** kon per·*mee*·so

Greetings

Hello./Hi.	Hola. *o*·la ¿Qué hubo? **(Chi)** ke *oo*·bo
Good day.	Buen día. bwen *dee*·a
Good morning.	Buenos días. *bwe*·nos *dee*·as
Good afternoon. (until 8pm)	Buenas tardes. *bwe*·nas *tar*·des
Good evening/night.	Buenas noches. *bwe*·nas *no*·ches
See you later.	Hasta luego. *as*·ta *lwe*·go
Goodbye.	¡Adiós! a·*dyos*
Bye.	Chao./Chaucito. chow/chow·*see*·to
Q How are you?	¿Cómo está? **sg pol** *ko*·mo es·*ta* ¿Cómo estás? **sg inf** *ko*·mo es·*tas* ¿Cómo están? **pl** *ko*·mo es·*tan*
A Fine, thank you. And you?	Bien, gracias. ¿Y Usted/tú? **pol/inf** byen *gra*·syas ee oos·*te*/too

Q What's your name?	¿Cómo se llama Usted? **pol** ko·mo se *ya*·ma oos·*te* ¿Cómo te llamas? **inf** *ko*·mo te *ya*·mas
A My name is ...	Me llamo ... me *ya*·mo ...
I'd like to introduce you to ...	Quisiera presentarle/te a ... **pol/inf** kee·*sye*·ra pre·sen·*tar*·le/te a ...

This is ...	Éste/Ésta es ... **m/f**	*es*·te/*es*·ta es ...

I'm pleased to meet you.	Mucho gusto. *moo*·cho *goos*·to

Titles & Addressing People

Women are mostly addressed as *Señora* se·*nyo*·ra regardless of age and marital status, although some older unmarried women may prefer to be called *Señorita* se·nyo·*ree*·ta. Men are usually addressed as *Señor* se·*nyor*. Professional titles are important and should be used before the surname when addressing someone directly.

Mr	Señor se·*nyor*
Ms/Mrs	Señora se·*nyo*·ra
Miss	Señorita se·nyo·*ree*·ta
Doctor (holder of a PhD or medical doctor)	Doctor(a) **m/f** dok·*tor*/dok·*to*·ra
Graduate	Licenciado/a **m/f** lee·sen·*sya*·do/a
Master (teacher or skilled musician/craftsman)	Maestro/a **m/f** ma·*es*·tro/a

Making Conversation

Do you live here?	¿Vive/Vives aquí? **pol/inf** *vee*·ve/*vee*·ves a·*kee*
Where are you going?	¿Adónde va/vas? **pol/inf** a·*don*·de va/vas
What are you doing?	¿Qué hace/haces? **pol/inf** *ke a*·se/*a*·ses
Are you waiting (for a bus)?	¿Está/Estás esperando (un autobús)? **pol/inf** es·*ta*/es·*tas* es·pe·*ran*·do (oon ow·to·*boos*)
Can I have a light?	¿Tiene/Tienes fuego? **pol/inf** *tye*·ne/*tye*·nes *fwe*·go
What's this called?	¿Cómo se llama esto? *ko*·mo se *ya*·ma *es*·to
What a beautiful baby!	¡Qué niño/a más lindo/a! **m/f** ke *nee*·nyo/a mas *leen*·do/a
That's (beautiful), isn't it?	Qué (precioso), ¿no? ke (pre·*syo*·so) no

LANGUAGE TIP

Polite & Informal

Spanish has two forms for the singular 'you'. With people you know well, your peers and children, use the informal form *tú* too. For addressing strangers, older people or people you've just met, use the polite form *Usted* oos·*te*. When your new-found friends feel it's time to switch to *tú*, they may say:

Let's use the 'tú' form.	Hablemos de tú.	a·*ble*·mos de too

See also **personal pronouns** in the **grammar** chapter (p21).

Q	**Do you like it here?**	¿Le/Te gusta estar aquí? **pol/inf** le/te *goos*·ta es·*tar* a·*kee*
A	**I love it here.**	Me encanta estar aquí. me en·*kan*·ta es·*tar* a·*kee*
Q	**How long are you here for?**	¿Cuánto tiempo se va a quedar? **pol** *kwan*·to *tyem*·po se va a ke·*dar* ¿Cuánto tiempo te vas a quedar? **inf** *kwan*·to *tyem*·po te vas a ke·*dar*
A	**I'm here for (four) weeks/days.**	Estoy aquí por (cuatro) semanas/días. es·*toy* a·*kee* por (*kwa*·tro) se·*ma*·nas/*dee*·as
Q	**Are you here on holiday?**	¿Está/Estás aquí de vacaciones? **pol/inf** es·*ta*/es·*tas* a·*kee* de va·ka·*syo*·nes
A	**I'm here ...**	Estoy aquí ... es·*toy* a·*kee* ...

for a holiday	de vacaciones	de va·ka·*syo*·nes
on business	en viaje de negocios	en *vya*·khe de ne·*go*·syos
to study	estudiando	es·too·*dyan*·do
with my family	con mi familia	kon mee fa·*mee*·lya
with my partner	con mi pareja **m&f**	kon mee pa·*re*·kha

Nationalities

Where are you from? (Q)	¿De dónde es/eres? **pol/inf** de *don*·de es/*e*·res
I'm from ... (A)	Soy de ... soy de ...

Australia	Australia	ow·*stra*·lya
Germany	Alemania	a·le·*ma*·nya
Scotland	Escocia	es·*ko*·sya
the USA	los Estados Unidos	los es·*ta*·dos oo·*nee*·dos

For more countries, see the **dictionary**.

Age

How old are you? (Q)	¿Cuántos años tiene/tienes? **pol/inf** *kwan*·tos *a*·nyos *tye*·ne/*tye*·nes
I'm ... years old. (A)	Tengo ... años. *ten*·go ... *a*·nyos
How old is your daughter? (Q)	¿Cuántos años tiene su/tu hija? **pol/inf** *kwan*·tos *a*·nyos tye·ne soo/too *ee*·kha
How old is your son? (Q)	¿Cuántos años tiene su/tu hijo? **pol/inf** *kwan*·tos *a*·nyos *tye*·ne soo/too *ee*·kho
He/She is ... years old. (A)	Tiene ... años. *tye*·ne ... *a*·nyos
Too old!	¡Demasiado viejo/a! **m/f** de·ma·*sya*·do *vye*·kho/a

LISTEN FOR

¡De ningún modo!	de neen·*goon mo*·do	No way!
¡Eh, tú!	e too	Hey!
¡Escucha (esto)!	es·*koo*·cha (*es*·to)	Listen (to this)!
Está bien.	es·*ta* byen	It's OK.
Estoy bien.	es·*toy* byen	I'm OK.
Macanudo. (Arg)	ma·ka·*noo*·do	Sure.
¡Mira!	*mee*·ra	Look!
¡Qué bárbaro!	ke *bar*·ba·ro	How cool!
¿Qué onda?	ke *on*·da	What's up?
¿Qué pasa?	ke *pa*·sa	What's up?
¿Qué pasó?	ke pa·*so*	What happened?
Quizás.	kee·*sas*	Maybe.
¡Se pasa! (Arg)	se *pa*·sa	How cool!
Te estoy cargando. (Arg)	te es·*toy* kar·*gan*·do	Just joking.
Te estoy tomando el pelo.	te es·*toy* to·*man*·do el *pe*·lo	Just joking.

I'm younger than I look. Soy más joven de lo que parezco.
soy mas *kho*·ven de lo ke pa·*res*·ko

For your age, see **numbers & amounts** (p32).

Occupations & Studies

Q What's your occupation? ¿A qué se dedica? pol
a ke se de·*dee*·ka
¿A qué te dedicas? inf
a ke te de·*dee*·kas

A I work in education. Trabajo en enseñanza.
tra·*ba*·kho en en·se·*nyan*·sa

A	**I work in hospitality.**	Trabajo en hostelería. tra·*ba*·kho en os·te·le·*ree*·a
A	**I'm self-employed.**	Soy trabajador/trabajadora autónomo/a. **m/f** soy tra·ba·kha·*dor*/ tra·ba·kha·*do*·ra ow·*to*·no·mo/a
A	**I'm retired.**	Estoy jubilado/a. **m/f** es·*toy* khoo·bee·*la*·do/a
A	**I'm unemployed.**	Estoy desempleado/a. **m/f** es·*toy* des·em·ple·*a*·do/a
Q	**What are you studying?**	¿Qué estudia/estudias? **pol/inf** ke es·*too*·dya/es·*too*·dyas
A	**I'm studying business.**	Estudio negocios. es·*too*·dyo ne·*go*·syos
A	**I'm studying languages.**	Estudio idiomas. es·*too*·dyo ee·*dyo*·mas
A	**I'm studying science.**	Estudio ciencias. es·*too*·dyo *syen*·syas

For more occupations and studies, see the **dictionary**.

Family

Q	**Do you have (a brother)?**	¿Tiene/Tienes (un hermano)? **pol/inf** *tye*·ne/*tye*·nes (oon er·*ma*·no)
A	**I have (a partner).**	Tengo (pareja). *ten*·go (pa·*re*·kha)
Q	**Do you live with (your family)?**	¿Vive/Vives con (su/tu familia)? **pol/inf** *vee*·ve/*vee*·ves kon (soo/too fa·*mee*·lya)
A	**I live with (my sister).**	Vivo con (mi hermana). *vee*·vo kon (mee er·*ma*·na)

Q **Are you married?**	¿Está casado/a? **m/f pol** es·*ta* ka·*sa*·do/a ¿Estás casado/a? **m/f inf** es·*tas* ka·*sa*·do/a
A **I live with someone.**	Vivo con alguien. *vee*·vo kon *al*·gyen
A **I'm single.**	Soy soltero/a. **m/f** soy sol·*te*·ro/a
A **I'm married.**	Estoy casado/a. **m/f** es·*toy* ka·*sa*·do/a
A **I'm separated.**	Estoy separado/a. **m/f** es·*toy* se·pa·*ra*·do/a

For more kinship terms, see the **dictionary**.

Talking with Children

When's your birthday?	¿Cuándo es tu cumpleaños? *kwan*·do es too koom·ple·*a*·nyos
What grade are you in?	¿En qué grado estás? en ke *gra*·do es·*tas*
Do you like school?	¿Te gusta el colegio? te *goos*·ta el ko·*le*·khyo
Do you like sport?	¿Te gusta el deporte? te *goos*·ta el de·*por*·te
What do you do after school?	¿Qué haces después del colegio? ke *a*·ses des·*pwes* del ko·*le*·khyo
Do you learn English?	¿Aprendes inglés? a·*pren*·des een·*gles*
Tell me how to play.	Dime cómo se juega. *dee*·me *ko*·mo se *khwe*·ga
Well done!	¡Muy bien! mooy byen

Farewells

Tomorrow is my last day here.	Mañana es mi último día aquí. ma·*nya*·na es mee *ool*·tee·mo *dee*·a a·*kee*
It's been great meeting you.	Me ha encantado conocerte. me a en·kan·*ta*·do ko·no·*ser*·te
I'll miss you.	Te voy a echar de menos. te voy a e·*char* de *me*·nos
Keep in touch!	¡Nos mantendremos en contacto! nos man·ten·*dre*·mos en kon·*tak*·to

Me encanta estar aquí.
me en·kan·ta es·tar a·kee
I love it here.

Q What's your ...?	¿Cuál es tu ...? kwal es too ...	
A Here's my ...	Éste/Ésta es mi ... m/f *es*·te/*es*·ta es mee ...	

address	dirección f	dee·rek·*syon*
email address	dirección f de email	dee·rek·*syon* de *ee*·mayl
mobile number	número m de móvil	*noo*·me·ro de *mo*·veel
phone number	número m de teléfono	*noo*·mero de te·*le*·fo·no

If you ever visit (Scotland) come and visit us.	Si algún día visitas (Escocia), ven a vernos. see al·*goon dee*·a vee·*see*·tas (es·*ko*·sya) ven a *ver*·nos
If you ever visit (the USA), you can stay with me.	Si algún día visitas (los Estados Unidos), te puedes quedar conmigo. see al·*goon dee*·a vee·*see*·tas (los es·*ta*·dos oo·*nee*·dos) te *pwe*·des ke·*dar* kon·*mee*·go

CULTURE TIP

Body Language

Personal space boundaries vary from culture to culture, and in Latin America they're set closer than in Anglo-Saxon countries. You'll probably find that when you're talking with someone they stand closer to you than you're used to, and may touch you on the arm or shoulder. Acquaintances always greet with a *beso be*·so (kiss), and good friends often add an *abrazo* a·*bra*·so (hug). It's also fairly common to see people of the same sex walking down the street arm-in-arm.

CULTURE TIP

Melting Pot

Latin American Spanish reflects the region's rich ethnic mix. One example of this are the words coined to refer to people with respect to their heritage. These terms aren't racially loaded labels, and people may use them to refer to themselves and their background.

criollo/a m/f kree·o·yo/a
person born in Latin America of Spanish ancestry. On the Caribbean Coast, a person of mixed African and European ancestry.

ladino/a m/f la·*dee*·no/a
Spanish-speaking person of mixed Indian and European ancestry

mestizo/a m/f mes·*tee*·so/a
person of mixed ancestry (usually Spanish and Indian)

zambo/a m/f *sam*·bo/a
person of mixed African and Indian ancestry

The term *indio/a* m/f *een*·dyo/a (Indian) can be offensive to indigenous people, so use *indígena* m&f een·*dee*·khe·na (indigenous person) instead.

I want to come and visit you.	Quiero venir a visitarte. *kye*·ro ve·*neer* a vee·see·*tar*·te
I'll send you copies of the photos.	Te enviaré copias de las fotos. te en·vya·*re ko*·pyas de las *fo*·tos

Interests

KEY PHRASES

What do you do in your spare time?	¿Qué te gusta hacer en tu tiempo libre?	ke te *goos*·ta a·*ser* en too *tyem*·po *lee*·bre
Do you like ...?	¿Te gusta/gustan ...? sg/pl	te *goos*·ta/*goos*·tan ...
I (don't) like ...	(No) Me gusta/gustan ... sg/pl	(no) me *goos*·ta/*goos*·tan ...

Common Interests

What do you do in your spare time?	¿Qué te gusta hacer en tu tiempo libre? ke te *goos*·ta a·*ser* en too *tyem*·po *lee*·bre
Q **Do you like ...?**	¿Te gusta/gustan ...? sg/pl te *goos*·ta/*goos*·tan ...
A **I (don't) like ...**	(No) Me gusta/gustan ... sg/pl (no) me *goos*·ta/*goos*·tan ...

board games	los juegos pl de tablero	los *khwe*·gos de ta·*ble*·ro
cooking	cocinar sg	ko·see·*nar*
films	el cine sg	el *see*·ne
travelling	viajar sg	vya·*khar*

For more hobbies and types of sports, see **sports** (p139), and the **dictionary**.

LANGUAGE TIP

Likes & Dislikes

In Spanish, in order to say you like something, you say *me gusta* me *goos*·ta (lit: me it-pleases). If what you're referring to is plural, use *me gustan* me *goos*·tan (lit: me they-please). If you're referring to an activity, eg cooking or travelling, use *me gusta* followed by the verb. You can negate any of these sentences by adding *no* no (not) to the beginning of the phrase.

I like this song.	Me gusta esta canción. me *goos*·ta *es*·ta kan·*syon*
I like soap operas.	Me gustan las telenovelas. me *goos*·tan las te·le·no·*ve*·las
I don't like dancing.	No me gusta bailar. no me *goos*·ta bai·*lar*

Music

Do you like to ...?	¿Te gusta ...? te *goos*·ta ...

dance	bailar	bai·*lar*
go to concerts	ir a conciertos	eer a kon·*syer*·tos
listen to music	escuchar música	es·koo·*char* *moo*·see·ka
play an instrument	tocar un instrumento	to·*kar* oon een·stroo·*men*·to
sing	cantar	kan·*tar*

Which bands do you like?	¿Qué grupos te gustan? ke *groo*·pos te *goos*·tan
Which music do you like?	¿Qué música te gusta? ke *moo*·see·ka te *goos*·ta

... music	música ... *moo*·see·ka ...

classical	clásica	*kla*·see·ka
electronic	electrónica	e·lek·*tro*·nee·ka
traditional	folclórica	fol·*klo*·ree·ka
world	étnica	*et*·nee·ka

Planning to go to a concert? See **buying tickets** (p42) and **going out** (p126).

Cinema & Theatre

I feel like going to a ...	Tengo ganas de ir a ... *ten*·go *ga*·nas de eer a ...

ballet	un ballet	oon ba·*le*
comedy	una comedia	*oo*·na ko·*me*·dya
film	una película	*oo*·na pe·*lee*·koo·la
play	una obra de teatro	*oo*·na *o*·bra de te·*a*·tro

What's showing at the cinema (tonight)?	¿Qué película dan en el cine (esta noche)? ke pe·*lee*·koo·la dan en el *see*·ne (*es*·ta *no*·che)
Is it in English/Spanish?	¿Es en inglés/castellano? es en een·*gles*/kas·te·*ya*·no
Does it have (English) subtitles?	¿Tiene subtítulos (en inglés)? *tye*·ne soob·*tee*·too·los (en een·*gles*)
Are those seats taken?	¿Están libres estos asientos? es·*tan lee*·bres *es*·tos a·*syen*·tos

Have you seen ...?	¿Has visto ...? as *vees*·to ...
Q **Who's in it?**	¿Quién actúa? kyen ak·*too*·a
A **It stars ...**	Actúa ... ak·*too*·a ...
Q **Did you like (the film)?**	Te gustó (la película)? te goos·*to* (la pe·*lee*·koo·la)
A **I thought it was crap.**	Pienso que fue una porquería. *pyen*·so ke fwe *oo*·na por·ke·*ree*·a
A **I thought it was excellent.**	Pienso que fue excelente. *pyen*·so ke fwe ek·se·*len*·te
animated films	películas **f pl** de dibujos animados pe·*lee*·koo·las de dee·*boo*·khos a·nee·*ma*·dos
comedies	comedias **f pl** ko·*me*·dyas
documentaries	documentales **m pl** do·koo·men·*ta*·les
film noir	cine **m** negro *see*·ne *ne*·gro
horror movies	cine **m** de terror *see*·ne de te·*ror*
Latin American cinema	cine **m** latinoamericano *see*·ne la·tee·no·a·me·ree·*ka*·no
sci-fi	cine **m** de ciencia ficción *see*·ne de *syen*·sya feek·*syon*
short films	cortos **m pl** *kor*·tos
thrillers	cine **m** de suspenso *see*·ne de soos·*pen*·so

Reading

Q What kind of books do you read?	¿Qué tipo de libros lees? ke *tee*·po de *lee*·bros *le*·es
Q Have you read ...?	¿Has leído a ...? as le·*ee*·do a ...
A I often read ...	Suelo leer ... *swe*·lo le·*er* ...
A I'm reading ...	Estoy leyendo ... es·*toy* le·*yen*·do ...
Q Which Latin American author do you recommend?	¿Qué autor latinoamericano recomiendas? ke ow·*tor* la·tee·no·a·me·ree·*ka*·no re·ko·*myen*·das
A I'd recommend ...	Recomiendo a ... re·ko·*myen*·do a ...
Where can I exchange books?	¿Dónde puedo cambiar libros? *don*·de *pwe*·do kam·*byar* *lee*·bros

For more on books, see **shopping** (p76).

Volunteering

I'd like to volunteer my skills.	Me gustaría ser voluntario. me goos·ta·*ree*·a ser vo·loon·*ta*·ryo
Are there any volunteer programs available in the area?	¿Hay programas para voluntarios en esta zona? ai pro·*gra*·mas *pa*·ra vo·loon·*ta*·ryos en *es*·ta *so*·na

Feelings & Opinions

KEY PHRASES

Are you ...?	¿Está/ Estás ...? pol/inf ¿Tiene/ Tienes ...? pol/inf	es·*ta*/ es·*tas* ... *tye*·ne/ *tye*·nes ...
I'm (not) ...	(No) Estoy ... (No) Tengo ...	(no) es·*toy* ... (no) *ten*·go ...
What did you think of it?	¿Qué pensó/ pensaste de eso? pol/inf	ke pen·*so*/ pen·*sas*·te de *e*·so
I thought it was OK.	Pienso que fue bien.	*pyen*·so ke fwe byen
How do people feel about ...?	¿Cómo se siente la gente con respecto a ...?	*ko*·mo se *syen*·te la *khen*·te kon res·*pek*·to a ...

Feelings

In Spanish feelings are described with either nouns or adjectives: the nouns use 'have' (eg 'I have hunger') and the adjectives use 'be' (as in English).

Are you (hungry)?	¿Tiene/Tienes (hambre)? pol/inf *tye*·ne/*tye*·nes (*am*·bre)
I'm (cold).	Tengo (frío). *ten*·go (*free*·o)
I'm not (hot).	No tengo (calor). no *ten*·go (ka·*lor*)

Are you (tired)?	¿Está (cansado/a)? **m/f pol** es·*ta* kan·*sa*·do/a
Are you (ready)?	¿Estás (listo/a)? **m/f inf** es·*tas* *lis*·to/a
I'm (annoyed).	Estoy (enojado/a). **m/f** es·*toy* (e·no·*kha*·do/a)
I'm not (embarrassed).	No estoy (avergonzado/a). **m/f** no es·*toy* (a·ver·gon·*sa*·do/a)
I'm a little (sad).	Estoy un poco (triste). es·*toy* oon *po*·ko (*trees*·te)
I'm quite (disappointed).	Estoy bastante (decepcionado/a). **m/f** es·*toy* bas·*tan*·te (de·sep·syo·*na*·do/a)

Opinions

Q **Did you like it?**	¿Le/Te gustó? **pol/inf** le/te goos·*to*
Q **What did you think of it?**	¿Qué pensó/pensaste de eso? **pol/inf** ke pen·*so*/pen·*sas*·te de *e*·so
A **I thought it was ...**	Pienso que fue ... *pyen*·so ke fwe ...
A **It's ...**	Es ... es ...

beautiful	bonito/a **m/f**	bo·*nee*·to/a
bizarre	raro/a **m/f**	*ra*·ro/a
crap	una porquería	*oo*·na por·ke·*ree*·ya
entertaining	entretenido/a **m/f**	en·tre·te·*nee*·do/a
excellent	fantástico/a **m/f**	fan·*tas*·tee·ko/a

Es fantástico.
es fan·tas·tee·ko
It's excellent.
Roland E-15

Politics & Social Issues

Q **Who do you vote for?**	¿A quién vota/votas? **pol/inf** a kyen *vo*·ta/*vo*·tas	
A **I support the ... party.**	Apoyo al partido ... a·*po*·yo al par·*tee*·do ...	

communist	comunista	ko·moo·*nees*·ta
conservative	conservador	kon·ser·va·*dor*
green	verde	*ver*·de
labour	laborista	la·bo·*rees*·ta
liberal	progresista	pro·gre·*sees*·ta
social democratic	social-demócrata	so·syal·de·*mo*·kra·ta
socialist	socialista	so·sya·*lees*·ta

LISTEN FOR

¡Anda ya!	*an*·da ya	In your dreams!
¡Eso no es verdad!	e·so no es ver·*da*	That's not true!
¡Exactamente!	ek·sak·ta·*men*·te	Exactly!
¡Por supuesto!	por soo·*pwes*·to	Absolutely!
¡Qué interesante!	ke een·te·re·*san*·te	How interesting!

Q Do you agree with it?	¿Está/Estás de acuerdo con eso? **pol/inf** es·*ta*/es·*tas* de a·*kwer*·do kon *e*·so
A I (don't) agree with ...	(No) Estoy de acuerdo con ... (no) es·*toy* de a·*kwer*·do kon ...
How do people feel about ...?	¿Cómo se siente la gente con respecto a ...? *ko*·mo se *syen*·te la *khen*·te kon res·*pek*·to a ...
Are you in favour of ...?	¿Está/Estás a favor de ...? **pol/inf** es·*ta*/es·*tas* a fa·*vor* de ...
Are you against ...?	¿Está/Estás en contra de ...? **pol/inf** es·*ta*/es·*tas* en *kon*·tra de ...
drugs	drogas **f pl** *dro*·gas
immigration	inmigración **f** een·mee·gra·*syon*
the economy	economía **f** e·ko·no·*mee*·a
the environment	medio **m** ambiente *me*·dyo am·*byen*·te

CULTURE TIP

Latin American Place Names

Many Latin American place names are linked to historical events. *Argentina* comes from the Latin *argentum* 'silver' allegedly because the first Europeans to arrive observed the indigenous people wearing silver jewellery. *Bolivia* is named after Simón Bolívar, the famous revolutionary general who helped liberate many Latin American countries from Spanish rule, then became Bolivia's first president. *Costa Rica* means 'rich coast' and was named by Christopher Columbus for the precious metals that the land was expected to yield. *Honduras* means 'depths' and was named by Columbus for the deep waters off the country's north coast. *Colombia* was named after Columbus, though not until the 19th century.

The Environment

Is there a/an (environmental) problem here?	¿Aquí hay un problema (con el medio ambiente)? a·*kee* ai oon pro·*ble*·ma (kon el *me*·dyo am·*byen*·te)
Is this a protected forest/park?	¿Es este bosque/parque protegido? es *es*·te *bos*·ke/*par*·ke pro·te·*khee*·do
Is this a protected species?	¿Es esta especie protegida? es *es*·ta es·*pe*·sye pro·te·*khee*·da
Where can I recycle this?	¿Dónde puedo reciclar ésto? *don*·de *pwe*·do re·see·*klar* *es*·to
pollution	contaminación **f** kon·ta·mee·na·*syon*
water supply	suministro **m** de agua soo·mee·*nees*·tro de *a*·gwa

Going Out

KEY PHRASES

What's on tonight?	¿Qué hay esta noche?	ke ai *es*·ta *no*·che
Where are the clubs?	¿Dónde hay clubs nocturnos?	*don*·de ai kloobs nok·*toor*·nos
Would you like to go for a coffee?	¿Te/Les gustaría ir a tomar un café? **sg/pl**	te/les goos·ta·*ree*·a eer a to·*mar* oon ka·*fe*
What time shall we meet?	¿A qué hora quedamos?	a ke o·ra ke·*da*·mos
Where will we meet?	¿Dónde quedamos?	*don*·de ke·*da*·mos

Where to Go

What's there to do in the evenings?	¿Qué se puede hacer por las noches? ke se *pwe*·de a·*ser* por las *no*·ches
What's on ...?	¿Qué hay ...? ke ai ...

locally	en la zona	en la *so*·na
this weekend	este fin de semana	*es*·te feen de se·*ma*·na
today	hoy	oy
tonight	esta noche	*es*·ta *no*·che

Where are the ...?	¿Dónde hay ...? *don*·de ai ...

clubs	clubs nocturnos	kloobs nok·*toor*·nos
gay venues	lugares gay	loo·*ga*·res gay
places to eat	lugares donde comer	loo·*ga*·res *don*·de ko·*mer*
pubs	bares	*ba*·res

Is there a local entertainment guide?	¿Hay una guía de espectáculos de la zona? ai *oo*·na *gee*·a de es·pek·*ta*·koo·los de la *so*·na
What's the cover charge?	¿Cuánto cuesta entrar? *kwan*·to *kwes*·ta en·*trar*
I feel like going to ...	Tengo ganas de ir ... *ten*·go *ga*·nas de eer ...

a bar	a un bar	a oon bar
a cafe	a una cafetería	a *oo*·na ka·fe·te·*ree*·a
a salsa dance club	a una salsoteca	a *oo*·na sal·so·*te*·ka
a tango club	a una milonga	a *oo*·na mee·*lon*·ga
the movies	al cine	al *see*·ne
the theatre	al teatro	al te·*a*·tro

Invitations

What are you doing this evening?	¿Qué haces/hacen esta noche? **sg/pl** ke *a*·ses/*a*·sen *es*·ta *no*·che

What are you doing this weekend?	¿Qué haces/hacen este fin de semana? sg/pl ke *a*·ses/*a*·sen *es*·te feen de se·*ma*·na
Would you like to go for a ...?	¿Te/Les gustaría ir a ...? sg/pl te/les goos·ta·*ree*·a eer a ...

coffee	tomar un café	to·*mar* oon ka·*fe*
drink	tomar unos tragos	to·*mar* *oo*·nos *tra*·gos
meal	comer	ko·*mer*
walk	pasear	pa·se·*ar*

I feel like going dancing.	Tengo ganas de ir a bailar. *ten*·go *ga*·nas de eer a bai·*lar*
Do you want to come to the concert with me?	¿Quieres/Quieren venir conmigo al concierto? sg/pl *kye*·res/*kye*·ren ve·*neer* kon·*mee*·go al kon·*syer*·to
Do you know a good restaurant?	¿Conoces/Conocen un buen restaurante? sg/pl ko·*no*·ses/ko·*no*·sen oon bwen res·tow·*ran*·te
We're having a party.	Vamos a dar una fiesta. *va*·mos a dar *oo*·na *fyes*·ta
You should come.	¿Por qué no vienes/vienen? sg/pl por ke no *vye*·nes/*vye*·nen

Responding to Invitations

Sure!	¡Por supuesto! por soo·*pwes*·to
Yes, I'd love to.	Me encantaría. me en·kan·ta·*ree*·a

LANGUAGE TIP

'Partying' Synonyms

Latin Americans know how to let down their hair and have a good time. Here are some expressions which all mean 'to go out drinking and partying', to help you get a slice of the action:

ir de copas	eer de *ko*·pas
ir de farra	eer de *fa*·ra
ir de fiesta	eer de *fyes*·ta
ir de juerga	eer de *khwer*·ga
ir de pachanga	eer de pa·*chan*·ga
ir de rumba	eer de *room*·ba

Yes, let's go.	Sí, vamos. see *va*·mos
No, I'm afraid I can't.	Lo siento pero no puedo. lo *syen*·to *pe*·ro no *pwe*·do
What about tomorrow?	¿Qué tal mañana? ke tal ma·*nya*·na
Sorry, I can't sing/dance.	Lo siento, no sé cantar/bailar. lo *syen*·to no se kan·*tar*/bai·*lar*

Arranging to Meet

Q **What time shall we meet?**	¿A qué hora quedamos? a ke *o*·ra ke·*da*·mos
A **Let's meet at (eight o'clock).**	Quedamos a las (ocho). ke·*da*·mos a las (*o*·cho)
Q **Where will we meet?**	¿Dónde quedamos? *don*·de ke·*da*·mos
A **Let's meet at the entrance.**	Quedamos en la entrada. ke·*da*·mos en la en·*tra*·da

I'll pick you up.	Paso a recogerte/ recogerles. sg/pl *pa*·so a re·ko·*kher*·te/ re·ko·*kher*·les
I'll be coming later.	Iré más tarde. ee·*re* mas *tar*·de
I'll see you then.	Nos vemos. nos *ve*·mos

CULTURE TIP

Latin American Rhythms

música f **Andina** *moo*·see·ka an·*dee*·na

Andean music incorporates the *quena* *ke*·na (reed flute), the *zampoña* sam·*po*·nya (pan flute), the *caja* *ka*·kha (tambourine-like drums) and the ukulele-like *charango* cha·*ran*·go.

música f **criolla** *moo*·see·ka kree·o·ya

With its roots in Spain and Africa, the main instruments of Creole music are guitars and a *cajón* ka·*khon* (wooden box drum).

música f **de los llanos** *moo*·see·ka de los *ya*·nos

A Venezuelan and Colombian song style accompanied by a *cuatro* *kwa*·tro (harp) and maracas.

reggae m *re*·gay

The reggae influence is strongly felt along the Caribbean coast of Central America.

salsa f *sal*·sa

This immensely popular dance style originated in New York but spread through the Caribbean in the 1960s.

tango m *tan*·go

Argentina is the birthplace of this style. A visit to a *club de tango* kloob de *tan*·go in Buenos Aires is an unforgettable experience.

LANGUAGE TIP

Masculine or Feminine?

In this book, when you see an m it means masculine, so the article you use should be either *un* oon or *el* el. When you see an f it means feminine, so the article should be either *una* *oo*·na or *la* la.

Where an *-o* ending and an *-a* ending mark masculine and feminine forms respectively, we've used a slash. For example, the two forms of the word 'beautiful', *lindo* *leen*·do and *linda* *leen*·da, are written *lindo/a.*

Where the only difference between masculine and feminine forms is the addition of an *-a* ending for the feminine form, we've used brackets. Hence the two forms of the word 'doctor', *doctor* dok·*tor* and *doctora* dok·*to*·ra, are abbreviated to *doctor(a).*

See also **gender** in the **grammar** chapter (p19).

If I'm not there by (nine), don't wait for me.	Si no estoy a las (nueve), no me esperes/esperen. sg/pl see no es·*toy* a las (*nwe*·ve) no me es·*pe*·res/es·*pe*·ren
Where will you be?	¿Dónde estarás/estarán? sg/pl *don*·de es·ta·*ras*/es·ta·*ran*
I'm looking forward to it.	Tengo muchas ganas de ir. *ten*·go *moo*·chas *ga*·nas de eer

Drugs

I don't take drugs.	No consumo ningún tipo de drogas. no kon·*soo*·mo neen·*goon* *tee*·po de *dro*·gas
I have ... occasionally.	Tomo ... de vez en cuando. *to*·mo ... de ves en *kwan*·do
Do you want to have a smoke?	¿Nos fumamos un porro? nos foo·*ma*·mos oon *po*·ro

Romance

KEY PHRASES

Would you like to do something?	¿Quieres hacer algo?	*kye*·res a·*ser* *al*·go
I love you.	Te quiero.	te *kye*·ro
Leave me alone!	¡Déjame en paz!	*de*·kha·me en pas

Asking Someone Out

Q **Would you like to do something (tonight)?**	¿Quieres hacer algo (esta noche)? *kye*·res a·*ser* *al*·go (*es*·ta *no*·che)
A **Yes, I'd love to.**	Me encantaría. me en·kan·ta·*ree*·a
A **No, I'm afraid I can't.**	Lo siento, pero no puedo. lo *syen*·to *pe*·ro no *pwe*·do

Pick-up Lines

Would you like a drink?	¿Puedo ofrecerte una copa? *pwe*·do o·fre·*ser*·te *oo*·na *ko*·pa
Do you have a light?	¿Tienes fuego? *tye*·nes *fwe*·go
You have a beautiful laugh.	Tienes una risa preciosa. *tye*·nes *oo*·na *ree*·sa pre·*syo*·sa
You have beautiful eyes.	Tienes unos ojos preciosos. *tye*·nes *oo*·nos *o*·khos pre·*syo*·sos

What star sign are you?	¿Cuál es tu signo del horóscopo? kwal es too *seeg*·no del o·*ros*·ko·po
Shall we get some fresh air?	¿Vamos a tomar el aire? *va*·mos a to·*mar* el *ai*·re

Rejections

I have a boyfriend/ girlfriend.	Tengo novio/a. m/f *ten*·go *no*·vyo/a
Excuse me, I have to go now.	Lo siento, pero me tengo que ir. lo *syen*·to *pe*·ro me *ten*·go ke eer
I'm not interested.	No estoy interesado/a. m/f no es·*toy* een·te·re·*sa*·do/a
I'm busy.	Estoy ocupado/a. m/f es·*toy* o·koo·*pa*·do/a
Your ego is out of control.	Tu ego está fuera de control. too *e*·go es·*ta fwe*·ra de kon·*trol*
Leave me alone!	¡Déjame en paz! *de*·kha·me en pas
Piss off!	¡Andate a la mierda! *an*·da·te a la *myer*·da

Getting Closer

You're very nice.	Eres muy simpático/a. m/f *e*·res mooy seem·*pa*·tee·ko/a
You're very attractive.	Eres muy guapo/a. m/f *e*·res mooy *gwa*·po/a
I'm interested in you.	Me fascinas mucho. me fa·*see*·nas *moo*·cho

Q Do you like me too?	¿Me tienes algo de cariño también? me *tye*·nes *al*·go de ka·*ree*·nyo tam·*byen*
A I like you very much.	Me gustas mucho. me *goos*·tas *moo*·cho
Can I kiss you?	¿Te puedo besar? te *pwe*·do be·*sar*
Will you take me home?	¿Me acompañas a casa? me a·kom·*pa*·nyas a *ka*·sa
Do you want to come inside for a while?	¿Quieres entrar a tomar algo? *kye*·res en·*trar* a to·*mar al*·go

Sex

I want to make love to you.	Quiero hacerte el amor. *kye*·ro a·*ser*·te el a·*mor*
Do you have a condom?	¿Tienes un condón? *tye*·nes oon kon·*don*
I won't do it without protection.	No lo haré sin preservativos. no lo a·*re* seen pre·ser·va·*tee*·vos
I think we should stop now.	Pienso que deberíamos parar. *pyen*·so ke de·be·*ree*·a·mos pa·*rar*
Let's go to bed!	¡Vamos a la cama! *va*·mos a la *ka*·ma
Kiss me!	¡Bésame! *be*·sa·me
I want you.	Te deseo. te de·*se*·o
Take this off.	Saca esto. *sa*·ka *es*·to

LANGUAGE TIP

Risqué Expressions

To say you like something, use the expression *me gusta* me *goos*·ta (lit: me it-pleases). Beware of using it for people though – to say *me gustas* me *goos*·tas (lit: me you-please) has erotic overtones. A less risqué way of saying that you enjoy someone's company is *me caes bien* me *ka*·es byen, which equates to the English 'I like you'.

Touch me here.	Tócame aquí. *to*·ka·me a·*kee*
Q **Do you like this?**	¿Esto te gusta? *es*·to te *goos*·ta
A **I (don't) like that.**	Esto (no) me gusta. *es*·to (no) me *goos*·ta
Please stop!	¡Para! *pa*·ra
Please don't stop!	¡No pares! no *pa*·res
That was amazing.	Eso fue increíble. *e*·so fwe een·kre·*ee*·ble
Can I stay over?	¿Puedo quedarme? *pwe*·do ke·*dar*·me

Love

I'm in love with you.	Estoy enamorado/a de ti. m/f es·*toy* e·na·mo·*ra*·do/a de tee
Q **Do you love me?**	¿Me quieres? me *kye*·res
A **I love you.**	Te quiero. te *kye*·ro
I think we're good together.	Creo que estamos bien juntos. *kre*·o ke es·*ta*·mos byen *khoon*·tos

Beliefs & Culture

KEY PHRASES

What's your religion?	¿Cuál es su/tu religión? **pol/inf**	kwal es soo/too re·lee·*khyon*
I'm ...	Soy ...	soy ...
I'm sorry, it's against my beliefs.	Lo siento, eso va en contra de mis creencias.	lo *syen*·to e·so va en *kon*·tra de mees kre·*en*·syas

Religion

Q **What's your religion?** ¿Cuál es su/tu religión? **pol/inf**
kwal es soo/too re·lee·*khyon*

A **I'm (not) ...** (No) Soy ...
(no) soy ...

an agnostic	agnóstico/a **m/f**	ag·*nos*·tee·ko/a
an atheist	ateo/a **m/f**	a·*te*·o/a
Buddhist	budista	boo·*dees*·ta
Catholic	católico/a **m/f**	ka·*to*·lee·ko/a
Christian	cristiano/a **m/f**	krees·*tya*·no/a
Hindu	hindú	een·*doo*
Jewish	judío/a **m/f**	khoo·*dee*·o/a
Muslim	musulmán **m** musulmana **f**	moo·sool·*man* moo·sool·*ma*·na
practising	practicante	prak·tee·*kan*·te
religious	religioso/a **m/f**	re·lee·*khyo*·so/a

I (don't) believe in God.	(No) Creo en Dios. (no) *kre*·o en dyos
I (don't) believe in fate.	(No) Creo en el destino. (no) *kre*·o en el des·*tee*·no
I'd like to go to (the) ...	Quisiera ir ... kee·*sye*·ra eer ...

church	a la iglesia	a la ee·*gle*·sya
mosque	a la mezquita	a la mes·*kee*·ta
synagogue	a la sinagoga	a la see·na·*go*·ga
temple	al templo	al *tem*·plo

Can I pray here?	¿Puedo rezar aquí? *pwe*·do re·*sar* a·*kee*
Where can I attend mass?	¿Dónde puedo asistir a la misa? *don*·de *pwe*·do a·sees·*teer* a la *mee*·sa

Cultural Differences

Is this a local custom?	¿Esto es una costumbre local? *es*·to es *oo*·na kos·*toom*·bre lo·*kal*
I'm not used to this.	No estoy acostumbrado/a a esto. m/f no es·*toy* a·kos·toom·*bra*·do/a a *es*·to
I'll try it.	Lo probaré. lo pro·ba·*re*
Sorry, I didn't mean to say/do anything wrong.	Lo siento, lo dije/hice sin querer. lo *syen*·to lo *dee*·khe/*ee*·se seen ke·*rer*

CULTURE TIP

Gringo Lingo

One word you might become well acquainted with is *gringo/a* m/f *green*·go/a. In Latin American Spanish this word has subtle nuances. It can simply be a neutral term meaning 'foreign' or 'foreigner', but it may be intended as pejorative in certain contexts. You'll notice this when it's combined with an unflattering word such as *pinche* *peen*·che (goddam) or said in an unfriendly tone of voice.

The term *gringo* can be used to refer to North Americans but also, in a broader sense, to visitors of European heritage. Blonde or fair-haired people are sometimes called *gringos* because they're marked out by their physical appearance. The word is thought to have originated from the Spanish word *griego* *grye*·go (Greek).

This is (very) different.	Esto es (muy) diferente. *es*·to es (mooy) dee·fe·*ren*·te
This is fun.	Esto es divertido. *es*·to es dee·ver·*tee*·do
This is interesting.	Esto es interesante. *es*·to es een·te·re·*san*·te
I don't mind watching, but I'd rather not join in.	No me importa mirar, pero prefiero no participar. no me eem·*por*·ta mee·*rar* *pe*·ro pre·*fye*·ro no par·tee·see·*par*
I'm sorry, it's against my beliefs.	Lo siento, eso va en contra de mis creencias. lo *syen*·to e·so va en *kon*·tra de mees kre·*en*·syas
I'm sorry, it's against my religion.	Lo siento, eso va en contra de mi religión. lo *syen*·to e·so va en *kon*·tra de mee re·lee·*khyon*

Sports

KEY PHRASES

Which sport do you play?	¿Qué deporte practicas?	ke de·*por*·te prak·*tee*·kas
Who's your favourite team?	¿Cuál es tu equipo favorito?	kwal es too e·*kee*·po fa·vo·*ree*·to
What's the score?	¿Cómo van?	*ko*·mo van

Sporting Interests

Q **Do you like (sport)?**	¿Te gustan (los deportes)? te *goos*·tan (los de·*por*·tes)
A **Yes, very much.**	Sí, mucho. see *moo*·cho
A **Not really.**	En realidad, no mucho. en re·a·lee·*da* no *moo*·cho
A **I like watching it.**	Me gusta mirar. me *goos*·ta mee·*rar*
Q **Which sport do you play?**	¿Qué deporte practicas? ke de·*por*·te prak·*tee*·kas
A **I play (tennis).**	Practico (el tenis). prak·*tee*·ko (el *te*·nees)
Who's your favourite athlete?	¿Quién es tu deportista favorito/a? m/f kyen es too de·por·*tees*·ta fa·vo·*ree*·to/a
Who's your favourite team?	¿Cuál es tu equipo favorito? kwal es too e·*kee*·po fa·vo·*ree*·to

Q **Which sport do you follow?**	¿A qué deporte eres aficionado/a? **m/f** a *ke* de·*por*·te e·res a·fee·syo·*na*·do/a
A **I follow (cycling).**	Soy aficionado/a al (ciclismo). **m/f** soy a·fee·syo·*na*·do/a al (see·*klees*·mo)

For more sports, see the **dictionary**.

Going to a Game

Would you like to go to a game?	¿Te gustaría ir a un partido? te goos·ta·*ree*·a eer a oon par·*tee*·do
Who are you supporting?	¿Con qué equipo vas? kon ke e·*kee*·po vas
Who's playing?	¿Quién juega? kyen *khwe*·ga
Who's winning?	¿Quién va ganando? kyen va ga·*nan*·do
How much time is left?	¿Cuánto tiempo queda? *kwan*·to *tyem*·po *ke*·da
Q **What's the score?**	¿Cómo van? *ko*·mo van
A **It's a draw.**	Empatados. em·pa·*ta*·dos
That was a bad/boring game!	¡Ese partido fue malo/aburrido! e·se par·*tee*·do fwe *ma*·lo/a·boo·*ree*·do
That was a great game!	¡Ese partido fue fabuloso/bárbaro! e·se par·*tee*·do fwe fa·boo·*lo*·so/*bar*·ba·ro

Playing Sport

Q **Do you want to play?**	¿Quieres jugar? *kye*·res khoo·*gar*
Q **Can I join in?**	¿Puedo jugar? *pwe*·do khoo·*gar*
A **Yes, that'd be great.**	Sí, me encantaría. see me en·kan·ta·*ree*·a
A **Not at the moment, thanks.**	Ahora mismo no, gracias. a·o·ra *mees*·mo no *gra*·syas
A **I have an injury.**	Tengo una lesion. *ten*·go *oo*·na le·*syon*
Thanks for the game.	Gracias por el partido. *gra*·syas por el par·*tee*·do

¿Con qué equipo vas?
kon ke e·*kee*·po vas
Who are you supporting?

LISTEN FOR

¡Qué atajada!	ke a·ta·*kha*·da	What a save!
¡Qué cabezazo!	ke ka·be·*sa*·so	What a header!
¡Qué chute!	ke *choo*·te	What a kick/shot!
¡Qué golazo!	ke go·*la*·so	What a goal!
¡Qué pase!	ke *pa*·se	What a pass!
¡Qué tiro!	ke *tee*·ro	What a hit!

You're a good player.	Juegas bien. *khwe*·gas byen
Where's the nearest gym?	¿Dónde está el gimnasio más cercano? *don*·de es·*ta* el kheem·*na*·syo mas ser·*ka*·no
Where's the best place to jog around here?	¿Cuál es el mejor sitio para hacer footing por aquí? kwal es el me·*khor see*·tyo *pa*·ra a·*ser foo*·teen por a·*kee*
Where's the nearest swimming pool?	¿Dónde está la piscina más cercana? *don*·de es·*ta* la pee·*see*·na mas ser·*ka*·na ¿Dónde está la pileta más cercana? **(Arg)** *don*·de es·*ta* la pee·*le*·ta mas ser·*ka*·na
Where's the nearest tennis court?	¿Dónde está la cancha de tenis más cercana? *don*·de es·*ta* la *kan*·cha de *te*·nees mas ser·*ka*·na
Do I have to be a member to attend?	¿Hay que ser socio/a para entrar? **m/f** ai ke ser *so*·syo/a *pa*·ra en·*trar*

What's the charge per ...?	¿Cúanto cobran por ...? *kwan*·to *ko*·bran por ...	

day	día	*dee*·a
game	partido	par·*tee*·do
hour	hora	*o*·ra
visit	visita	vee·*see*·ta

Can I hire a ...?	¿Es posible alquilar una ...? es po·*see*·ble al·kee·*lar oo*·na ...

ball	pelota	pe·*lo*·ta
bicycle	bicicleta	bee·see·*kle*·ta
court	cancha	*kan*·cha
racquet	raqueta	ra·*ke*·ta

Is there a women-only session?	¿Hay alguna sesión sólo para mujeres? ai al·*goo*·na se·syon *so*·lo *pa*·ra moo·*khe*·res
Where are the changing rooms?	¿Dónde están los vestuarios? *don*·de es·*tan* los ves·*twa*·ryos
Can I have a locker?	¿Puedo usar una lócker? *pwe*·do oo·*sar oo*·na *lo*·ker

LISTEN FOR

¡Pásamelo!	*pa*·sa·me·lo	Kick/Pass it to me!
Mi/Tu punto.	mee/too *poon*·to	My/Your point.

LISTEN FOR

amonestación f	a·mo·ne·sta·*syon*	warning
arquero/a m/f (Arg)	ar·*ke*·ro/a	goalkeeper
delantero/a m/f	de·lan·*te*·ro/a	striker
jugador m	khoo·ga·*dor*	player
jugadora f	khoo·ga·*do*·ra	player
marcar	mar·*kar*	score (a goal)
portero/a m/f	por·*te*·ro/a	goalkeeper
saque m	*sa*·ke	kickoff
saque m **de banda**	*sa*·ke de *ban*·da	throw-in
tarjeta f **roja/ amarilla**	tar·*khe*·ta *ro*·kha/ a·ma·*ree*·ya	red/yellow card
tiro m **libre**	*tee*·ro *lee*·bre	free kick

Football/Soccer

Which team is at the top of the league?	¿Qué equipo está en primera posición en la tabla de clasificaciones? ke e·*kee*·po es·*ta* en pree·*me*·ra po·see·*syon* en la *ta*·bla de kla·see·fee·ka·*syo*·nes
Who plays for ...?	¿Quién juega para el ...? kyen *khwe*·ga *pa*·ra el ...
He's a great (player).	Es un (jugador) bárbaro. es oon (khoo·ga·*dor*) *bar*·ba·ro
He played brilliantly in the match against (Brazil).	Jugó fenomenal en el partido contra (Brasil). khoo·*go* fe·no·me·*nal* en el par·*tee*·do *kon*·tra (bra·*seel*)
What a terrible team!	¡Qué equipo más malo! ke e·*kee*·po mas *ma*·lo

Outdoors

KEY PHRASES

Where can I buy supplies?	¿Dónde se puede comprar víveres?	*don*·de se *pwe*·de kom·*prar* *vee*·ve·res
Do we need a guide?	¿Se necesita un guía?	se ne·se·*see*·ta oon *gee*·a
Is it safe?	¿Es seguro?	es se·*goo*·ro
I'm lost.	Estoy perdido/a. m/f	es·*toy* per·*dee*·do/a
What's the weather like?	¿Qué tiempo hace?	ke *tyem*·po *a*·se

Hiking & Mountaineering

Where can I ...? ¿Dónde se puede ...? *don*·de se *pwe*·de ...

buy supplies	comprar víveres	kom·*prar* *vee*·ve·res
find someone who knows this area	encontrar a alguien que conozca el área	en·kon·*trar* a *al*·gyen ke ko·*nos*·ka el *a*·re·a
get a map	obtener un mapa	ob·te·*ner* oon *ma*·pa
hire hiking gear	alquilar equipo para ir de excursión	al·kee·*lar* e·*kee*·po *pa*·ra eer de eks·koor·*syon*
hire mountaineering gear	alquilar equipo de alpinismo	al·kee·*lar* e·*kee*·po de al·pee·*nees*·mo

How long is the trail?	¿Cómo es de largo el camino? *ko*·mo es de *lar*·go el ka·*mee*·no
How high is the climb?	¿A qué altura se escala? a ke al·*too*·ra se es·*ka*·la
Is the path open?	¿Está la ruta abierta? es·*ta* la *roo*·ta a·*byer*·ta
Is it safe?	¿Es seguro? es se·*goo*·ro
Is there a hut there?	¿Hay una cabaña allí? ai *oo*·na ka·*ba*·nya a·*yee*
When does it get dark?	¿A qué hora oscurece? a ke *o*·ra os·koo·*re*·se
Do we need a guide?	¿Se necesita un guía? se ne·se·*see*·ta oon *gee*·a
Are there guided treks/ climbs?	¿Se organizan excursiones/ escaladas guiadas? se or·ga·*nee*·san eks·koor·*syo*·nes/ es·ka·*la*·das gee·*a*·das
Do we need to take bedding?	¿Se necesita llevar algo en que dormir? se ne·se·*see*·ta ye·*var al*·go en ke dor·*meer*
Do we need to take food/water?	¿Se necesita llevar comida/agua? se ne·se·*see*·ta ye·*var* ko·*mee*·da/*a*·gwa
Is the track (well) marked?	¿Es (bien) marcado el sendero? es (byen) mar·*ka*·do el sen·*de*·ro
Is the track scenic?	¿Es pintoresco el sendero? es peen·to·*res*·ko el sen·*de*·ro

LISTEN FOR

Cuidado con la corriente.	kwee·*da*·do kon la ko·*ryen*·te	Be careful of the undertow.
¡Es peligroso!	es pe·lee·*gro*·so	It's dangerous!
altura f	al·*too*·ra	altitude
escarpado/a m/f	es·kar·*pa*·do/a	steep
refugio m **de montaña**	re·*foo*·khyo de mon·*ta*·nya	mountain hut
subir de hielo	soo·*beer* de *ye*·lo	ice-climbing

Which is the easiest/ shortest route?	¿Cuál es el camino más fácil/corto? kwal es el ka·*mee*·no mas *fa*·seel/*kor*·to
Where have you come from?	¿De dónde vienes? de *don*·de *vye*·nes
How long did it take?	¿Cuánto has tardado? *kwan*·to as tar·*da*·do
Does this path go to ...?	¿Este camino va a ...? *es*·te ka·*mee*·no va a ...
Where's the nearest village?	¿Dónde está el pueblo más cercano? *don*·de es·*ta* el *pwe*·blo mas ser·*ka*·no
Where are we on this map?	¿Dónde estamos aquí en el mapa? *don*·de es·*ta*·mos a·*kee* en el *ma*·pa
I'm lost.	Estoy perdido/a. m/f es·*toy* per·*dee*·do/a
Is the water OK to drink?	¿Se puede beber el agua? se *pwe*·de be·*ber* el *a*·gwa

At the Beach

Where's the nearest beach?	¿Dónde está la playa más cercana? *don*·de es·*ta* la *pla*·ya mas ser·*ka*·na
Where's the nicest beach?	¿Dónde está la playa más bonita? *don*·de es·*ta* la *pla*·ya mas bo·*nee*·ta
Where's the nudist beach?	¿Dónde está la playa nudista? *don*·de es·*ta* la *pla*·ya noo·*dees*·ta
Are there any reefs?	¿Hay arrecifes? ai a·re·*see*·fes
Are there any rips?	¿Hay corrientes? ai ko·*ryen*·tes
Are there any water hazards?	¿Hay peligros en el agua? ai pe·*lee*·gros en el *a*·gwa
Is it safe to dive/swim here?	¿Es seguro bucear/nadar aquí? es se·*goo*·ro boo·se·*ar*/na·*dar* a·*kee*
What time is high/low tide?	¿A qué hora es la marea alta/baja? a ke *o*·ra es la ma·*re*·a *al*·ta/*ba*·kha
Where are the showers/ toilets?	¿Dónde hay duchas/baños? *don*·de ai *doo*·chas/*ba*·nyos

LOOK FOR

Prohibido Nadar	pro·ee·*bee*·do na·*dar*	No Swimming

Weather

Q	**What's the weather like?**	¿Qué tiempo hace? ke *tyem*·po *a*·se
A	**It's raining.**	Llueve. *ywe*·ve
A	**It's snowing.**	Nieva. *nye*·va
A	**It's ...**	Hace ... *a*·se ...

cold	frío	*free*·o
freezing	un frío que pela	oon *free*·o ke *pe*·la
hot	calor	ka·*lor*
sunny	sol	sol
warm	calor	ka·*lor*
windy	viento	*vyen*·to

Q	**Will it be (cold) tomorrow?**	¿Mañana hará (frío)? ma·*nya*·na a·*ra* (*free*·o)
A	**It will rain (tomorrow).**	(Mañana) Lloverá. (ma·*nya*·na) yo·ve·*ra*
A	**It will snow (tomorrow).**	(Mañana) Nevará. (ma·*nya*·na) ne·va·*ra*
	Where can I buy a rain jacket?	¿Dónde puedo comprar un impermeable? *don*·de *pwe*·do kom·*prar* oon eem·per·me·*a*·ble
	Where can I buy an umbrella?	¿Dónde puedo comprar un paraguas? *don*·de *pwe*·do kom·*prar* oon pa·*ra*·gwas

Where can I buy sunblock?	¿Dónde puedo comprar crema solar? *don*·de *pwe*·do kom·*prar* *kre*·ma so·*lar*
dry season	época **f** seca *e*·po·ka *se*·ka
rainy season	época **f** de lluvias *e*·po·ka de *yoo*·vyas

Flora & Fauna

What ... is that?	¿Qué ... es ése/ésa? **m/f** ke ... es *e*·se/*e*·sa

animal	animal **m**	a·nee·*mal*
flower	flor **f**	flor
plant	planta **f**	*plan*·ta
tree	árbol **m**	*ar*·bol

Is it ...?	¿Es ...? es ...

common	común	ko·*moon*
dangerous	peligroso/a **m/f**	pe·lee·*gro*·so/a
poisonous	venenoso/a **m/f**	ve·ne·*no*·so/a
protected	protegido/a **m/f**	pro·te·*khee*·do/a

Is it endangered?	¿Está en peligro de extinción? es·*ta* en pe·*lee*·gro de ek·steen·*syon*
What's it used for?	¿Para qué se usa? *pa*·ra ke se *oo*·sa
Can you eat it?	¿Se puede comerlo? se *pwe*·de ko·*mer*·lo

For names of plants and animals, see the **dictionary**.

Safe Travel

Emergencies

KEY PHRASES

Help!	¡Socorro!	so·*ko*·ro
There's been an accident.	Ha habido un accidente.	a a·*bee*·do oon ak·see·*den*·te
It's an emergency.	Es una emergencia.	es *oo*·na e·mer·*khen*·sya

Help!	¡Socorro! so·*ko*·ro
Stop!	¡Pare! *pa*·re
Go away!	¡Váyase! *va*·ya·se
Thief!	¡Ladrón! la·*dron*
Fire!	¡Fuego! *fwe*·go
Watch out!	¡Cuidado! kwee·*da*·do
Call the police!	¡Llame a la policía! *ya*·me a la po·lee·*see*·a
Call a doctor!	¡Llame a un médico! *ya*·me a oon *me*·dee·ko
Call an ambulance!	¡Llame a una ambulancia! *ya*·me a *oo*·na am·boo·*lan*·sya
There's been an accident.	Ha habido un accidente. a a·*bee*·do oon ak·see·*den*·te

LOOK FOR

Comisaría de Policía	ko·me·sa·*ree*·a de po·lee·*see*·a	Police Station
Policía	po·lee·*see*·a	Police
Urgencias	oor·*khen*·syas	Casualty

It's an emergency.	Es una emergencia. es *oo*·na e·mer·*khen*·sya
Could you help me, please?	¿Me puede ayudar, por favor? me *pwe*·de a·yoo·*dar* por fa·*vor*
I have to use the telephone.	Necesito usar el teléfono. ne·se·*see*·to oo·*sar* el te·*le*·fo·no
I'm lost.	Estoy perdido/a. m/f es·*toy* per·*dee*·do/a
Where are the toilets?	¿Dónde están los baños? *don*·de es·*tan* los *ba*·nyos
Is it safe ...?	¿Es seguro ...? es se·*goo*·ro ...

at night	por la noche	por la *no*·che
for foreigners	para los extranjeros	*pa*·ra los ek·stran·*khe*·ros
for gay travellers	para viajeros gay	*pa*·ra vya·*khe*·ros gay
for women travellers	para viajeras	*pa*·ra vya·*khe*·ras

Police

KEY PHRASES

Where's the police station?	¿Dónde está la comisaría?	*don*·de es·*ta* la ko·mee·sa·*ree*·a
I want to contact my embassy/ consulate.	Quiero ponerme en contacto con mi embajada/ consulado.	*kye*·ro po·*ner*·me en kon·*tak*·to kon mee em·ba·*kha*·da/ kon·soo·*la*·do
My bag was stolen.	Mi bolso fue robado.	mee *bol*·so fwe ro·*ba*·do

Where's the police station?	¿Dónde está la comisaría? *don*·de es·*ta* la ko·mee·sa·*ree*·a
I want to report an offence.	Quiero denunciar un delito. *kye*·ro de·noon·*syar* oon de·*lee*·to
(My bag) was stolen.	(Mi bolso) fue robado. (mee *bol*·so) fwe ro·*ba*·do
I've lost (my wallet).	He perdido (mi cartera). e per·*dee*·do (mee kar·*te*·ra)
I've been robbed.	Me han robado. me an ro·*ba*·do
I've been raped.	He sido violado/a. **m/f** e *see*·do vyo·*la*·do/a
I have a prescription for this drug.	Tengo receta para este medicamento. *ten*·go re·*se*·ta *pa*·ra *es*·te me·dee·ka·*men*·to

This drug is for personal use.	Esta droga es para uso personal. *es·ta dro·ga es pa·ra oo·so per·so·nal*
Can I call a lawyer?	¿Puedo llamar a un abogado? *pwe·do ya·mar a oon a·bo·ga·do*
I need a lawyer who speaks English.	Necesito un abogado que hable inglés. *ne·se·see·to oon a·bo·ga·do ke a·ble een·gles*
I want to contact my embassy/consulate.	Quiero ponerme en contacto con mi embajada/consulado. *kye·ro po·ner·me en kon·tak·to kon mee em·ba·kha·da/ kon·soo·la·do*
What am I accused of?	¿De qué me acusan? *de ke me a·koo·san*
I'm innocent.	Soy inocente. *soy ee·no·sen·te*

LISTEN FOR

alterar el orden público	*al·te·rar el or·den poo·blee·ko*	disturbing the peace
asalto m	*a·sal·to*	assault
exceso m **de velocidad**	*ek·se·so de ve·lo·see·da*	speeding
hurto m **en tiendas**	*oor·to en tyen·das*	shoplifting
posesión f **(de sustancias ilegales)**	*po·se·syon (de soos·tan·syas ee·le·ga·les)*	possession (of illegal substances)
robo m	*ro·bo*	theft
violación f	*vyo·la·syon*	rape

Health

KEY PHRASES

Where's the nearest hospital?	¿Dónde está el hospital más cercano?	*don*·de es·*ta* el os·pee·*tal* mas ser·*ka*·no
I'm sick.	Estoy enfermo/a. **m/f**	es·*toy* en·*fer*·mo/a
I need a doctor.	Necesito un médico.	ne·se·*see*·to oon *me*·dee·ko
I'm on medication for ...	Estoy bajo medicación para ...	es·*toy ba*·kho me·dee·ka·*syon pa*·ra ...
I'm allergic to ...	Soy alérgico/a a ... **m/f**	soy a·*ler*·khee·ko/a a ...

Doctor

Where's the nearest ...? ¿Dónde está ... más cercano/a? **m/f** *don*·de es·*ta* ... mas ser·*ka*·no/a

(night) chemist	la farmacia **f** (de guardia); la droguería **f** (de guardia) **(Col)**	la far·*ma*·sya (de *gwar*·dya); la dro·ge·*ree*·a (de *gwar*·dya)
dentist	el dentista **m**	el den·*tees*·ta
doctor	el médico **m**	el *me*·dee·ko
hospital	el hospital **m**	el os·pee·*tal*
optometrist	el oculista **m**	el o·koo·*lees*·ta

I need a doctor (who speaks English).	Necesito un médico (que hable inglés).	ne·se·*see*·to oon *me*·dee·ko (ke *a*·ble een·*gles*)
Could I see a female doctor?	¿Puede examinarme una médica?	*pwe*·de ek·sa·mee·*nar*·me *oo*·na *me*·dee·ka
Can the doctor come here?	¿Puede visitarme el médico?	*pwe*·de vee·see·*tar*·me el *me*·dee·ko
I've been vaccinated against ...	Estoy vacunado/a contra ... **m/f**	es·*toy* va·koo·*na*·do/a *kon*·tra ...

(yellow) fever	la fiebre (amarilla)	la *fye*·bre (a·ma·*ree*·ya)
hepatitis A/B/C	la hepatitis A/B/C	la e·pa·*tee*·tees a/be/se
tetanus	el tétano	el *te*·ta·no
typhoid	la tifus	la *tee*·foos

I need new glasses.	Necesito anteojos nuevos.	ne·se·*see*·to an·te·*o*·khos *nwe*·vos
I need new contact lenses.	Necesito lentes de contacto nuevas.	ne·se·*see*·to *len*·tes de kon·*tak*·to *nwe*·vas
I've run out of my medication.	Se me terminaron los medicamentos.	se me ter·mee·*na*·ron los me·dee·ka·*men*·tos

LISTEN FOR

¿Dónde le duele?	*don*·de le *dwe*·le	Where does it hurt?
¿Tiene fiebre?	*tye*·ne *fye*·bre	Do you have a temperature?
¿Desde cuándo se siente así?	*des*·de *kwan*·do se *syen*·te a·*see*	How long have you been like this?
¿Ha tenido esto antes?	a te·*nee*·do *es*·to *an*·tes	Have you had this before?

Can I have a receipt for my insurance?	¿Puede darme un recibo para mi seguro médico?	*pwe*·de *dar*·me oon re·*see*·bo *pa*·ra mee se·*goo*·ro *me*·dee·ko

Symptoms & Conditions

I'm sick.	Estoy enfermo/a. **m/f**	es·*toy* en·*fer*·mo/a
It hurts here.	Me duele aquí.	me *dwe*·le a·*kee*
I've been injured.	He sido herido.	e *see*·do e·*ree*·do
I've been vomiting.	He estado vomitando.	e es·*ta*·do vo·mee·*tan*·do
I'm dehydrated.	Estoy deshidratado/a. **m/f**	es·*toy* des·ee·dra·*ta*·do/a
I can't sleep.	No puedo dormir.	no *pwe*·do dor·*meer*
I feel hot and cold.	Tengo escalofríos.	*ten*·go es·ka·lo·*free*·os
I feel breathless.	Tengo falta de aliento.	*ten*·go *fal*·ta de a·*lyen*·to

I feel ...	Me siento ... me *syen*·to ...

dizzy	mareado/a **m/f**	ma·re·*a*·do/a
nauseous	con nauseas	kon *now*·se·as
shivery	destemplado/a **m/f**	des·tem·*pla*·do/a
weak	débil	*de*·beel

I'm asthmatic.	Soy asmático/a. **m/f** soy as·*ma*·tee·ko/a
I'm diabetic.	Soy diabético/a. **m/f** soy dya·*be*·tee·ko/a
I'm epileptic	Soy epiléptico/a. **m/f** soy e·pee·*lep*·tee·ko/a
I have (a fever).	Tengo (fiebre). *ten*·go (*fye*·bre)
I have a cold.	Estoy resfriado/a. **m/f** es·*toy* res·free·*a*·do/a Tengo un resfrío. **(SAm)** *ten*·go oon res·*free*·o
I've (recently) had ...	(Hace poco) He tenido ... (*a*·se *po*·ko) e te·*nee*·do ...

LISTEN FOR

¿Tiene Usted alergias?	*tye*·ne oos·*te* a·*ler*·khyas Are you allergic to anything?
¿Se encuentra bajo medicación?	se en·*kwen*·tra *ba*·kho me·dee·ka·*syon* Are you on medication?
¿Usted bebe/fuma?	oos·*te* *be*·be/*foo*·ma Do you drink/smoke?
¿Usted toma drogas?	oos·*te* *to*·ma *dro*·gas Do you take drugs?

I'm on medication for ...	Estoy bajo medicación para ... es·*toy* *ba*·kho me·dee·ka·*syon* *pa*·ra ...

For more symptoms and conditions, see the **dictionary**.

Women's Health

(I think) I'm pregnant.	(Creo que) Estoy embarazada. (*kre*·o ke) es·*toy* em·ba·ra·*sa*·da
I'm on the Pill.	Tomo la píldora. *to*·mo la *peel*·do·ra
I haven't had my period for (five) weeks.	Hace (cinco) semanas que no me viene la regla. *a*·se (*seen*·ko) se·*ma*·nas ke no me *vye*·ne la *re*·gla
I've noticed a lump here.	Me he fijado que tengo un bulto aquí. me e fee·*kha*·do ke *ten*·go oon *bool*·to a·*kee*
I need contraception.	Quisiera usar algún método anticonceptivo. kee·*sye*·ra oo·*sar* al·*goon* *me*·to·do an·tee·kon·sep·*tee*·vo
I need the morning-after pill.	Quisiera tomar la píldora del día siguiente. kee·*sye*·ra to·*mar* la *peel*·do·ra del *dee*·a see·*gyen*·te
I need a pregnancy test.	Quisiera una prueba de embarazo. kee·*sye*·ra *oo*·na *prwe*·ba de em·ba·*ra*·so

LISTEN FOR

¿Es usted sexualmente activa?	es oos·*te* sek·swal·*men*·te ak·*tee*·va Are you sexually active?
¿Usa anticonceptivos?	*oo*·sa an·tee·kon·sep·*tee*·vos Are you using contraception?
¿Tiene la menstruación?	*tye*·ne la mens·trwa·*syon* Are you menstruating?
¿Cuándo le vino la regla por última vez?	*kwan*·do le *vee*·no la *re*·gla por *ool*·tee·ma ves When did you last have your period?
¿Está embarazada?	es·*ta* em·ba·ra·*sa*·da Are you pregnant?
Está embarazada.	es·*ta* em·ba·ra·*sa*·da You're pregnant.

Allergies

I'm allergic to (anti-inflammatories).	Soy alérgico/a a (los antiinflamatorios). m/f *soy a·ler·khee·ko/a a (los an·teen·fla·ma·to·ryos)*
I have hay fever.	Tengo alergia al polen. *ten·go a·ler·khya al po·len*
I have a skin allergy.	Tengo una alergia en la piel. *ten·go oo·na a·ler·khya en la pyel*
I think it's the medication I'm on.	Me parece que son los medicamentos que estoy tomando. *me pa·re·se ke son los me·dee·ka·men·tos ke es·toy to·man·do*

For food-related allergies, see **vegetarian & special meals** (p186).

Parts of the Body

My (knee) hurts.	Me duele (la rodilla). me *dwe*·le (la ro·*dee*·ya)
I can't move (my ankle).	No puedo mover (el tobillo). no *pwe*·do mo·*ver* (el to·*bee*·yo)
I have a cramp (in my foot).	Tengo calambres (en el pie). *ten*·go ka·*lam*·bres (en el pye)
(My arm) is swollen.	Se me hinchó (el brazo). se me een·*cho* (el *bra*·so)

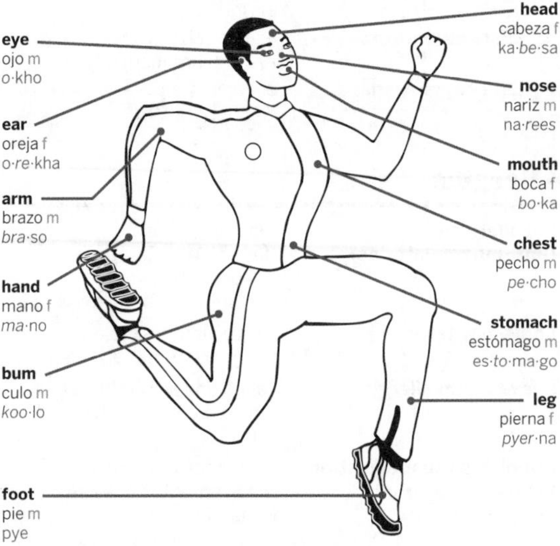

Chemist

I need something for (diarrhoea).	Necesito algo para (diarrea). ne·se·*see*·to al·go *pa*·ra (dee·a·*re*·a)
Do I need a prescription for (antihistamines)?	¿Necesito receta para (antihistamínicos)? ne·se·*see*·to re·*se*·ta *pa*·ra (an·tee·ees·ta·*mee*·nee·kos)
I have a prescription.	Tengo receta médica. *ten*·go re·*se*·ta *me*·dee·ka
This is my usual medicine.	Éste es mi medicamento habitual. es·te es mee me·dee·ka·*men*·to a·bee·*twal*
How many times a day?	¿Cuántas veces al día? *kwan*·tas *ve*·ses al *dee*·a
Will it make me drowsy?	¿Me producirá somnolencia? me pro·doo·see·*ra* som·no·*len*·sya

LISTEN FOR

¿Ha tomado esto antes?	a to·*ma*·do *es*·to *an*·tes Have you taken this before?
Debe terminar el tratamiento.	*de*·be ter·mee·*nar* el tra·ta·*myen*·to You must complete the course.
Dos veces al día (con la comida).	dos *ve*·ses al *dee*·a (kon la ko·*mee*·da) Twice a day (with food).
Estará listo en (veinte minutos).	es·ta·*ra lees*·to en (*vayn*·te mee·*noo*·tos) It'll be ready in (20 minutes).

Dentist

I have a broken tooth.	Se me ha roto un diente. se me a *ro*·to oon *dyen*·te
I have a cavity.	Tengo una caries. *ten*·go *oo*·na *ka*·ryes
I have a toothache.	Me duele una muela. me *dwe*·le *oo*·na *mwe*·la
I've lost a filling.	Se me ha caído un empaste. se me a ka·*ee*·do oon em·*pas*·te
I need a filling.	Necesito un empaste. ne·se·*see*·to oon em·*pas*·te
My dentures are broken.	Se me han roto los dientes postizos. se me an *ro*·to los *dyen*·tes pos·*tee*·sos
My gums hurt.	Me duelen las encías. me *dwe*·len las en·*see*·as
I don't want it extracted.	No quiero que me lo arranque. no *kye*·ro ke me lo a·*ran*·ke
I need an anaesthetic.	Necesito anestesia. ne·se·*see*·to a·nes·*te*·sya

LISTEN FOR

Abra.	*a*·bra	Open wide.
Enjuague.	en·*khwa*·ge	Rinse.
Muerda esto.	*mwer*·da *es*·to	Bite down on this.

Food

Eating Out

KEY PHRASES

Can you recommend a restaurant?	¿Puede recomendar un restaurante?	*pwe*·de re·ko·men·*dar* oon res·tow·*ran*·te
A table for two people, please.	Una mesa para dos, por favor.	*oo*·na *me*·sa *pa*·ra dos por fa·*vor*
I'd like the menu, please.	Quisiera el menú, por favor.	kee·*sye*·ra el me·*noo* por fa·*vor*
I'd like a beer, please.	Quisiera una cerveza, por favor.	kee·*sye*·ra *oo*·na ser·*ve*·sa por fa·*vor*
Please bring the bill.	Por favor nos trae la cuenta.	por fa·*vor* nos *tra*·e la *kwen*·ta

Basics

breakfast	desayuno **m** de·sa·*yoo*·no
lunch	almuerzo **m** al·*mwer*·so
dinner	cena **f** *se*·na
snack	tentempié **m** ten·tem·*pye*
eat	comer ko·*mer*
drink	beber be·*ber*

Finding a Place to Eat

Can you recommend a cafe?	¿Puede recomendar una cafetería? *pwe*·de re·ko·men·*dar oo*·na ka·fe·te·*ree*·a
Can you recommend a restaurant?	¿Puede recomendar un restaurante? *pwe*·de re·ko·men·*dar* oon res·tow·*ran*·te
Where would you go for (a) ...?	¿Adónde se va para ...? a·*don*·de se va *pa*·ra ...

business lunch	una comida de negocios	*oo*·na ko·*mee*·da de ne·*go*·syos
celebration	festejar	fes·te·*khar*
cheap meal	comer una comida barata	ko·*mer oo*·na ko·*mee*·da ba·*ra*·ta
local specialities	comer comida típica	ko·*mer* ko·*mee*·da *tee*·pee·ka

I'd like to reserve a table for (eight) o'clock.	Quisiera reservar una mesa para las (ocho). kee·*sye*·ra re·ser·*var oo*·na *me*·sa *pa*·ra las (*o*·cho)
I'd like to reserve a table for (two) people.	Quisiera reservar una mesa para (dos) personas. kee·*sye*·ra re·ser·*var oo*·na *me*·sa *pa*·ra (dos) per·*so*·nas

For two, please.	Para dos, por favor.	*pa*·ra dos por fa·*vor*

CULTURE TIP

Eateries

In Latin America there's no shortage of eateries where you can snack on the run or dine out at. Here are some of the typical establishments you may come across:

bar m — bar
many offer cheap light meals

chifa f — *chee*·fa
term for Chinese restaurant in various countries

churrasquería f — choo·ras·ke·*ree*·a
restaurant serving mainly barbecued meat

fuente f **de soda** — *fwen*·te de *so*·da
(lit: fountain of soda) cafe-style establishment serving snacks in addition to ice creams and soft drinks

lonchería f — lon·che·*ree*·a
cheap snack bar or diner

parrillada f — pa·ree·*ya*·da
Argentine steakhouse – a carnivore's delight

restaurante m **chino** — res·tow·*ran*·te *chee*·no
popular and cheap Chinese restaurant serving bowls of *tallarines* ta·ya·*ree*·nes (noodles) with chopped meat

Are you still serving food?	¿Siguen sirviendo comida? *see*·gen seer·*vyen*·do ko·*mee*·da
How long is the wait?	¿Cuánto hay que esperar? *kwan*·to ai ke es·pe·*rar*

LISTEN FOR

Hemos cerrado.	e·mos se·*ra*·do We're closed.
Estamos llenos.	es·*ta*·mos *ye*·nos We're fully booked.
No tenemos mesas.	no te·*ne*·mos *me*·sas We have no tables.
¿Dónde le gustaría sentarse?	*don*·de le goos·ta·*ree*·a sen·*tar*·se Where would you like to sit?

At the Restaurant

I'd like a/the ..., please.	Quisiera ..., por favor. kee·*sye*·ra ... por fa·*vor*

drink list	la lista de bebidas	la *lees*·ta de be·*bee*·das
menu	el menú	el me·*noo*
(non)smoking section	(no) fumadores	(no) foo·ma·*do*·res
table for (two)	una mesa para (two)	*oo*·na *me*·sa *pa*·ra (dos)

Menu, please.	El menú, por favor.	el me·*noo* por fa·*vor*

Do you have children's meals?	¿Tienen comidas para niños? *tye*·nen ko·*mee*·das *pa*·ra *nee*·nyos
Do you have a menu in English?	¿Tienen un menú en inglés? *tye*·nen oon me·*noo* en een·*gles*

LISTEN FOR

¿En qué le puedo servir?	en ke le *pwe*·do ser·*veer*	What can I get for you?
¿Cómo lo quiere preparado?	*ko*·mo lo *kye*·re pre·pa·*ra*·do	How would you like that cooked?
Recomiendo ...	re·ko·*myen*·do ...	I suggest the ...
Aquí tiene.	a·*kee tye*·ne	Here you go!
¡Que aproveche!	ke a·pro·*ve*·che	Enjoy your meal.

Is it self-serve?	¿Es de autoservicio?	es de ow·to·ser·*vee*·syo
What would you recommend?	¿Qué me recomienda?	ke me re·ko·*myen*·da
I'll have what they're having.	Tomaré lo mismo que ellos.	to·ma·*re* lo *mees*·mo ke *e*·yos
I'd like a local speciality.	Quisiera un plato típico.	kee·*sye*·ra oon *pla*·to *tee*·pee·ko
What's in that dish?	¿De qué es ese plato?	de ke es *e*·se *pla*·to
Does it take long to prepare?	¿Se tarda mucho en prepararlo?	se *tar*·da *moo*·cho en pre·pa·*rar*·lo
Are these complimentary?	¿Éstos son gratis?	*es*·tos son *gra*·tees

Eating Out

Can I see the menu, please?

¿Puedo ver el menú, por favor?
pwe·do ver el me·*noo* por fa·*vor*

What would you recommend for ...?

¿Qué recomienda para ...?
ke re·ko·*myen*·da *pa*·ra ...

the main meal
el plato principal
el *pla*·to preen·see·*pal*

dessert
el postre
el *pos*·tre

drinks
beber
be·*ber*

Can you bring me some ..., please?

Por favor me trae ...
por fa·*vor* me *tra*·e ...

I'd like the bill, please.

Quisiera la cuenta, por favor.
kee·*sye*·ra la *kwen*·ta por fa·*vor*

Requests

Is there any (tomato sauce)?	¿Hay (salsa de tomate)? ai (*sal*·sa de to·*ma*·te)
Please bring a ...	Por favor nos trae ... por fa·*vor* nos *tra*·e ...

cloth	un trapo	oon *tra*·po
glass	un vaso	oon *va*·so
serviette	una servilleta	*oo*·na ser·vee·*ye*·ta
wineglass	una copa de vino	*oo*·na *ko*·pa de *vee*·no

I'd like it ...	Lo quisiera ... lo kee·*sye*·ra ...
I don't want it ...	No lo quiero ... no lo *kye*·ro ...

boiled	hervido	er·*vee*·do
deep-fried	frito en aceite abundante	*free*·to en a·*say*·te a·boon·*dan*·te
fried	frito	*free*·to
grilled	a la parilla	a la pa·*ree*·ya
medium	no muy hecho	no mooy *e*·cho
rare	vuelta y vuelta	*vwel*·ta ee *vwel*·ta
reheated	recalentado	re·ka·len·*ta*·do
steamed	al vapor	al va·*por*
well done	muy hecho	mooy *e*·cho
with the dressing on the side	con el aliño aparte	kon el a·*lee*·nyo a·*par*·te
without (chilli)	sin (chile)	seen (*chee*·le)

LOOK FOR

Abrebocas	a·bre·*bo*·kas	Appetisers
Sopas	*so*·pas	Soups
De Entrada	de en·*tra*·da	Starters
Ensaladas	en·sa·*la*·das	Salads
Comidas Ligeras	ko·*mee*·das lee·*khe*·ras	Light Meals
Segundos Platos	se·*goon*·dos *pla*·tos	Main Courses
Postres	*pos*·tres	Desserts
Bebidas	be·*bee*·das	Drinks
Aperitivos	a·pe·ree·*tee*·vos	Aperitifs
Licores	lee·*ko*·res	Spirits
Cervezas	ser·*ve*·sas	Beers
Gaseosas	ga·se·*o*·sas	Soft Drinks
Vinos Blancos	*vee*·nos *blan*·kos	White Wines
Vinos de la Casa	*vee*·nos de la *ka*·sa	House Wines
Vinos del Lugar	*vee*·nos del loo·*gar*	Local Wines
Vinos Espumosos	*vee*·nos es·poo·*mo*·sos	Sparkling Wines
Vinos Rosados	*vee*·nos ro·*sa*·dos	Roses
Vinos Tintos	*vee*·nos *teen*·tos	Red Wines
Vinos Dulces	*vee*·nos *dool*·ses	Dessert Wine
Digestivos	dee·khes·*tee*·vos	Digestifs

For more words you might see on a menu, see the **menu decoder** (p189).

Compliments & Complaints

That was delicious!	¡Estaba buenísimo! es·*ta*·ba bwe·*nee*·see·mo
My compliments to the chef.	Felicitaciones al cocinero. fe·lee·see·ta·*syo*·nes al ko·see·*ne*·ro
I'm full.	Estoy satisfecho/a. **m/f** es·*toy* sa·tees·*fe*·cho/a
I love this dish.	Me encanta este plato. me en·*kan*·ta *es*·te *pla*·to
I love the local cuisine.	Me encanta la comida típica de la zona. me en·*kan*·ta la ko·*mee*·da *tee*·pee·ka de la *so*·na
This is ...	Esto está ... *es*·to es·*ta* ...

burnt	quemado	ke·*ma*·do
cold	frío	*free*·o
hot	caliente	ka·*lyen*·te
(too) spicy	(demasiado) picante	(de·ma·*sya*·do) pee·*kan*·te
superb	exquisito	ek·skee·*see*·to

Paying the Bill

Please bring the bill.	Por favor nos trae la cuenta. por fa·*vor* nos *tra*·e la *kwen*·ta

Bill, please.	La cuenta, por favor.	la *kwen*·ta por fa·*vor*

LANGUAGE TIP

Regionalisms

The main meal of the day in Latin America is lunch, known as *el almuerzo* el al·*mwer*·so or *la comida* la ko·*mee*·da. Many restaurants in Latin America provide a set menu for lunch, usually consisting of soup, a main course and a drink. This cheap and popular option goes under the following guises:

Argentina, Central America, Chile	almuerzo m completo; comida f corrida	al·*mwer*·so kom·*ple*·to; ko·*mee*·da ko·*ree*·da
Colombia	almuerzo m corriente	al·*mwer*·so ko·*ryen*·te
Costa Rica	casado m	ka·*sa*·do
Guatemala, Mexico, Peru	menú m (del día)	me·*noo* (del *dee*·a)

Is service included in the bill?	¿La cuenta incluye el servicio? la *kwen*·ta een·*kloo*·ye el ser·*vee*·syo
There's a mistake in the bill.	Hay un error en la cuenta. ai oon e·*ror* en la *kwen*·ta

Nonalcoholic Drinks

Latin Americans drink prodigious quantities of sweet, fizzy drinks. The general term for 'soft drink' is *gaseosa* ga·se·*o*·sa, but in Chile they are *bebidas* be·*bee*·das, in Panama *refrescos* re·*fres*·kos or *sodas* *so*·das, and in Ecuador *colas* *ko*·las.

boiled water	agua f hervida *a*·gwa er·*vee*·da
coffee (without sugar)	café m (sin azúcar) ka·*fe* (seen a·*soo*·kar)

(orange) juice	jugo m (de naranja) *khoo*·go (de na·*ran*·kha)
lemonade	limonada f lee·mo·*na*·da
milk	leche f *le*·che
(fruit) milkshake	licuado m (de frutas) lee·*kwa*·do (de *froo*·tas)
tea (with milk)	té m (con leche) te (kon *le*·che)
sparkling mineral water	agua f mineral con gas *a*·gwa mee·ne·*ral* kon gas
still mineral water	agua f mineral sin gas *a*·gwa mee·ne·*ral* seen gas

LANGUAGE TIP

Regionalisms

Visitors to Latin America who are expecting out-of-this-world coffee might be surprised to learn that the best beans are shipped overseas to earn export dollars. It's still a popular drink though, and here's some vocabulary to help you order what you want:

black coffee	un café negro; un café tinto (Col)	oon ka·*fe ne*·gro; oon ka·*fe teen*·to
coffee with milk	un café con leche; un cortado (Arg)	oon ka·*fe* kon *le*·che; oon kor·*ta*·do
instant coffee	un nescafé	oon nes·ka·*fe*
milk coffee	un café con leche; un perico (Col)	oon ka·*fe* kon *le*·che; oon pe·*ree*·ko
small cup of coffee	un cafecito; un café chico (Arg)	oon ka·fe·*see*·to; oon ka·*fe chee*·ko

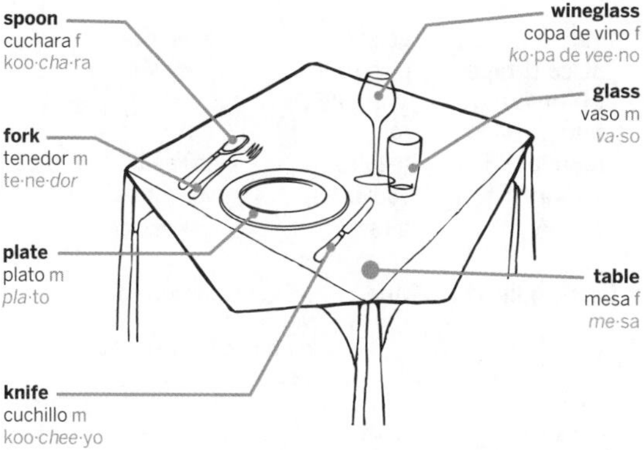

Alcoholic Drinks

brandy	coñac m ko·*nyak*
champagne	champán m cham·*pan*
cocktail	combinado m kom·bee·*na*·do
draught beer	cerveza f de baril ser·*ve*·sa de ba·*reel*

a shot of ... un trago de ...
oon *tra*·go de ...

gin	ginebra	khee·*ne*·bra
pisco (grape brandy)	pisco	*pees*·ko
rum	ron	ron
tequila	tequila	te·*kee*·la
vodka	vodka	*vod*·ka
whisky	güisqui	*gwees*·kee

a bottle/glass of ... wine una botella/copa de vino ...
oo·na bo·*te*·ya/*ko*·pa de *vee*·no ...

dessert	dulce	*dool*·se
red	tinto	*teen*·to
rose	rosado	ro·*sa*·do
sparkling	espumoso	es·poo·*mo*·so
white	blanco	*blan*·ko

a ... of beer ... de cerveza
... de ser·*ve*·sa

glass	un vaso	oon *va*·so
jug	una jarra; un chop **(SAm)**	*oo*·na *kha*·ra; oon chop
large bottle	una litrona	*oo*·na lee·*tro*·na
pint	una pinta	*oo*·na *peen*·ta
small bottle	un botellín	oon bo·te·*yeen*

In the Bar

Excuse me!	¡Oiga! *oy*·ga
I'm next.	¡Ahora voy yo! a·*o*·ra voy yo
Q **What would you like?**	¿Qué quiere/quieres tomar? **pol/inf** ke *kye*·re/*kye*·res to·*mar*
A **I'll have a glass of red wine.**	Para mí, una copa de vino tinto. *pa*·ra mee *oo*·na *ko*·pa de *vee*·no *teen*·to
A **I'd like a beer, please.**	Quisiera una cerveza, por favor. kee·*sye*·ra *oo*·na ser·*ve*·sa por fa·*vor*
Same again, please.	Otra de lo mismo. *o*·tra de lo *mees*·mo
No ice, thanks.	Sin hielo, gracias. seen *ye*·lo *gra*·syas
I'd like it straight, please.	Solo, por favor. *so*·lo por fa·*vor*
I'll buy you a drink.	Le/Te invito a una copa. **pol/inf** le/te een·*vee*·to a *oo*·na *ko*·pa
It's my round.	Es mi ronda. es mee *ron*·da
You can get the next one.	La próxima la pagas tú. **inf** la *prok*·see·ma la *pa*·gas too
Do you serve meals here?	¿Sirven comidas aquí? *seer*·ven ko·*mee*·das a·*kee*

LOOK FOR

Baños	*ba*·nyos	Toilets
Caballeros	ka·ba·*ye*·ros	Men
Damas	*da*·mas	Women
Hombres	*om*·bres	Men
Mujeres	moo·*khe*·res	Women
Señoras	se·*nyo*·ras	Women
Servicios	ser·*vee*·syos	Toilets
Varones	va·*ro*·nes	Men

Drinking Up

Cheers!	¡Salud! sa·*loo*
This is hitting the spot.	Me lo estoy pasando muy bien. me lo es·*toy* pa·*san*·do mooy byen
Thanks, but I don't feel like it.	Lo siento, pero no me apetece. lo *syen*·to *pe*·ro no me a·pe·*te*·se
I don't drink alcohol.	No bebo alcohol. no *be*·bo al·*kol*
I'm feeling drunk.	Esto me está subiendo mucho. *es*·to me es·*ta* soo·*byen*·do *moo*·cho
I think I've had one too many.	Creo que he tomado una de más. *kre*·o ke e to·*ma*·do *oo*·na de mas
I'm pissed.	Estoy borracho/a. **m/f** es·*toy* bo·*ra*·cho/a

Self-Catering

KEY PHRASES

What's the local speciality?	¿Cuál es la especialidad de la zona?	kwal es la es·pe·sya·lee·*da* de la *so*·na
Where can I find the ... section?	¿Dónde está la sección de ...?	*don*·de es·*ta* la sek·*syon* de ...
I'd like some ...	Déme unos/unas ... **m/f**	*de*·me *oo*·nos/*oo*·nas ...

Buying Food

What's the local speciality?	¿Cuál es la especialidad de la zona? kwal es la es·pe·sya·lee·*da* de la *so*·na
Do you sell locally produced food?	¿Vende productos locales? *ven*·de pro·*dook*·tos lo·*ka*·les
Do you sell organic produce?	¿Vende productos orgánicos? *ven*·de pro·*dook*·tos or·*ga*·nee·kos
What's that?	¿Qué es eso? ke es *e*·so
What's that called?	¿Cómo se llama eso? *ko*·mo se *ya*·ma *e*·so
Can I taste it?	¿Puedo probarlo/a? **m/f** *pwe*·do pro·*bar*·lo/a
Do you have other kinds?	¿Tiene otros tipos? *tye*·ne *ot*·ros *tee*·pos

How much is (a kilo of cheese)?	¿Cuánto vale (un kilo de queso)? *kwan*·to *va*·le (oon *kee*·lo de *ke*·so)
Do you have anything cheaper?	¿Tiene algo más barato? *tye*·ne *al*·go mas ba·*ra*·to
I'd like ...	Déme ... *de*·me ...

(200) grams	(doscientos) gramos	(do·*syen*·tos) *gra*·mos
a bottle	una botella	*oo*·na bo·*te*·ya
a dozen	una docena	*oo*·na do·*se*·na
a jar	una jarra	*oo*·na *kha*·ra
a kilo	un kilo	oon *kee*·lo
(two) kilos	(dos) kilos	(dos) *kee*·los
a packet	un paquete	oon pa·*ke*·te
a piece	un trozo	oon *tro*·so
(three) pieces	(tres) trozos	(tres) *tro*·sos
a slice	una loncha	*oo*·na *lon*·cha
(six) slices	(seis) lonchas	(says) *lon*·chas
a tin	una lata	*oo*·na *la*·ta
some ...	unos ... **m pl** unas ... **f pl**	*oo*·nos ... *oo*·nas ...
that one	ése/ésa **m/f**	*e*·se/*e*·sa
this one	éste/ésta **m/f**	*es*·te/*es*·ta

Enough.	Ya. ya
A bit more.	Un poco más. oon *po*·ko mas
Less.	Menos. *me*·nos

LOOK FOR

Carnicería	kar·nee·se·*ree*·a	Butcher
Fiambrería	fyam·bre·*ree*·a	Delicatessen
Frutería	froo·te·*ree*·a	Fruit Shop
Heladería	e·la·de·*ree*·a	Ice-Cream Parlour
Lechería	le·che·*ree*·a	Dairy Shop
Mercado	mer·*ka*·do	Market
Panadería	pa·na·de·*ree*·a	Baker
Pastelería	pas·te·le·*ree*·a	Cake Shop
Pescadería	pes·ka·de·*ree*·a	Fish Shop
Pollería	po·ye·*ree*·a	Poultry Shop
Supermercado	soo·per·mer·*ka*·do	Supermarket
Tabaquero	ta·ba·*ke*·ro	Tobacconist
Verdulería	ver·doo·le·*ree*·a	Greengrocer

Can I have a bag, please?	¿Me da una bolsa, por favor? me da *oo*·na *bol*·sa por fa·*vor*
Where can I find the ... section?	¿Dónde está la sección de ...? *don*·de es·*ta* la sek·*syon* de ...

dairy	productos lácteos	pro·*dook*·tos *lak*·te·os
frozen goods	productos congelados	pro·*dook*·tos kon·khe·*la*·dos
fruit and vegetable	frutas y verduras	*froo*·tas ee ver·*doo*·ras
meat	carne	*kar*·ne
poultry	aves	*a*·ves

Cooking

cooked	cocido/a **m/f** ko·*see*·do/a
dried	seco/a **m/f** *se*·ko/a
fresh	fresco/a **m/f** *fres*·ko/a
frozen	congelado/a **m/f** kon·khe·*la*·do/a
powdered	en polvo en *pol*·vo
raw	crudo/a **m/f** *kroo*·do/a
vacuum-packed	envasado/a **m/f** al vacío en·va·*sa*·do/a al va·*see*·o

LOOK FOR

apropriado/a m/f para cocinar en microondas	a·pro·*prya*·do/a *pa*·ra ko·see·*nar* en mee·kro·*on*·das microwaveable
consúmase antes del ...	kon·*soo*·ma·se *an*·tes del ... use by ...
consúmase dentro de (cuatro) días de abierto	kon·*soo*·ma·se *den*·tro de (*kwa*·tro) *dee*·as de a·*byer*·to consume within (four) days of opening
manténgase en el refrigerador	man·*ten*·ga·se en el re·free·khe·ra·*dor* keep refrigerated

¿Cuánto vale ...?
kwan·to va·le ...
How much is ...?

BRENT WINEBRENNER / LONELY PLANET IMAGES ©

Could I please borrow (a bottle opener)?	¿Me puede prestar (un abrebotellas)? me *pwe*·de pres·*tar* (oon a·bre·bo·*te*·yas)
Where's (a can opener)?	¿Dónde hay (un abrelatas)? *don*·de ai (oon a·bre·*la*·tas)

For more cooking implements, see the **dictionary**.

Vegetarian & Special Meals

KEY PHRASES

Do you have vegetarian food?	¿Tienen comida vegetariana?	*tye*·nen ko·*mee*·da ve·khe·ta·*rya*·na
Could you prepare a meal without ...?	¿Me puede preparar una comida sin ...?	me *pwe*·de pre·pa·*rar oo*·na ko·*mee*·da seen ...
I'm allergic to ...	Soy alérgico/a a ... m/f	soy a·*ler*·khee·ko/a a ...

Special Diets & Allergies

Is there a halal restaurant near here?	¿Hay un restaurante halal por aquí? ai oon res·tow·*ran*·te a·*lal* por a·*kee*
Is there a kosher restaurant near here?	¿Hay un restaurante kosher por aquí? ai oon res·tow·*ran*·te *ko*·sher por a·*kee*
Is there a vegetarian restaurant near here?	¿Hay un restaurante vegetariano por aquí? ai oon res·tow·*ran*·te ve·khe·ta·*rya*·no por a·*kee*
I'm vegan.	Soy vegetariano/a estricto/a. m/f soy ve·khe·ta·*rya*·no/a es·*treek*·to/a
I'm on a special diet.	Estoy a dieta especial. es·*toy* a *dye*·ta es·pe·*syal*

I'm allergic to ...	Soy alérgico/a ... m/f soy a·*ler*·khee·ko/a ...

dairy produce	a los productos lácteos	a los pro·*dook*·tos *lak*·te·os
eggs	a los huevos	a los *we*·vos
fish	al pescado	al pes·*ka*·do
gelatin	a la gelatina	a la khe·la·*tee*·na
honey	a la miel	a la myel
nuts	a las nueces	a las *nwe*·ses
peanuts	al maní	al ma·*nee*
seafood	al marisco	al ma·*rees*·ko

Ordering Food

Do you have (vegetarian) food?	¿Tienen comida (vegetariana)? *tye*·nen ko·*mee*·da (ve·khe·ta·*rya*·na)
I don't eat (red meat).	No como (carne roja). no *ko*·mo (*kar*·ne *ro*·kha)
Is it cooked in/with ...?	¿Está cocinado en/con ...? es·*ta* ko·see·*na*·do en/kon ...
Could you prepare a meal without ...?	¿Me puede preparar una comida sin ...? me *pwe*·de pre·pa·*rar* *oo*·na ko·*mee*·da seen ...

butter	mantequilla	man·te·*kee*·ya
meat/fish stock	caldo de carne/ pescado	*kal*·do de *kar*·ne/ pes·*ka*·do
pork	cerdo	*ser*·do
poultry	aves	*a*·ves

LISTEN FOR

Le preguntaré al cocinero.	le pre·goon·ta·*re* al ko·see·*ne*·ro I'll check with the cook.
¿Puede comer ...?	*pwe*·de ko·*mer* ... Can you eat ...?
Todo lleva (carne).	*to*·do *ye*·va (*kar*·ne) It all has (meat) in it.

Is this ...? ¿Esto es ...? *es*·to es ...

cholesterol-free	sin colesterol	seen ko·les·te·*rol*
decaffeinated	sin cafeína	seen ka·fe·*ee*·na
free of animal produce	sin productos de animales	seen pro·*dook*·tos de a·nee·*ma*·les
free-range	de corral	de ko·*ral*
genetically modified	transgénico/a **m/f**	trans·*khe*·nee·ko/a
gluten-free	sin gluten	seen *gloo*·ten
low-fat	bajo/a **m/f** en grasas	*ba*·kho/a en *gra*·sas
low in sugar	bajo/a **m/f** en azúcar	*ba*·kho/a en a·*soo*·kar
organic	orgánico/a **m/f**	or·*ga*·nee·ko/a
salt-free	sin sal	seen sal

Menu DECODER

léxico culinario

This miniguide to Latin American cuisine lists dishes and ingredients in Spanish alphabetical order (see **alphabet**, p13). Spanish nouns have their gender indicated by ⓜ or ⓕ. If it's a plural noun, you'll also see pl.

~ A ~

a la plancha a la *plan*·cha grilled
a punto a *poon*·to medium (steak)
aceite ⓜ a·*say*·te oil
aceitunas ⓕ pl a·say·*too*·nas olives
— alinadas (Cub) a·lee·*na*·das olives marinated in cummin, hot pepper, lemon, garlic & vinegar
— rellenas re·*ye*·nas stuffed olives
achicoria ⓕ a·chee·*ko*·rya chicory • endive
achuras ⓕ pl a·*choo*·ras offal
adobo ⓜ a·*do*·bo paste of garlic, oregano, paprika, peppercorn, salt, olive, lime juice & vinegar for seasoning meat
agua ⓕ *a*·gwa water
— de canilla de ka·*nee*·ya tap water
— de jamaica (CAm) de kha·*mai*·ka sweet, red, iced tea made from hibiscus flowers
— de la llave de la *ya*·ve tap water
— de panel (Col) de pa·*nel* unrefined sugar melted in hot water
— de vertiente de ver·*tyen*·te spring water
— del tubo del *too*·bo tap water
— mineral mee·ne·*ral* mineral water
aguacate ⓜ a·gwa·*ka*·te avocado
— salsa (Cub) *sal*·sa avocado sauce containing tomato, capsicum, olive, tomato & white rum
aguardiente ⓜ (Col) a·gwar·*dyen*·te spirit flavoured with anise
ahumado/a ⓜ/ⓕ a·oo·*ma*·do/a smoked
ají ⓜ a·*khee* chilli sauce • red chilli
ajiaco ⓜ a·*khya*·ko spicy potato stew • in Colombia, soup with chicken & three varieties of potato, served with corn & capers
ajili-mójili ⓜ (Pue) a·*khee*·lee *mo*·khee·lee tangy garlic sauce
ajillo, al a·*khee*·yo, al in garlic
ajo ⓜ *a*·kho garlic
ajoporro ⓜ a·kho·*po*·ro leek
al ajillo al a·*khee*·yo in garlic
al horno al *or*·no baked
al vapor al va·*por* steamed
albahaca ⓕ al·*ba*·ka basil
albóndigas ⓕ pl al·*bon*·dee·gas meatballs
alcachofa ⓕ al·ka·*cho*·fa artichoke
alcaparra ⓕ al·ka·*pa*·ra caper
alcaucil ⓜ (SAm) al·*kow*·seel artichoke
alcohol ⓜ al·*kol* alcohol

aliado ⓜ (Chi) a·*lya*·do sandwich with cold ham & cheese
alita ⓕ a·*lee*·ta wing (bird or poultry)
allioli ⓜ al·*yo*·lee garlic sauce
almejas ⓕ pl al·*me*·khas clams
almendra ⓕ al·*men*·dra almond
almuerzo ⓜ al·*mwer*·so lunch
alubias ⓕ pl a·*loo*·byas kidney beans
amarillos ⓜ pl (Pue) a·ma·*ree*·yos fried ripe plantains coated with cinnamon, sugar & wine sauce
ananá(s) ⓜ a·na·*na(s)* pineapple
anca ⓜ *an*·ka haunch
anchoas ⓕ pl an·*cho*·as anchovies
anguila ⓜ an·*gee*·la eel
anís ⓜ a·*nees* anise • aniseed
anticucho ⓜ (Bol, Chi, Per) an·tee·*koo*·cho kebab
apio ⓜ *a*·pyo celery
arenque ⓜ a·*ren*·ke herring
arepa ⓕ (Col, Ven) a·*re*·pa small toasted or fried maize pancake
areperas ⓕ (Ven) a·re·*pe*·ras snack bars selling **arepas**
arreglados ⓜ pl (Cos) a·re·*gla*·dos savoury filled puff pastries
arrollado ⓜ a·ro·*ya*·do rolled pork
arroz ⓜ a·*ros* rice
— con habichuelas (Pue) kon a·bee·*chwe*·las dish of rice & beans
— con leche kon *le*·che rice pudding
— con pollo kon *po*·yo dish of rice & chicken
arveja ⓕ (Ecu) ar·*ve*·kha pea stew
— seca *se*·ka split pea
arvejas ⓕ pl ar·*ve*·khas peas
asado ⓜ (SAm) a·*sa*·do mixed grill
— al espiedo al es·*pye*·do spit roast
asado/a ⓜ/ⓕ a·*sa*·do/a roasted
— al horno al *or*·no oven-roasted
asopao ⓜ **de pollo** (Pue) a·so·*pa*·o de po·*yo* chicken stew with **adobo** seasoning
atún ⓜ a·*toon* tuna
— con ron (Cub) kon ron tuna with a rum sauce
auyama ⓕ (Col, Ven) ow·*ya*·ma pumpkin
ave ⓜ *a*·ve fowl • poultry
avellana ⓜ a·ve·*ya*·na hazelnut
azafran ⓜ a·sa·*fran* saffron
azucar ⓜ a·*soo*·kar sugar

~ B ~

bacalao ⓜ ba·ka·*la*·o (salted) cod
baho ⓜ (Nic) *ba*·o stew of beef, various types of plantains & **yuca**
baleadas ⓕ pl (Hon) ba·le·*a*·das white-flour tortillas filled with refried beans, cream & crumbled cheese
banana ⓕ (Arg, Per) ba·*na*·na banana
banano ⓜ (CAm,Col) ba·*na*·no banana
bandeja ⓕ (Col) ban·*de*·kha main course
— paisa (Col) *pai*·sa traditional dish consisting of ground beef, sausage, red beans, rice, green banana, egg, salt, pork & avocado
baracoa ⓜ **special** (Cub) ba·ra·*ko*·a spe·*syal* cocktail of rum , coconut cream, grapefruit juice & limejuice
Barros Jarpa ⓜ (Chi) *ba*·ros *khar*·pa sandwich with cold ham & melted cheese, named after a Chilean painter
Barros Luco ⓜ (Chi) *ba*·ros *loo*·ko steak sandwich with melted cheese, named after a Chilean president
batata ⓕ ba·*ta*·ta sweet potato
bebida ⓕ be·*bee*·da drink (beverage)
beicon ⓜ **con queso** *bay*·kon kon *ke*·so cold bacon with cheese
berberechos ⓜ pl ber·be·*re*·chos cockles
berenjena ⓕ be·ren·*khe*·na aubergine • eggplant
berro ⓜ *be*·ro watercress
besugo ⓜ be·*soo*·go bream
betarraga ⓕ (Bol, Chi) ba·ta·*ra*·ga beetroot

bien asado/a ⓜ/ⓕ byen a·*sa*·do/a well-done
bien hecho/a ⓜ/ⓕ byen *e*·cho/a well-done
bife ⓜ (Arg, Par, Uru) *bee*·fe steak
— a caballo a ka·*ba*·yo steak served with two eggs & chips
— asado a·*sa*·do roast beef
— de chorizo de cho·*ree*·so rump steak
— de costilla de kos·*tee*·ya T-bone steak (also called **chuleta**)
— de lomo ⓜ de *lo*·mo tenderloin
bistec ⓜ bees·*tek* steak
— con patatas kon pa·*ta*·tas steak & chips
blanco ⓜ *blan*·ko white (wine)
bocadillo ⓜ (Cub) bo·ka·*dee*·yo sandwich filled with ham or cheese
bocaditos ⓜ pl (Cub) bo·ka·*dee*·tos substantial snack dishes
bocas ⓕ pl (Cos, Pan) *bo*·kas savoury side dishes served at bars
bollos ⓜ pl *bo*·yos bread rolls
boniatillo ⓜ (Cub) bo·nya·*tee*·yo dessert made from sweet potato, sugar, cinnamon, lime, egg yolks & sherry
boniato ⓜ (Arg) bo·*nya*·to sweet potato
bori-bori ⓜ (Par) *bo*·ree *bo*·ree chicken soup with corn meal balls
botella ⓕ bo·*te*·ya bottle
breva ⓕ *bre*·va fig
brócoli ⓜ *bro*·ko·lee broccoli
budín ⓜ boo·*deen* pudding
buey ⓜ bway ox

~ C ~

caballa ⓕ ka·*ba*·ya mackerel
cabeza ⓜ ka·*be*·sa head
cabra ⓕ *ka*·bra goat
cacao ⓜ ka·*ka*·o cocoa
cachapa ⓕ (Ven) ka·*cha*·pa large round corn pancake often served with cheese, ham or both
cachito ⓜ (Ven) ka·*chee*·to a type of hot croissant filled with chopped ham
café ⓜ ka·*fe* coffee
— chico (Arg) *chee*·ko small cup of coffee
— doble *do*·ble long black coffee
— marrón (Ven) ma·*ron* coffee consisting of half coffee & half milk
— negro *ne*·gro black coffee
— tinto (Col) *teen*·to black coffee
— solo ⓜ *so*·lo black coffee
cafecito ⓜ ka·fe·*see*·to small cup of coffee
cajeta ⓕ (Cos) ka·*khe*·ta similar to **dulce de leche**
calabacín ⓜ ka·la·ba·*seen* courgette • zucchini
calabaza ⓕ ka·la·*ba*·sa gourd • marrow • pumpkin
calamares ⓜ pl ka·la·*ma*·res calamari • squid
caldereta ⓕ kal·de·*re*·ta stew
caldillo ⓜ **cubano** (Cub) kal·*dee*·yo koo·*ba*·no hotpot made with steak, onions, tomatoes, potatoes, hot pepper, garlic, brown sugar & cumin
caldo ⓜ *kal*·do broth • stock
— de gallina de ga·*yee*·na chicken soup
— de patas (Ecu) de *pa*·tas soup made of boiled cattle hooves
caliente ka·*lyen*·te hot
callampas ⓕ (Chi) ka·*yam*·pas mushrooms
camarón ⓜ ka·ma·*ron* shrimp • small prawn
cambur ⓜ (Ven) kam·*boor* banana
camomila ⓕ ka·mo·*mee*·la camomile tea
camote ⓜ ka·*mo*·te sweet potato
caña ⓕ *ka*·nya **aguardiente** • cane alcohol
— de azúcar de a·*soo*·kar sugar cane
canela ⓕ ka·*ne*·la cinnamon
canelones ⓜ pl ka·ne·*lo*·nes cannelloni
cangrejo ⓜ kan·*gre*·kho crab
— de río de *ree*·o crayfish

cañita ⓕ (Pue) ka·*nyee*·ta homemade, illegal rum
capitán ⓜ (Chi) ka·pee·*tan* vermouth
capón ⓜ (SAm) ka·*pon* mutton
carabinero ⓜ ka·ra·bee·*ne*·ro large prawn
caracol ⓜ ka·ra·*kol* snail
carbonada ⓕ (Arg) kar·bo·*na*·da beef stew of rice, potatoes, maize, squash, apples & peaches
carimañola ⓕ (Pan) ka·ree·ma·*nyo*·la deep-fried roll filled with meat, made from ground & boiled **yuca**
carne ⓕ *kar*·ne meat
— de caballo de ka·*ba*·yo horsemeat
— de vaca de *va*·ka beef
— fría *free*·a cold meat
— mechada (Pue) me·*cha*·da roast beef
— molida mo·*lee*·da minced meat
carnicería ⓕ kar·nee·se·*ree*·a butcher's shop
carpa ⓕ *kar*·pa carp
casado ⓜ (Cos) ka·*sa*·do platter of rice, black beans, plantain, meat or fish, cabbage, an egg or avocado
— vegetariano (Cos) ve·khe·ta·*rya*·no vegetarian version of **casado**
casamiento ⓜ (Sal) ka·sa·*myen*·to rice & beans mixed together
castaña ⓕ kas·*ta*·nya chestnut
— de Pará de pa·*ra* brazil nut
cave ⓜ (Hon) *ka*·ve a type of coffee liqueur
caza ⓕ *ka*·sa game (meat)
— de temporada de tem·po·*ra*·da game in season
cazuela ⓕ ka·*swe*·la casserole • fish stew (Arg)
— de mariscos (Chi) de ma·*rees*·kos shellfish soup
cebada ⓕ se·*ba*·da barley
cebolla ⓕ se·*bo*·ya onion
cerdo ⓜ *ser*·do pig • pork
cereales ⓜ pl se·re·*a*·les cereal
cereza ⓕ se·*re*·sa cherry
cerveza ⓕ ser·*ve*·sa beer
— de barril de ba·*reel* beer on tap • draught beer
— de malta de *mal*·ta dark beer
— lager *la*·ger lager beer
— negra *ne*·gra stout
ceviche ⓜ se·*vee*·che raw fish marinated in lemon juice, chilli or onions or both
chacarero ⓜ (Chi) cha·ka·*re*·ro beefsteak with tomato & vegetables
chairo ⓜ (Bol) *chai*·ro mutton or beef soup served with **chuños**, fresh potato & dried maize
chajchu ⓜ (Bol) *chakh*·choo beef with freeze-dried potatoes, hard-boiled egg, cheese & hot red-pepper sauce
chalote ⓜ cha·*lo*·te shallot • spring onion
champán ⓜ cham·*pan* champagne
champiñones ⓜ pl cham·pee·*nyo*·nes mushrooms
— al ajillo al a·*khee*·yo garlic mushrooms
chapalele ⓜ (Chi) cha·pa·*le*·le boiled potato & flour bread
chaque ⓜ (Bol) *cha*·ke similar to **chupe** but much thicker & with more grain
charque ⓜ (Bol) *char*·ke dried beef, llama or other red meat
— kan kan **charque** served with mashed hominy
chauchas ⓕ pl *chow*·chas string beans
chicha ⓕ (Bol, Per) *chee*·cha maize beer associated with ceremonial & ritual occasions in Peru
chicharrón ⓜ chee·cha·*ron* fried pork fat
chifa ⓕ (Bol, CAm, Per) *chee*·fa Chinese restaurant
chilcano ⓜ (Chi, Per) cheel·*ka*·no ginger ale (may be served with **pisco**)

chile ⓜ *chee*·le pimento (small red pepper)
chimichurri ⓜ (Arg, Uru) chee·mee·*choo*·ree strong olive oil, parsley & garlic barbecue sauce
chinchulines ⓜ pl cheen·choo·*lee*·nes small intestines – a common **asado** dish
chipa ⓕ **de almidón** (Par) *chee*·pa de al·mee·*don* like **chipa guazú** but made with manioc flour rather than corn meal
chipa ⓕ **guazú** (Par) *chee*·pa gwa·*soo* dish resembling a cheese souffle containing corn meal
chipirón ⓜ chee·pee·*ron* small squid
chirimoya ⓕ chee·ree·*mo*·ya custard apple
chispa tren ⓕ (Cub) *chees*·pa tren 'train sparks' – Cuban firewater
chivito ⓜ (Uru) chee·*vee*·to tasty & filling steak sandwich with a variety of additions including cheese, lettuce, tomato & bacon
— al plato al *pla*·to steak served with a fried egg, potato salad, green salad & French fries
chivo ⓜ *chee*·vo baby goat • kid
choclo ⓜ *cho*·klo corn on the cob • maize
choco ⓜ *cho*·ko cuttlefish
chocolate ⓜ cho·ko·*la*·te chocolate
— caliente ka·*lyen*·te hot chocolate drink
— santafereño (Col) san·ta·fe·*re*·nyo cup of hot chocolate accompanied by a piece of cheese & bread
chola ⓕ (Bol) *cho*·la bread roll filled with meat, onion, tomato & **escabeche**
chop ⓜ chop draught beer
choripán ⓜ (Arg) cho·ree·*pan* spicy sausage sandwich
chorizo ⓜ cho·*ree*·so spicy pork sausage
— al horno al *or*·no spicy baked sausage
chorlito ⓜ chor·*lee*·to plover (small game bird)
chuleta ⓕ choo·*le*·ta chop • cutlet • T-bone steak (Arg)
— de puerco de *pwer*·ko pork chop
chuños ⓜ pl (Bol) *choo*·nyos freeze-dried potatoes made by leaving potatoes out in the winter cold
chupe ⓜ *choo*·pe soup • stew • in Bolivia, a vegetable, meat & grain soup with a clear broth flavoured with **ají**, tomato, cumin or onion
— de camarones (Per) de ka·ma·*ro*·nes prawn soup
— de cóngrio (Chi) de *kon*·gryo conger-eel stew
— de locos (Chi) de *lo*·kos abalone stew
churrasco ⓜ choo·*ras*·ko rib steak • in Ecuador, a hearty dish of rice, fried beef, fried eggs, vegetables, fried potatoes, a slice of avocado, tomato & rice
ciruela ⓕ see·*rwe*·la plum
— seca *se*·ka prune
ckocko ⓜ (Bol) *ko*·ko spicy chicken cooked in wine or **chicha** & served with maize, olives, raisins & aromatic condiments
clericó ⓜ (Uru) kle·ree·*ko* usually a mixture of white wine, fruit juice, a liqueur, fruit salad, ice & a carbonated soft drink or cider
cocina ⓕ ko·*see*·na cuisine • kitchen
cocinado/a ⓜ/ⓕ ko·see·*na*·do/a cooked
cocinar ko·see·*nar* to cook
cocinero/a ⓜ/ⓕ ko·see·*ne*·ro/a chef
coco ⓜ *ko*·ko coconut
codorniz ⓕ ko·dor·*nees* quail
coles ⓜ pl **de Bruselas** *ko*·les de broo·*se*·las Brussels sprouts
coliflor ⓜ ko·lee·*flor* cauliflower
combinado ⓜ kom·bee·*na*·do cocktail

completo ⓜ (Chi) kom·*ple*·to a hot dog with the lot
con gas kon gas fizzy
con leche kon *le*·che with milk
coñac ⓜ ko·*nyak* brandy
conejo ⓜ ko·*ne*·kho rabbit
confitería ⓕ kon·fee·te·*ree*·a candy store • sweet shop
confites ⓜ pl (Bol) kon·*fee*·tes festive candies consisting of coloured sugar syrup, nuts, aniseed, fruits, biscuit or coconut
copa ⓕ *ko*·pa glass
corazón ⓜ ko·ra·*son* heart
cordero ⓜ kor·*de*·ro lamb
cortado ⓜ (Arg) kor·*ta*·do coffee with a little milk
costilla ⓕ kos·*tee*·ya loin • spare rib
— de cerdo de *ser*·do pork chop
costillar ⓜ **de cordero** kos·tee·*yar* de kor·*de*·ro rack of lamb
crema ⓕ *kre*·ma cream
— batida ba·*tee*·da whipped cream
croquetas ⓕ pl (Cub) kro·*ke*·tas fried ham or chicken croquettes
crudo/a ⓜ/ⓕ *kroo*·do/a raw
crustáceos ⓜ pl kroos·*ta*·se·os shellfish
cuadril ⓜ kwa·*dreel* rump steak
cubo ⓜ **de hielo** *koo*·bo de *ye*·lo ice cube
curanto ⓜ (Chi) koo·*ran*·to hearty stew of fish, shellfish, chicken, pork, lamb, beef & potato
curtido ⓜ (Sal) koor·*tee*·do mixture of pickled beets, cabbage & carrots served with **pupusas**
cuy ⓜ kooy grilled or roasted guinea pig

~ D ~

damasco ⓜ da·*mas*·ko apricot
dátil ⓜ *da*·teel date
descafeinado/a ⓜ/ⓕ des·ka·fay·*na*·do/a decaffeinated
desnatado/a ⓜ/ⓕ des·na·*ta*·do/a low-fat
digestivo ⓜ dee·khes·*tee*·vo digestif
dorado/a ⓜ/ⓕ do·*ra*·do/a browned
dulce ⓜ **de leche** (Arg) *dool*·se de *le*·che caramelised condensed milk • filling in sweet pastries
dulce *dool*·se sweet
dulces ⓜ pl *dool*·ses sweets

~ E ~

(de) elaboración propia (de) e·la·bo·ra·*syon pro*·pya made on the premises
elote ⓜ (CAm) e·*lo*·te corn • corn on the cob
empanada ⓕ em·pa·*na*·da stuffed meat & vegetable turnover
empanadilla ⓕ (Pue) em·pa·na·*dee*·ya pocket of plantain or **yuca** dough stuffed with meat
empanadillas ⓕ pl **de jueyes** (Pue) em·pa·na·*dee*·yas de *khwe*·yes highly seasoned land crab meat baked into an **empanadilla** of cassava paste
empana ⓕ (Cub) em·*pa*·na meat or vegetable pattie
en escabeche (Pue) en es·ka·*be*·che way of preparing seafood by frying, then chilling & pickling it
en rodajas en ro·*da*·khas sliced
enchilladas ⓕ pl (Hon, Mex) en·chee·*ya*·das crisp fried tortilla topped with spicy meat, salad & crumbled cheese
endulzado/a ⓜ/ⓕ en·dool·*sa*·do/a sweetened
eneldo ⓜ e·*nel*·do dill
ensalada ⓕ en·sa·*la*·da salad • in El Salvador, a mixed fruit juice served with fruit salad floating on top
— mixta *meeks*·ta mixed salad
— rusa *roo*·sa vegetable salad with mayonnaise
— verde *ver*·de green salad

entremeses ⓕ pl en·tre·*me*·ses hors-d'oeuvres
erizos ⓜ pl (Chi) e·*ree*·sos sea urchins
escabeche ⓜ (Bol) es·ka·*be*·che vegetables, onion & peppers preserved in vinegar
espagueti ⓜ pl es·pa·*ge*·tee spaghetti
espárrago ⓜ es·*pa*·ra·go asparagus
especialidad ⓕ es·pe·sya·lee·*da* speciality
— de la casa de la *ka*·sa speciality of the house
— del día del *dee*·a speciality of the day
espinacas ⓜ pl es·pee·*na*·kas spinach
espumoso/a ⓜ/ⓕ es·poo·*mo*·so/a sparkling
estofado ⓜ es·to·*fa*·do stew
estofado/a ⓜ/ⓕ es·to·*fa*·do/a braised
estragón ⓜ es·tra·*gon* tarragon

~ F ~

faba ⓜ *fa*·ba type of dried bean
facturas ⓕ pl (Arg) fak·*too*·ras buns • cakes
faisán ⓜ fai·*san* pheasant
falso conejo ⓜ (Bol) *fal*·so ko·*ne*·kho 'false rabbit' – greasy, glutinous meat-based dish
fideos ⓜ pl fee·*de*·os noodles
filete ⓜ fee·*le*·te fillet of meat or fish
— de bife de *bee*·fe beef fillet
flan ⓜ flan creme caramel • egg custard
frambuesa ⓕ fram·*bwe*·sa raspberry
fresa ⓕ *fre*·sa strawberry
fresco/a ⓜ/ⓕ *fres*·ko/a fresh
frescos ⓜ pl (Hon) *fres*·kos fruit drinks blended with water & sugar
fricasés ⓜ (Bol) free·ka·*ses* pork or chicken stew with maize grits
frijol ⓜ free·*khol* bean
— blanco *blan*·ko large butter bean
frijoles ⓜ pl free·*kho*·les beans
— con arroz (Gua) kon *a*·ros beans & rice
frío/a ⓜ/ⓕ *free*·o/a cold
fritada ⓕ free·*ta*·da scraps of fried or roast pork
fritanga ⓕ free·*tan*·ga hotpot or stew • in Bolivia, spicy hot pork with mint & hominy
frito/a ⓜ/ⓕ *free*·to/a fried
— a la sartén a la sar·*ten* pan-fried
fruta ⓕ *froo*·ta fruit
frutilla ⓕ froo·*tee*·ya strawberry
fuerte *fwer*·te strong

~ G ~

galleta ⓕ ga·*ye*·ta biscuit • cookie
gallina ⓕ ga·*yee*·na chicken
gallito ⓜ ga·*yee*·to cockerel
gallo ⓜ *ga*·yo rooster
gallo ⓜ **pinto** (Cos, Nic, Pan) *ga*·yo *peen*·to lightly spiced mixture of rice & black beans traditionally served for breakfast, sometimes with **natilla** or fried eggs
gallos ⓜ pl (Cos) *ga*·yos tortilla sandwiches containing meat, beans or cheese
gambas ⓕ pl **rebozadas** *gam*·bas re·bo·*sa*·das batter-fried scampi (large prawns)
ganso ⓜ *gan*·so goose
garbanzo ⓜ gar·*ban*·so chickpea
gaseoso/a ⓜ/ⓕ ga·se·*o*·so/a fizzy
gazpacho ⓜ ga·*spa*·cho cold tomato & vegetable soup
ginebra ⓕ **bols** (Arg) khee·*ne*·bra bols alcoholic drink similar to gin
girasol ⓜ khee·ra·*sol* sunflower
glaseado/a ⓜ/ⓕ gla·se·*a*·do/a glazed • iced
gol ⓜ (Chi) gol translucent alcoholic mixture of butter, sugar & milk

granada Ⓕ gra·*na*·da pomegranate
grande *gran*·de big • large
grasa Ⓕ *gra*·sa fat • grease
gratinado/a Ⓜ/Ⓕ gra·tee·*na*·do/a au gratin
grosella Ⓕ gro·*se*·ya redcurrant
— espinosa es·pee·*no*·sa gooseberry
— negra *ne*·gra blackcurrant
guífiti Ⓜ (Hon) *gi*·fee·tee mix of **aguardiente** with aromatic & marine plants – a Garífuna specialty
guinda Ⓕ (Per) *geen*·da sweet cherry brandy
guindado Ⓜ (Chi) geen·*da*·do fermented alcoholic drink made from a cherry-like fruit, brandy, cinnamon & cloves
guindilla Ⓕ geen·*dee*·ya hot chilli
guisantes Ⓜ pl gee·*san*·tes peas
guiso Ⓜ (Cos) *gee*·so stew
güisqui Ⓜ *gwees*·kee whisky

~ H ~

haba Ⓕ *a*·ba broad bean • Lima bean
hallaca Ⓕ (Ven) a·*ya*·ka chopped pork, beef and/or chicken with vegetables & olives, all folded in a maize dough, wrapped in banana leaves & steamed
hamburguesa Ⓕ am·boor·*ge*·sa hamburger
harina Ⓕ a·*ree*·na flour
hecho/a Ⓜ/Ⓕ *e*·cho/a made • prepared
heladería Ⓕ e·la·de·*ree*·a ice-cream parlour
helado/a Ⓜ/Ⓕ e·*la*·do/a chilled • iced
helado Ⓜ e·*la*·do ice cream
hervido/a Ⓜ/Ⓕ er·*vee*·do/a boiled
— a fuego lento a *fwe*·go *len*·to simmered
hervir er·*veer* boil
hierba Ⓕ *yer*·ba herb
hierbabuena Ⓕ yer·ba·*bwe*·na mint
hígado Ⓜ *ee*·ga·do liver
higo Ⓜ *ee*·go fig
hocico Ⓜ o·*see*·ko snout
hongo Ⓜ *on*·go button mushroom
horchata Ⓕ (Cos) or·*cha*·ta rice-based drink flavoured with cinnamon
— de cebada (Sal) de se·*ba*·da sweet barley-based beverage spiced with cinnamon
hormiga Ⓕ **culona** (Col) or·*mee*·ga koo·*lo*·na large fried ants – unique to Santander
horneado/a Ⓜ/Ⓕ or·ne·*a*·do/a baked
hornear or·ne·*ar* bake
horno Ⓜ *or*·no oven
horno, al *or*·no, al oven-baked
hortalizas Ⓕ pl or·ta·*lee*·sas vegetables
hueso Ⓜ *we*·so bone
huevos Ⓜ pl *we*·vos eggs
— cocidos ko·*see*·dos boiled eggs
— de paslama de pas·*la*·ma turtle eggs – a popular dish in Nicaragua though ecologically suspect
— duros *doo*·ros hard-boiled eggs
— estrellados es·tre·*ya*·dos fried eggs
— fritos *free*·tos fried eggs
— pericos pe·*ree*·kos scrambled eggs with fried onions
— revueltos re·*vwel*·tos scrambled eggs
humitas Ⓕ pl (Bol) oo·*mee*·tas corn **tamales** filled with spiced beef, vegetables & potatoes
— en chala (Chi) en *cha*·la popular & tasty snack of steamed **tamales** wrapped in corn husks
húngaros Ⓜ pl (Uru) *oon*·ga·ros spicy sausages on a hot-dog roll

~ I ~

infusión Ⓕ een·foo·*syon* herbal tea

~ J ~

jabalí ⓜ kha·ba·*lee* wild boar
jamón ⓜ kha·*mon* ham
— dulce *dool*·se boiled ham
— serrano se·*ra*·no cured ham
jengibre ⓜ khen·*khee*·bre ginger
jochi ⓜ *kho*·chee agouti (a rodent prized for its meat)
jolque ⓜ (Bol) *khol*·ke kidney soup
jueyes ⓜ pl (Pue) *khwe*·yes land crabs – an island staple
jugo ⓜ *khoo*·go juice
— exprimido ⓜ ek·spree·*mee*·do freshly squeezed juice
jugoso/a ⓜ/ⓕ khoo·*go*·so/a succulent

~ K ~

kala purkha ⓕ (Bol) *ka*·la *poor*·ka soup made from maize cooked in a ceramic dish by adding a steaming chunk of heavy pumice
kosher *ko*·sher kosher
kuchen ⓜ (Chi) *koo*·chen pastries filled with local fruit, baked by Chileans of German descent

~ L ~

lager *la*·ger lager • light-coloured or pale beer
langosta ⓕ lan·*gos*·ta spiny lobster
langostino ⓜ lan·gos·*tee*·no lobster • prawn
lawa ⓕ (Bol) *la*·wa soup made from a broth thickened with corn starch or wheat flour
leche ⓕ *le*·che milk
— desnatada des·na·*ta*·da skimmed milk
lechón ⓜ le·*chon* suckling pig – a speciality of Cochabamba in Bolivia
lechona ⓕ (Col) le·*cho*·na pig carcass stuffed with its own meat, rice & dried peas & baked in an oven
lechuga ⓕ le·*choo*·ga lettuce
legumbre ⓕ le·*goom*·bre pulse
lengua ⓕ *len*·gwa tongue
lenguado ⓜ len·*gwa*·do dab • lemon sole
lenteja ⓕ len·*te*·kha lentil • in Ecuador, a lentil stew
lentejas ⓕ pl len·*te*·khas lentils
licuados ⓜ pl lee·*kwa*·dos milk-blended fruit drinks
lima ⓕ *lee*·ma lime
limón ⓜ lee·*mon* lemon
limonadas ⓕ pl lee·mo·*na*·das lemonade made with lime or lemon juice, water & sugar
lista ⓕ **de vinos** *lees*·ta de *vee*·nos wine list
llajhua ⓕ (Bol) *ya*·khwa hot **salsa** made from tomatoes & hot-pepper pods
llano/a ⓜ/ⓕ *ya*·no/a plain
llapingachos ⓜ pl (Ecu) ya·peen·*ga*·chos fried pancakes made from mashed potato & cheese, often served with **fritada**
llaucha ⓕ pl **paceña** (Bol) *yow*·cha pa·*se*·nya doughy cheese bread
locotos ⓜ pl (Bol) lo·*ko*·tos small hot-pepper pods
locro ⓜ *lo*·kro in Argentina & Paraguay, a maize stew • in Ecuador, potato soup with corn & avocado or cheese topping
lomo ⓜ *lo*·mo loin
— a lo pobre (Chi) a lo *po*·bre huge slab of beef topped with two fried eggs & served with French fries
— con pimientos kon pee·*myen*·tos pork sausage with peppers
— de cerdo de *ser*·do pork loin • sausage
— saltado (Per) sal·*ta*·do chopped steak fried with onions, tomatoes, potatoes & served with rice
longaniza ⓕ lon·ga·*nee*·sa dark pork sausage

~ M ~

M

macarrones Ⓜ pl *ma·ka·ro·nes* macaroni
maíz Ⓜ *ma·ees* corn • maize • sweet corn
mallorca Ⓕ (Pue) *ma·yor·ka* sweet pastry covered with powdered sugar
malta Ⓕ (Pue) *mal·ta* nonalcoholic, vitamin-fortified malt beverage
mandarina Ⓕ *man·da·ree·na* tangerine
mango Ⓜ *man·go* mango
maní Ⓜ *ma·nee* peanut
mantequilla Ⓕ *man·te·kee·ya* butter
manzana Ⓕ *man·sa·na* apple
maracuyá Ⓕ *ma·ra·koo·ya* passionfruit
marinado/a Ⓜ/Ⓕ *ma·ree·na·do/a* marinated
mariscos Ⓜ pl *ma·rees·kos* seafood • shellfish
masaco Ⓜ (Bol) *ma·sa·ko* llama **charque** served with mashed plantain or **yuca**
matambre Ⓜ **relleno** (Arg) *ma·tam·bre re·ye·no* stuffed & rolled flank steak, baked or eaten cold as an appetiser
mate Ⓜ *ma·te* tea prepared from **yerba mate** – the most popular hot beverage in Argentina, Paraguay & Uruguay
— de coca (Bol, Per) *de ko·ka* coca-leaf tea
mavi Ⓜ (Pue) *ma·vee* a root beer–like drink made from the bark of the ironwood tree
mayonesa Ⓕ *ma·yo·ne·sa* mayonnaise
mazamorro Ⓜ *ma·sa·mo·ro* in Costa Rica, a pudding made from corn starch • in Paraguay, corn mush
mazapan Ⓜ *ma·sa·pan* almond paste • marzipan
mazorca Ⓕ *ma·sor·ka* corn on the cob
mbaipy heé Ⓜ (Par) *mba·ee·pee e·e* dessert of corn, milk & molasses
mbaipy soó Ⓜ (Par) *mba·ee·pee so·o* hot maize pudding with meat chunks
mbeyú Ⓜ (Par) *mbe·yoo* grilled manioc pancake
medialunas Ⓕ pl *me·dya·loo·nas* 'half moons' – small croissants (a popular breakfast food in Argentine cafes)
mediana Ⓕ *me·dya·na* bottle (third of a litre)
medianoche Ⓜ (Pue) *me·dya·no·che* ham, pork & cheese sandwich
medio y medio Ⓜ (Uru) *me·dyo ee me·dyo* mixture of sparkling wine & white wine
mejilla Ⓕ *me·khee·ya* cheek
mejillones Ⓜ pl *me·khee·yo·nes* mussels
— al vapor *al va·por* steamed mussels
melocotón Ⓜ *me·lo·ko·ton* peach
melón Ⓜ *me·lon* melon
membrillo Ⓜ *mem·bree·yo* quince
menta Ⓜ *men·ta* mint
menú Ⓜ *me·noo* menu
menudencias Ⓕ pl (SAm) *me·noo·den·syas* giblets
menudo Ⓜ **de pollo** *me·noo·do de po·yo* gizzard • poultry entrails
mercado Ⓜ *mer·ka·do* market
merengadas Ⓕ pl (Ven) *me·ren·ga·das* milkshake with juice
merluza Ⓕ *mer·loo·sa* hake – in Argentina, it's served batter-fried with mashed potatoes
— a la plancha Ⓕ *a la plan·cha* grilled hake
mermelada Ⓕ *mer·me·la·da* jam
miel Ⓕ *myel* honey
migas Ⓕ pl *mee·gas* fried breadcrumb dish
mil hojas Ⓕ pl (Pue) *meel o·khas* 'a thousand leaves' – layers of thin pastry filled with almond & honey paste

milanesa ⓕ mee·la·*ne*·sa schnitzel
milcao ⓜ (Chi) meel·*kow* potato bread
mojama ⓕ mo·*kha*·ma cured tuna
mojo ⓜ **isleño** (Pue) *mo*·kho ees·*le*·nyo piquant sauce of vinegar, tomato sauce, olive oil, onions, capers, pimentos, olives, bay leaves & garlic – often served with fried fish
molleja ⓕ mo·*ye*·kha sweetbread
mondongo ⓜ (Ven) mon·*don*·go seasoned tripe cooked in bouillon with maize, potatoes & other vegetables
montado ⓜ mon·*ta*·do tiny sandwich served as an appetiser
mora ⓕ *mo*·ra blackberry
morcilla ⓕ mor·*see*·ya blood sausage – a common **asado** dish
moros y cristianos ⓜ pl (Cub) *mo*·ros ee krees·*tya*·nos 'Moors & Christians' – dish of black beans & rice
mostaza ⓕ mos·*ta*·sa mustard
mosto ⓜ (Par) *mos*·to sugar-cane juice
mote ⓜ **con huesillo** (Chi) *mo*·te kon we·*see*·yo peach nectar with barley kernels
muchacho ⓜ (Ven) moo·*cha*·cho roast loin of beef served in sauce
muslo ⓜ *moos*·lo thigh
muy hecho/a ⓜ/ⓕ mooy e·cho/a well-done

~ N ~

nabo ⓜ *na*·bo turnip
nacatamales ⓜ pl (Nic) na·ka·ta·*ma*·les cornmeal, meat, vegetables & herbs wrapped in banana leaves
naranja ⓕ na·*ran*·kha orange
naranjadas ⓕ pl na·ran·*kha*·das lemonades made with orange juice
nata ⓕ *na*·ta cream
natilla ⓕ (Cos) na·*tee*·ya sour cream
natillas ⓕ pl na·*tee*·yas creamy milk dessert • custard
nuez ⓜ nwes nut • walnut

~ O ~

ocas ⓕ pl (Bol) *o*·kas tough, purple, potato-like tubers
ojo ⓜ **de bife** o·kho de *bee*·fe eye of round steak
olímpicos ⓜ pl (Uru) o·*leem*·pee·kos club sandwiches
oporto ⓜ o·*por*·to port
orejón ⓜ o·re·*khon* dried apricot
orgánico/a ⓜ/ⓕ or·ga·nee·ko/a organic
ostión ⓜ os·*tyon* scallop
ostiones ⓜ pl (Cub) os·*tyo*·nes drink or appetiser containing mussels or oysters, rum, lime juice, salt & pepper
ostras ⓕ pl *os*·tras oysters
oveja ⓕ o·*ve*·kha ewe

~ P ~

pabellón ⓜ (Ven) pa·be·*yon* main course consisting of shredded beef, rice, beans & fried plantain – Venezuela's national dish
pacumutas ⓕ pl (Bol) pa·koo·*moo*·tas enormous chunks of grilled meat accompanied by **yuca**, onions & other trimmings
paila ⓕ **marina** (Chi) *pai*·la ma·*ree*·na fish & shellfish chowder
pajarito ⓜ pa·kha·*ree*·to small bird
paleta ⓕ pa·*le*·ta shoulder
palmitos ⓜ pl (Cos) pal·*mee*·tos hearts of palm – usually served in a vinegar dressing
paloma ⓕ pa·*lo*·ma pigeon
palta ⓕ (SAm) *pal*·ta avocado
— a la jardinera (Per) a la khar·dee·*ne*·ra avocado stuffed with cold vegetables & mayonnaise
— a la reina (Per) a la *ray*·na avocado stuffed with chicken salad

pan Ⓜ pan bread
— de coco (Hon) de *ko*·ko coconut bread
panapen Ⓜ (Pue) pa·*na*·pen breadfruit
panchos Ⓜ pl (Arg, Uru) *pan*·chos mild sausages on a hot-dog roll
panes Ⓜ pl (Sal) *pa*·nes French breads sliced open & stuffed with chicken or turkey
papas Ⓕ pl *pa*·pas potatoes
— fritas *free*·tas chips • French fries
— rellenas (Bol) re·*ye*·nas stuffed potatoes – a speciality from the central highlands
papitas Ⓕ pl pa·*pee*·tas crisps • potato chips
parrilla Ⓕ pa·*ree*·ya grill
parrillada Ⓕ pa·ree·*ya*·da mixed grill – huge slabs of grilled meat prepared over hot coals, served with spicy sauces & vegetables • steak house – an institution in Argentina
pasa Ⓜ *pa*·sa raisin
pasankalla Ⓕ (Bol) pa·san·*ka*·ya puffed maize with caramel – very sticky & chewy concoction
pasta Ⓕ *pas*·ta pasta
pastel Ⓜ pas·*tel* cake • pastry • in Puerto Rico, a sweeter version of an **empanadilla** with a stuffing of raisins, beans, fish or pork
— de choclo (Chi) de *cho*·klo maize casserole filled with vegetables, chicken & beef
pastelillos Ⓜ pl (Pue) pas·te·*lee*·yos smaller version of a **pastel** stuffed with meat & cheese
patacones Ⓜ pl (Cos, Pan) pa·ta·*ko*·nes fried green plantains cut into thin pieces, salted, then pressed & fried
patita Ⓕ **de cerdo** pa·*tee*·ta de *ser*·do pig's trotter
pato Ⓜ *pa*·to duck
pavo Ⓜ *pa*·vo turkey
pebre Ⓜ (Chi) *pe*·bre tasty condiment made from chopped tomatoes, onion, garlic, chilli peppers, coriander & parsley
pechuga Ⓕ pe·*choo*·ga breast meat
pedido Ⓜ pe·*dee*·do order
pejibaye Ⓜ (Cos) pe·khee·*ba*·ye starchy palm fruit also eaten as a salad
pepinillo Ⓜ pe·pee·*nee*·yo gherkin
pepino Ⓜ pe·*pee*·no cucumber
pera Ⓕ *pe*·ra pear
perca Ⓕ *per*·ka perch
perdiz Ⓕ per·*dees* partridge
perejil Ⓜ pe·re·*kheel* parsley
perico Ⓜ (Col) pe·*ree*·ko small milk coffee
pescadilla Ⓕ pes·ka·*dee*·ya whiting
pescado Ⓜ pes·*ka*·do fish
— de agua dulce de *a*·gwa *dool*·se freshwater fish
— de mar Ⓜ de mar saltwater fish
pescaíto Ⓜ pes·ka·*ee*·to tiny fried fish
pez Ⓜ **espada** pes es·*pa*·da swordfish
picada Ⓕ (Arg) pee·*ka*·da snack
picadillo Ⓜ pee·ka·*dee*·yo minced meat • in Cuba, ground beef hash with capsicum, raisins, ham, spices, olives & rice
picante pee·*kan*·te spicy
pierna Ⓕ *pyer*·na leg
pil pil Ⓜ peel peel often spicy garlic sauce
pimentón Ⓜ pee·men·*ton* paprika
pimienta Ⓕ pee·*myen*·ta pepper
pimiento Ⓜ pee·*myen*·to bell pepper • capsicum
piña Ⓕ *pee*·nya pineapple
pinchita Ⓕ (Pue) peen·*chee*·ta homemade, illegal rum
pincho Ⓜ *peen*·cho kebab
piñón Ⓜ pee·*nyon* pine nut
pintado Ⓜ (Col) peen·*ta*·do small milk coffee

piononos ⓜ pl (Pue) pyo·*no*·nos deep-fried cones made from plantains stuffed with cheese (or meat) & coated with egg batter
pipas ⓕ pl (Cos) *pee*·pas green coconuts with a straw to drink the milk
pique ⓜ **a lo macho** (Bol) *pee*·ke a lo *ma*·cho chunked grilled beef & sausage served with French fries, lettuce, tomatoes, onions, capsicum & **locotos**
pisco ⓜ (Chi, Per) *pees*·ko grape brandy – often served as a **pisco sauer** with egg white, lemon juice & powdered sugar
pistacho ⓜ pees·*ta*·cho pistachio
plancha ⓕ *plan*·cha grill
plátano ⓜ *pla*·ta·no banana • plantain
— maduro (Pan) ma·*doo*·ro slices of ripe plantains baked or broiled with butter, brown sugar & cinnamon
platija ⓕ pla·*tee*·kha flounder
plato ⓜ *pla*·to dish • plate
poché po·*che* poached
poco hecho/a ⓜ/ⓕ *po*·ko e·cho/a rare
pollo ⓜ *po*·yo chicken
— a la canasta (Bol) a la ka·*nas*·ta 'chicken in a basket' – chicken served with mustard, fries or **yuca** & **ají**
polvo ⓜ *pol*·vo powder
pomelo ⓜ po·*me*·lo grapefruit
porotos ⓜ pl po·*ro*·tos beans
porrón ⓜ **de cerveza** po·*ron* de ser·*ve*·sa bottled beer
postre ⓜ *pos*·tre dessert
potaje ⓜ po·*ta*·khe stew
primer ⓜ **plato** pree·*mer pla*·to entree • first course
puchero ⓜ (Arg) poo·*che*·ro casserole with beef, chicken, bacon, sausage, blood sausage, maize, peppers, tomatoes, onions, cabbage, sweet potatoes & squash
puerros ⓜ pl *pwe*·ros leek
pukacapa ⓕ (Bol) poo·ka·*ka*·pa circular **empanada** filled with cheese, olives, onions & hot-pepper sauce
pulpo ⓜ *pool*·po octopus
— a la gallega a la ga·*ye*·ga octopus in sauce
punto, a *poon*·to, a medium (steak)
pupusas ⓕ pl (Sal) poo·*poo*·sas cornmeal pastry stuffed with farmer's cheese, refried beans, **chicharrón,** or all three (called **revuelta**)

~ Q ~

queque ⓜ *ke*·ke cake
— seco *se*·ko pound cake
quesillos ⓜ pl (Nic) ke·*see*·yos soft cheese & onions folded in a **tortilla**
quesito ⓜ (Pue) ke·*see*·to sweet baked shell stuffed with cheese & topped with honey
queso ⓜ *ke*·so cheese
— fruta bomba (Cub) *froo*·ta *bom*·ba appetiser of warm papaya & cheese
quinoa ⓜ (Bol) kee·*no*·a nutritious indigenous grain high in protein & used to thicken stews
quinto ⓜ *keen*·to very small bottle

~ R ~

rábano ⓜ *ra*·ba·no radish
rabo ⓜ *ra*·bo tail
ración ⓕ ra·*syon* small tapas plate or dish
rancio/a ⓜ/ⓕ *ran*·syo/a stale
ranga ⓕ (Bol) *ran*·ga potato soup with chopped liver
rape ⓜ *ra*·pe monkfish
raspados ⓜ pl (Pan) ras·*pa*·dos cones made of shaved ice topped with fruit syrup & sweetened condensed milk
refresco ⓜ (Bol) re·*fres*·ko fruit-based juice with a dried peach in it
refrescos ⓜ pl re·*fres*·kos soft drinks

relleno ⓜ re·*ye*·no stuffing • in Bolivia, a stuffed corn fritter similar to **humitas**
relleno/a ⓜ/ⓕ re·*ye*·no/a stuffed
remolacha ⓕ re·mo·*la*·cha beetroot
repollo ⓜ re·*po*·yo cabbage
revoltijo ⓜ re·vol·*tee*·kho scrambled egg
revuelta ⓕ (Sal) re·*vwel*·ta cornmeal pastry stuffed with farmer's cheese, refried beans and fried pork fat
riñón ⓜ ree·*nyon* kidney
rodaja ⓕ ro·*da*·kha slice
romero ⓜ ro·*me*·ro rosemary
ron ⓜ ron rum
rondón ⓜ (Cos) ron·*don* thick seafood-based soup blended with coconut milk
ropa ⓕ **vieja** (Pan) *ro*·pa *vye*·kha 'old clothes' – spicy shredded-beef combination served over rice
rosado ⓜ ro·*sa*·do rosé
rostro ⓜ **asado** (Bol) *ros*·tro a·*sa*·do roasted sheep's head
ruibarbo ⓜ rooy·*bar*·bo rhubarb

~ S ~

sal ⓕ sal salt
salado/a ⓜ/ⓕ sa·*la*·do salted • salty
salchichas ⓕ pl sal·*chee*·chas sausages similar to hot dogs
salmón ⓜ sal·*mon* salmon
salpicón ⓜ (Cub) sal·pee·*kon* salad made from cold meat, potatoes, olives, capers, onion, lettuce, pineapple, capsicum & vinegar
salsa ⓕ *sal*·sa sauce
— de carne de *kar*·ne gravy
salteado/a ⓜ/ⓕ sal·te·*a*·do/a sauteed
salteñas ⓕ pl (Bol) sal·te·*nyas* delicious rugby ball–shaped meat & vegetable pasties that originated in Salta, Argentina
salvaje sal·*va*·khe wild
sancocho ⓜ san·*ko*·cho in Panama, a spicy chicken & vegetable stew • in Puerto Rico, vegetable soup containing plantains, tomatoes, green pepper, chilli pepper, cilantro leaves, onion & corn kernels • in Venezuela, vegetable stew with meat, fish or chicken
sandía ⓕ san·*dee*·a watermelon
sangre ⓕ *san*·gre blood
sangría ⓕ san·*gree*·a red-wine punch
sardina ⓕ sar·*dee*·na sardine
seco ⓜ (Ecu) *se*·ko 'dry' – meat stew served with rice
seco/a ⓜ/ⓕ *se*·ko/a dried • dry
segundo ⓜ **plato** se·*goon*·do *pla*·to main course
sémola ⓕ *se*·mo·la semolina
sepia ⓕ *se*·pya cuttlefish
sésamo ⓜ *se*·sa·mo sesame
sesos ⓜ pl *se*·sos brains
sidra ⓕ *see*·dra cider
silpancho ⓜ (Bol) seel·*pan*·cho a thin greasy schnitzel
sin cubierto seen koo·*byer*·to no cover charge
sin gas seen gas still
sin grasa seen *gra*·sa lean
sobrasada ⓕ so·bra·sa·da soft pork sausage
sofrito ⓜ (Pue) so·*free*·to seasoning consisting of garlic, onions & pepper browned in olive oil, then flavoured with annatto seeds
soja ⓕ *so*·kha soya
solomillo ⓜ so·lo·*mee*·yo sirloin
sooyo sopy ⓜ (Par) *soo*·yo *so*·pee thick soup of ground meat, accompanied by rice or noodles
sopa ⓕ *so*·pa soup
— a la criolla (Per) a la kree·*o*·ya lightly spiced noodle soup with beef, egg, milk & vegetables
— de caracol (Hon) de ka·*ra*·kol conch soup made with coconut

— de mariscos (Chi) de ma·*rees*·kos shellfish soup
— de mondongo (Hon) de mon·*don*·go tripe soup – reputed to be a good hangover remedy
— de pescado de pes·*ka*·do fish soup
— paraguaya ⓕ (Par) pa·ra·*gwa*·ya corn bread with cheese & onion
sopaipa ⓕ (Chi) so·*pai*·pa dark-brown unbaked wheat & flour bread
sopaipillas ⓕ (Bol) so·pai·*pee*·yas sweet fried breads
sopón ⓜ **de pescado** (Pue) so·*pon* de pes·*ka*·do fish soup flavoured with garlic, onions & sherry
submarino ⓜ (Arg) soob·ma·*ree*·no breakfast beverage consisting of a semisweet chocolate bar dissolved in steamed milk
suflé ⓜ soo·*fle* souffle

~ T ~

tajadas ⓕ pl (Nic, Pan, Ven) ta·*kha*·das sliced plantains served as a base for grilled meat & cabbage salad
tajaditas ⓕ pl (Hon) ta·kha·*dee*·tas crispy, fried banana chips
tallarines ⓜ pl ta·ya·*ree*·nes noodles mixed with pork, chicken, beef or vegetables sold at **chifas**
tamales ⓜ pl ta·*ma*·les cornmeal dough filled with spiced beef, vegetables & potatoes, wrapped in a maize husk & fried, grilled or baked • in Colombia, chopped pork with rice & vegetables folded in a maize dough, wrapped in banana leaves & steamed
— asados (Cos) a·*sa*·dos sweet cornmeal cakes
tarta ⓕ *tar*·ta cake
tasajo ⓜ (Pan) ta·*sa*·kho dried meat cooked with vegetables
tatú ⓜ ta·*too* armadillo
tawa-tawas ⓜ (Bol) ta·wa·*ta*·was type of doughnut
té ⓜ te tea
— con leche kon *le*·che tea with milk
— con limón kon lee·*mon* tea with lemon
— de menta de *men*·ta mint tea
— sin leche seen *le*·che black tea
tembleque ⓜ (Pue) tem·*ble*·ke pudding-like concoction of coconut milk & cinnamon
tereré ⓜ (Par) te·re·*re* ice-cold **mate**
ternera ⓕ ter·*ne*·ra veal
thimpu ⓜ (Bol) *teem*·poo spicy lamb & vegetable stew
tibio/a ⓜ/ⓕ *tee*·byo/a warm
timochenko ⓜ (Hon) tee·mo·*chen*·ko **aguardiente** mixed with aromatic plants of the region
tinto ⓜ *teen*·to red (wine) • in Colombia, a small cup of black coffee
tira ⓕ **de asado** *tee*·ra de a·*sa*·do a narrow strip of rib roast
tocino ⓜ to·*see*·no bacon
— ahumado a·oo·*ma*·do smoked bacon
— con queso kon *ke*·so cold bacon with cheese
tojorí ⓜ (Bol) to·kho·*ree* oatmeal-like concoction of mashed corn,cinnamon & sugar
tomatada ⓕ **de cordero** (Bol) to·ma·*ta*·da de kor·*de*·ro lamb stew with tomato sauce
tomate ⓜ to·*ma*·te tomato
torta ⓕ *tor*·ta cake • flan • tart
tortilla ⓕ tor·*tee*·ya omelette
— de maíz (Ecu, Pan) de ma·*ees* thick, fried cornmeal tortilla
tortillas ⓕ pl **con quesillo** (Hon) tor·*tee*·yas kon ke·*see*·lyo two crisp fried tortillas with melted white cheese between them
tortuga ⓕ tor·*too*·ga turtle
tostada ⓕ tos·*ta*·da toast
tostones ⓜ pl (Pue) tos·*to*·nes fried green plantains

trigo ⓜ *tree*·go wheat
tripa ⓕ *tree*·pa tripe
— gorda *gor*·da large intestine (a common **asado** dish)
tripas ⓕ pl *tree*·pas offal
trozo ⓜ *tro*·so piece • slice
trucha ⓕ *troo*·cha trout
trufa ⓕ *troo*·fa truffle
tubo ⓜ *too*·bo tall glass
tucumana ⓕ (Bol) too·koo·*ma*·na heavily spiced puff-pastry shell packed with egg, potatoes, chicken & onions
tuétano ⓜ *twe*·ta·no bone marrow
turrón ⓜ too·*ron* almond nougat

~ U ~

ubre ⓕ *oo*·bre udder
uva ⓕ *oo*·va grape

~ V ~

vaca ⓕ *va*·ka beef
vacío ⓜ va·*see*·o flank steak – textured & chewy, but tasty
vainilla ⓕ vai·*nee*·ya vanilla
vapor ⓜ va·*por* steam
vapor, al va·*por*, al steamed
vaso ⓜ *va*·so glass
vegetal ⓜ ve·khe·*tal* vegetable
vegetariano/a ⓜ/ⓕ ve·khe·ta·*rya*·no/a vegetarian
venado ⓜ ve·*na*·do venison
venera ⓕ ve·*ne*·ra scallop
verduras ⓕ pl ver·*doo*·ras green vegetables
vigorón ⓜ (Nic) vee·go·*ron* cassava steamed & topped with fried pork rind & cabbage salad, usually served on a banana leaf
vinagre ⓜ vee·*na*·gre vinegar
vino ⓜ *vee*·no wine
— de la casa de la *ka*·sa house wine
— espumoso es·poo·*mo*·so sparkling wine
— (muy) seco (mooy) *se*·ko (very) dry wine

~ W ~

wafle ⓜ *wa*·fle waffle
witu ⓜ (Bol) *gwee*·too beef stew with pureed tomatoes

~ Y ~

yaguarlocro ⓜ (Ecu) ya·gwar·*lo*·kro potato soup with chunks of barely congealed blood sausage floating in it
yerba ⓕ **mate** *yer*·ba *ma*·te dried chopped leaf of Ilex Paraguayensis which is made into a tea in Argentina, Uruguay & Paraguay
yogur ⓜ yo·*goor* yogurt
yuca ⓕ *yoo*·ka cassava – a common staple in Latin American cuisine

~ Z ~

zanahoria ⓕ sa·na·o·rya carrot
zapallo ⓜ (SAm) sa·*pa*·yo pumpkin
zarzuela ⓕ **de marisco** sar·*swe*·la de ma·*rees*·ko seafood stew

Dictionary

ENGLISH *to* SPANISH

inglés – español

Nouns in the dictionary have their gender indicated by ⓜ or ⓕ. If it's a plural noun, you'll also see pl. When a word that could be either a noun or a verb has no gender indicated, it's a verb.

A

(be) able poder po·*der*
aboard a bordo a *bor*·do
abortion aborto ⓜ a·*bor*·to
about sobre *so*·bre
above arriba a·*ree*·ba
abroad en el extranjero en el ek·stran·*khe*·ro
accept aceptar a·sep·*tar*
accident accidente ⓜ ak·see·*den*·te
accommodation alojamiento ⓜ a·lo·kha·*myen*·to
across a través a tra·*ves*
activist activista ⓜ&ⓕ ak·tee·*vees*·ta
acupuncture acupuntura ⓕ a·koo·poon·*too*·ra
adaptor adaptador ⓜ a·dap·ta·*dor*
addicted adicto/a ⓜ/ⓕ a·*deek*·to/a
address dirección ⓕ dee·rek·*syon*
administration administración ⓕ ad·mee·nees·tra·*syon*
admission price precio ⓜ de entrada *pre*·syo de en·*tra*·da
admit (accept) admitir ad·mee·*teer*
admit (acknowledge) reconocer re·ko·no·*ser*
admit (allow to enter) dejar entrar de·*khar* en·*trar*
adult adulto/a ⓜ/ⓕ a·*dool*·to/a
advertisement anuncio ⓜ a·*noon*·syo
advice consejo ⓜ kon·*se*·kho
advise aconsejar a·kon·se·*khar*
after después de des·*pwes* de
aftershave loción ⓕ para después del afeitado lo·*syon* *pa*·ra des·*pwes* del a·fay·*ta*·do
again otra vez *o*·tra ves
age edad ⓕ e·*da*
aggressive agresivo/a ⓜ/ⓕ a·gre·*see*·vo/a
agree estar de acuerdo es·*tar* de a·*kwer*·do
agriculture agricultura ⓕ a·gree·kool·*too*·ra
AIDS SIDA ⓜ *see*·da
air aire ⓜ *ai*·re
(by) airmail por vía aérea por *vee*·a a·e·re·a
air-conditioned con aire acondicionado kon *ai*·re a·kon·dee·syo·*na*·do
airline aerolínea ⓕ a·e·ro·*lee*·ne·a
airport aeropuerto ⓜ a·e·ro·*pwer*·to
airport tax tasa ⓕ del aeropuerto *ta*·sa del a·e·ro·*pwer*·to

aisle (plane, train) pasillo ⓜ pa·*see*·yo
alarm clock despertador ⓜ des·per·ta·*dor*
all (singular) todo/a ⓜ/ⓕ sg *to*·do/a
all (plural) todos/as ⓜ/ⓕ pl *to*·dos/as
allergy alergia ⓕ a·*ler*·khya
allow permitir per·mee·*teer*
almond almendra ⓕ al·*men*·dra
almost casi *ka*·see
alone solo/a ⓜ/ⓕ *so*·lo/a
already ya ya
also también tam·*byen*
altitude altura ⓕ al·*too*·ra
altitude sickness soroche ⓜ so·*ro*·che
always siempre *syem*·pre
ambassador embajador(a)ⓜ/ⓕ em·ba·kha·*dor*/em·ba·kha·*do*·ra
ambulance ambulancia ⓕ am·boo·*lan*·sya
among entre *en*·tre
amount cantidad ⓕ kan·tee·*da*
anarchist anarquista ⓜ&ⓕ a·nar·*kees*·ta
ancient antiguo/a ⓜ/ⓕ an·*tee*·gwo/a
and y ee
angry enojado/a ⓜ/ⓕ e·no·*kha*·do/a
animal animal ⓜ a·nee·*mal*
animal rights derechos ⓜ pl de animales de·*re*·chos de a·nee·*ma*·les
ankle tobillo ⓜ to·*bee*·yo
annoyed fastidiado/a ⓜ/ⓕ fas·tee·*dya*·do/a
answer respuesta ⓕ res·*pwes*·ta
answering machine contestador ⓜ automático kon·tes·ta·*dor* ow·to·*ma*·tee·ko
ant hormiga ⓕ or·*mee*·ga
antibiotics antibióticos ⓜ pl an·tee·*byo*·tee·kos
antihistamines antihistaminicos ⓜ pl an·tee·ees·ta·*mee*·nee·kos
antimalarial tablets pastillas ⓕ pl antipalúdicas pas·*tee*·yas an·tee·pa·*loo*·dee·kas
antique antigüedad ⓕ an·tee·gwe·*da*
antiseptic antiséptico ⓜ an·tee·*sep*·tee·ko
any (singular) alguno/a ⓜ/ⓕ sg al·*goo*·no/a
any (plural) algunos/as ⓜ/ⓕ pl al·*goo*·nos/as
appendix apéndice ⓜ a·*pen*·dee·se
apple manzana ⓕ man·*sa*·na
appointment cita ⓕ *see*·ta
apricot ⓜ damasco da·*mas*·ko
archaeological arqueológico/a ⓜ/ⓕ ar·ke·o·*lo*·khee·ko/a
architect arquitecto/a ⓜ/ⓕ ar·kee·*tek*·to/a
architecture arquitectura ⓕ ar·kee·tek·*too*·ra
Argentina Argentina ⓕ ar·khen·*tee*·na
argue discutir dees·koo·*teer*
arm brazo ⓜ *bra*·so
armadillo armadillo ⓜ ar·ma·*dee*·yo
army ejercito ⓜ e·*kher*·see·to
arrest detener de·te·*ner*
arrivals llegadas ⓕ pl ye·*ga*·das
arrive llegar ye·*gar*
art arte ⓜ *ar*·te
art gallery museo ⓜ de arte moo·*se*·o de *ar*·te
artist artista ⓜ&ⓕ ar·*tees*·ta
ashtray cenicero ⓜ se·nee·*se*·ro
ask (a question) preguntar pre·goon·*tar*
ask (for something) pedir pe·*deer*
aspirin aspirina ⓕ as·pee·*ree*·na
asthma asma ⓜ *as*·ma
athletics atletismo ⓜ at·le·*tees*·mo
atmosphere atmósfera ⓕ at·*mos*·fe·ra
aubergine berenjena ⓕ be·ren·*khe*·na

aunt tía ⓕ *tee*·a
automatic automático/a ⓜ/ⓕ ow·to·*ma*·tee·ko/a
ATM cajero ⓜ automático ka·*khe*·ro ow·to·*ma*·tee·ko
autumn otoño ⓜ o·*to*·nyo
avenue avenida ⓕ a·ve·*nee*·da
avocado palta ⓕ *pal*·ta

B

B&W (film) blanco y negro *blan*·ko ee *ne*·gro
baby bebé ⓜ&ⓕ be·*be*
baby food comida ⓕ de bebé ko·*mee*·da de be·*be*
baby powder talco ⓜ *tal*·ko
back (body) espalda ⓕ es·*pal*·da
backpack mochila ⓕ mo·*chee*·la
bacon tocino ⓜ to·*see*·no
bad malo/a ⓜ/ⓕ *ma*·lo/a
bag (general) bolso ⓜ *bol*·so
bag (shopping) bolsa ⓕ (de compras) *bol*·sa (de *kom*·pras)
baggage equipaje ⓜ e·kee·*pa*·khe
baggage allowance límite ⓜ de equipaje *lee*·mee·te de e·kee·*pa*·khe
baggage claim recogida ⓕ de equipajes re·ko·*khee*·da de e·kee·*pa*·khes
bakery panadería ⓕ pa·na·de·*ree*·a
balance (account) saldo ⓜ *sal*·do
balcony balcón ⓜ bal·*kon*
ball pelota ⓕ pe·*lo*·ta
ballpoint pen bolígrafo ⓜ bo·*lee*·gra·fo
banana (CAm) plátano ⓜ *pla*·ta·no
banana (SAm) banana ⓕ ba·*na*·na
banana (Ven) cambur ⓜ kam·*boor*
band (music) grupo ⓜ *groo*·po
bandage vendaje ⓜ ven·*da*·khe
Band-Aids curitas ⓕ pl koo·*ree*·tas
bank (money) banco ⓜ *ban*·ko
bank account cuenta ⓕ bancaria *kwen*·ta ban·*ka*·rya
banknotes billetes ⓜ pl de banco bee·*ye*·tes de *ban*·ko
baptism bautizo ⓜ bow·*tee*·so
barber barbero ⓜ bar·*be*·ro
basket canasta ⓕ ka·*nas*·ta
bath baño ⓜ *ba*·nyo
bath tub bañera ⓕ ba·*nye*·ra
bathing suit malla ⓕ de baño • traje ⓜ de baño *ma*·ya de *ba*·nyo • *tra*·khe de *ba*·nyo
bathroom baño ⓜ *ba*·nyo
battery (car) batería ⓕ ba·te·*ree*·a
battery (general) pila ⓕ *pee*·la
be estar • ser es·*tar* • ser
beach playa ⓕ *pla*·ya
beans frijoles ⓜ pl free·*kho*·les
beautician esteticista ⓜ&ⓕ es·te·tee·*sees*·ta
beautiful bello/a ⓜ/ⓕ *be*·yo/a
beauty salon salón ⓜ de belleza sa·*lon* de be·*ye*·sa
because porque *por*·ke
bed cama ⓕ *ka*·ma
bedding ropa ⓕ de cama *ro*·pa de *ka*·ma
bedroom habitación ⓕ a·bee·ta·*syon*
bee abeja ⓕ a·*be*·kha
beef carne ⓕ de vaca *kar*·ne de *va*·ka
beer cerveza ⓕ ser·*ve*·sa
beetroot remolacha ⓕ re·mo·*la*·cha
before antes *an*·tes
beggar mendigo/a ⓜ/ⓕ men·*dee*·go/a
begin comenzar ko·men·*sar*
behind detrás de de·*tras* de
bell pepper pimiento ⓜ pee·*myen*·to
below abajo a·*ba*·kho
Belize Belice ⓕ be·*lee*·se
best mejor me·*khor*
bet apuesta ⓕ a·*pwes*·ta
better mejor me·*khor*
between entre *en*·tre
bible biblia ⓕ *bee*·blya
bicycle bicicleta ⓕ bee·see·*kle*·ta
big grande *gran*·de
bike bici ⓕ *bee*·see
bike chain cadena ⓕ de bici ka·*de*·na de *bee*·see

bike path camino ⓜ de bici ka·*mee*·no de *bee*·see
bill (account) cuenta ⓕ *kwen*·ta
biography biografía ⓕ byo·gra·*fee*·a
bird pájaro ⓜ *pa*·kha·ro
birth certificate partida ⓕ de nacimiento par·*tee*·da de na·see·*myen*·to
birthday cumpleaños ⓜ koom·ple·*a*·nyos
biscuit galleta ⓕ ga·*ye*·ta
bite (dog) mordedura ⓕ mor·de·*doo*·ra
bite (insect) picadura ⓕ pee·ka·*doo*·ra
black negro/a ⓜ/ⓕ *ne*·gro/a
blanket frazada ⓕ fra·*sa*·da
blind ciego/a ⓜ/ⓕ *sye*·go/a
blister ampolla ⓕ am·*po*·ya
blocked atascado/a ⓜ/ⓕ a·tas·*ka*·do/a
blood sangre ⓕ *san*·gre
blood group grupo ⓜ sanguíneo *groo*·po san·*gee*·ne·o
blood pressure presión ⓕ arterial pre·*syon* ar·te·*ryal*
blood test análisis ⓜ de sangre a·*na*·lee·sees de *san*·gre
blue azul a·*sool*
board (plane, ship) embarcarse em·bar·*kar*·se
boarding house pensión ⓕ pen·*syon*
boarding pass tarjeta ⓕ de embarque tar·*khe*·ta de em·*bar*·ke
boat barco ⓜ *bar*·ko
body cuerpo ⓜ *kwer*·po
Bolivia Bolivia ⓕ bo·*lee*·vya
bomb bomba ⓕ *bom*·ba
bone hueso ⓜ *we*·so
book libro ⓜ *lee*·bro
book (reserve) reservar re·ser·*var*
booked out lleno/a ⓜ/ⓕ *ye*·no/a
bookshop librería ⓕ lee·bre·*ree*·a
boots botas ⓕ pl *bo*·tas
border (frontier) frontera ⓕ fron·*te*·ra
borders (photography) marcos ⓜ pl *mar*·kos
(be) bored (estar) aburrido/a ⓜ/ⓕ (es·*tar*) a·boo·*ree*·do/a
boring aburrido/a ⓜ/ⓕ a·boo·*ree*·do/a
borrow pedir pe·*deer*
botanic garden jardín ⓜ botánico khar·*deen* bo·*ta*·nee·ko
both ambos/as ⓜ/ⓕ pl *am*·bos/as
bottle botella ⓕ bo·*te*·ya
bottle opener abrebotellas ⓜ a·bre·bo·*te*·yas
(at the) bottom (al) fondo (de) (al) *fon*·do (de)
bowl bol ⓜ bol
box caja ⓕ *ka*·kha
boxing boxeo ⓜ bok·*se*·o
boy chico ⓜ *chee*·ko
boyfriend novio ⓜ *no*·vyo
bra corpiño ⓜ kor·*pee*·nyo
brake freno ⓜ pl *fre*·no
brandy coñac ⓜ ko·*nyak*
brave valiente va·*lyen*·te
Brazil Brasil ⓜ bra·*seel*
bread pan ⓜ pan
bread rolls bollos ⓜ pl *bo*·yos
break romper rom·*per*
break down descomponerse des·kom·po·*ner*·se
breakfast desayuno ⓜ de·sa·*yoo*·no
breast (poultry) pechuga ⓕ pe·*choo*·ga
breasts senos ⓜ pl *se*·nos
breathe respirar res·pee·*rar*
bribe (CAm) mordida ⓕ mor·*dee*·da
bribe (SAm) coima ⓕ *koy*·ma
bribe coimear koy·me·*ar*
bridge puente ⓜ *pwen*·te
briefcase maletín ⓜ ma·le·*teen*
brilliant briliante bree·*lyan*·te
bring traer tra·*er*
broken roto/a ⓜ/ⓕ *ro*·to/a
broken down (machine) averiado/a ⓜ/ⓕ a·ve·*rya*·do/a
brother hermano ⓜ er·*ma*·no

brown marrón ma·*ron*
bruise moretón ⓜ mo·re·*ton*
bucket balde ⓜ *bal*·de
budget presupuesto ⓜ pre·soo·*pwes*·to
Buddhist budista ⓜ&ⓕ boo·*dees*·ta
bug bicho ⓜ *bee*·cho
build construir kons·troo·*eer*
building edificio ⓜ e·dee·*fee*·syo
bulb bombillo ⓜ bom·*bee*·yo
bulb (Ecu, Per) foco ⓜ *fo*·ko
bull toro ⓜ *to*·ro
bullfight corrida ⓕ ko·*ree*·da
bullring plaza ⓕ de toros *pla*·sa de *to*·ros
bum (body) culo ⓜ *koo*·lo
burn quemadura ⓕ ke·ma·*doo*·ra
burn quemar ke·*mar*
bus (city) autobús ⓜ ow·to·*boos*
bus (intercity) ómnibus ⓜ *om*·nee·boos
bus station (city) estación ⓕ de autobuses es·ta·*syon* de ow·to·*boo*·ses
bus station (intercity) estación ⓕ de ómnibuses es·ta·*syon* de *om*·nee·boo·ses
bus stop (city) parada ⓕ de autobús pa·*ra*·da de ow·to·*boos*
bus stop (intercity) parada ⓕ de ómnibus pa·*ra*·da de *om*·nee·boos
business negocio ⓜ ne·*go*·syo
business class clase ⓕ preferente *kla*·se pre·fe·*ren*·te
business person comerciante ⓜ&ⓕ ko·mer·*syan*·te
busker artista callejero/a ⓜ/ⓕ ar·*tees*·ta ka·ye·*khe*·ro/a
busy ocupado/a ⓜ/ⓕ o·koo·*pa*·do/a
but pero *pe*·ro
butcher's shop carnicería ⓕ kar·nee·se·*ree*·a
butter mantequilla ⓕ man·te·*kee*·ya
butterfly mariposa ⓕ ma·ree·*po*·sa
button botón ⓜ bo·*ton*
buy comprar kom·*prar*
buzzard gallinazo ⓜ ga·yee·*na*·so

C

cabbage repollo ⓜ re·*po*·yo
cable cable ⓜ *ka*·ble
cable car teleférico ⓜ te·le·*fe*·ree·ko
cafe cafetería ⓕ ka·fe·te·*ree*·a
cake torta ⓕ *tor*·ta
cake shop pastelería ⓕ pas·te·le·*ree*·a
calculator calculadora ⓕ kal·koo·la·*do*·ra
calendar calendario ⓜ ka·len·*da*·ryo
call llamar ya·*mar*
camera cámara ⓕ (fotográfica) *ka*·ma·ra (fo·to·*gra*·fee·ka)
camera shop tienda ⓕ de fotografía *tyen*·da de fo·to·gra·*fee*·a
camp acampar a·kam·*par*
campsite cámping ⓜ *kam*·peen
camping store tienda ⓕ de provisiones de cámping *tyen*·da de pro·vee·*syo*·nes de *kam*·peen
can (tin) lata ⓕ *la*·ta
can (be able) poder po·*der*
can opener abrelatas ⓜ a·bre·*la*·tas
cancel cancelar kan·se·*lar*
candle vela ⓕ *ve*·la
candy dulces ⓜ pl *dool*·ses
cantaloupe cantalupo ⓜ kan·ta·*loo*·po
capsicum pimiento ⓜ pee·*myen*·to
car carro ⓜ *ka*·ro
car hire alquiler ⓜ de carro al·kee·*ler* de *ka*·ro
car owner's title papeles ⓜ pl del auto pa·*pe*·les del *ow*·to
car park parking ⓜ *par*·keen
car registration matrícula ⓕ ma·*tree*·koo·la
caravan caravana ⓕ ka·ra·*va*·na
cards cartas ⓕ pl *kar*·tas
care (about something) preocuparse por pre·o·koo·*par*·se por
care (for someone) cuidar de kwee·*dar* de
caring bondadoso/a ⓜ/ⓕ bon·da·*do*·so/a

C

carriage (train) vagón ⓜ va·*gon*
carpenter carpintero ⓜ kar·peen·*te*·ro
carrot zanahoria ⓕ sa·na·o·rya
carry llevar ye·*var*
cash dinero ⓜ en efectivo dee·*ne*·ro en e·fek·*tee*·vo
cash (a cheque) cobrar (un cheque) ko·*brar* (oon *che*·ke)
cash register caja ⓕ registradora *ka*·kha re·khees·tra·*do*·ra
cashew castaña ⓕ de cajú kas·*ta*·nya de ka·*khoo*
cashier cajero/a ⓜ/ⓕ ka·*khe*·ro/a
castle castillo ⓜ kas·*tee*·yo
casual work trabajo ⓜ eventual tra·*ba*·kho e·ven·*twal*
cat gato/a ⓜ/ⓕ *ga*·to/a
cathedral catedral ⓕ ka·te·*dral*
Catholic católico/a ⓜ/ⓕ ka·*to*·lee·ko/a
cauliflower coliflor ko·lee·*flor*
cave cueva ⓕ *kwe*·va
cavity (tooth) caries ⓕ *ka*·ryes
CD cómpact ⓜ *kom*·pak
celebration celebración ⓕ se·le·bra·*syon*
cell phone teléfono ⓜ móvil te·*le*·fo·no *mo*·veel
cemetery cementerio ⓜ se·men·*te*·ryo
cent centavo ⓜ sen·*ta*·vo
centimetre centímetro ⓜ sen·*tee*·me·tro
Central America Centroamérica ⓕ sen·tro·a·*me*·ree·ka
Central American centroaméricano/a ⓜ/ⓕ sen·tro·a·me·ree·*ka*·no/a
central heating calefacción ⓕ central ka·le·fak·*syon* sen·*tral*
centre centro ⓜ *sen*·tro
ceramic cerámica ⓕ se·*ra*·mee·ka
cereal cereales ⓜ pl se·re·*a*·les
certificate certificado ⓜ ser·tee·fee·*ka*·do
chain cadena ⓕ ka·*de*·na
chair silla ⓕ *see*·ya
chance oportunidad ⓕ o·por·too·nee·*da*
change (money) cambio ⓜ *kam*·byo
change cambiar kam·*byar*
changing room vestuario ⓜ ves·*twa*·ryo
charming encantador(a) ⓜ/ⓕ en·kan·ta·*dor*/en·kan·ta·*do*·ra
chat up tratar de ligar tra·*tar* de lee·*gar*
cheap barato/a ⓜ/ⓕ ba·*ra*·to/a
cheat tramposo/a ⓜ/ⓕ tram·*po*·so/a
check (bill) cuenta ⓕ *kwen*·ta
check revisar re·vee·*sar*
check-in (airport) facturación ⓕ fak·too·ra·*syon*
check-in (baggage) facturación ⓕ de equipaje fak·too·ra·*syon* de e·kee·*pa*·khe
check-in (hotel) registrar re·khees·*trar*
checkpoint control ⓜ kon·*trol*
cheese queso ⓜ *ke*·so
chef cocinero/a ⓜ/ⓕ ko·see·*ne*·ro/a
chemist (shop) farmacia ⓕ far·*ma*·sya
chemist (person) farmacéutico/a ⓜ/ⓕ far·ma·see·*oo*·tee·ko/a
cheque cheque ⓜ *che*·ke
chess ajedrez ⓜ a·khe·*dres*
chest pecho ⓜ *pe*·cho
chewing gum chicle ⓜ *chee*·kle
chicken pollo ⓜ *po*·yo
chickpeas garbanzos ⓜ pl gar·*ban*·sos
child niño/a ⓜ/ⓕ *nee*·nyo/a
child's car seat asiento ⓜ de seguridad para bebés a·*syen*·to de se·goo·ree·*da pa*·ra be·*bes*
childminding service guardería ⓕ gwar·de·*ree*·a
Chile Chile ⓕ *chee*·le

chilli ají ⓜ a·*khee*
chilli sauce salsa ⓕ de ají *sal*·sa de a·*khee*
chocolate chocolate ⓜ cho·ko·*la*·te
choose escoger es·ko·*kher*
chopping board tabla ⓕ de cortar *ta*·bla de kor·*tar*
Christian cristiano/a ⓜ/ⓕ krees·*tya*·no/a
Christmas Navidad ⓕ na·vee·*da*
church iglesia ⓕ ee·*gle*·sya
cider sidra ⓕ *see*·dra
cigar cigarro ⓜ see·*ga*·ro
cigarette cigarillo ⓜ see·ga·*ree*·yo
cigarette lighter mechero ⓜ me·*che*·ro
cigarette paper papel ⓜ de fumar pa·*pel* de foo·*mar*
cinema cine ⓜ *see*·ne
circus circo ⓜ *seer*·ko
citizenship ciudadanía ⓕ syoo·da·da·*nee*·a
city ciudad ⓕ syoo·*da*
city centre centro ⓜ de la ciudad *sen*·tro de la syoo·*da*
civil rights derechos ⓜ pl civiles de·*re*·chos see·*vee*·les
classical clásico/a ⓜ/ⓕ *kla*·see·ko/a
clean limpio/a ⓜ/ⓕ *leem*·pyo/a
cleaning limpieza ⓕ leem·*pye*·sa
client cliente/a ⓜ/ⓕ *klyen*·te/a
cliff acantilado ⓜ a·kan·tee·*la*·do
climb subir soo·*beer*
cloak capote ⓜ ka·*po*·te
cloakroom guardarropa ⓜ gwar·da·*ro*·pa
clock reloj ⓜ re·*lokh*
close (nearby) cerca *ser*·ka
close (shut) cerrar se·*rar*
closed cerrado/a ⓜ/ⓕ se·*ra*·do/a
clothes line cuerda ⓕ para tender la ropa *kwer*·da *pa*·ra ten·*der* la *ro*·pa
clothing ropa ⓕ *ro*·pa
clothing store tienda ⓕ de ropa *tyen*·da de *ro*·pa
cloud nube ⓕ *noo*·be
cloudy nublado/a ⓜ/ⓕ noo·*bla*·do/a
clutch embrague ⓜ em·*bra*·ge
coach (sport) entrenador(a) ⓜ/ⓕ en·tre·na·*dor*/en·tre·na·*do*·ra
coast costa ⓕ *kos*·ta
coat saco ⓜ *sa*·ko
coke (drug) coca ⓕ *ko*·ka
cocaine cocaína ⓕ ko·ka·*ee*·na
coca plant coca ⓕ *ko*·ka
cockroach cucaracha ⓕ koo·ka·*ra*·cha
cocoa cacao ⓜ ka·*kow*
coconut coco ⓜ *ko*·ko
coconut palm palma ⓕ de coco *pal*·ma de *ko*·ko
codeine codeína ⓕ ko·de·*ee*·na
coffee café ⓜ ka·*fe*
coins monedas ⓕ pl mo·*ne*·das
coke (drug) coca ⓕ *ko*·ka
cold frío/a ⓜ/ⓕ *free*·o/a
(have a) cold (tener) resfrío (te·*ner*) res·*free*·o
colleague colega ⓜ&ⓕ ko·*le*·ga
collect call llamada ⓕ a cobro revertido ya·*ma*·da a *ko*·bro re·ver·*tee*·do
college (hall of residence) residencia ⓕ de estudiantes re·see·*den*·sya de es·too·*dyan*·tes
college (school) colegio ⓜ ko·*le*·khyo
college (university) universidad ⓕ oo·nee·ver·see·*da*
Colombia Colombia ⓕ ko·*lom*·bya
colour color ⓜ ko·*lor*
comb peine ⓜ *pay*·ne
come venir ve·*neer*
comedy comedia ⓕ ko·*me*·dya
comfortable cómodo/a ⓜ/ⓕ *ko*·mo·do/a
communion comunión ⓕ ko·moo·*nyon*
communist comunista ⓜ&ⓕ ko·moo·*nees*·ta
companion compañero/a ⓜ/ⓕ kom·pa·*nye*·ro/a

company compañía ⓕ kom·pa·*nyee*·a
compass brújula ⓕ *broo*·khoo·la
complain quejarse ke·*khar*·se
computer computadora ⓕ kom·poo·ta·*do*·ra
computer game juego ⓜ de computadora *khwe*·go de kom·poo·ta·*do*·ra
concert concierto ⓜ kon·*syer*·to
conditioner acondicionador ⓜ a·kon·dee·syo·na·*dor*
condom condón ⓜ kon·*don*
confession confesión ⓕ kon·fe·*syon*
confirm confirmar kon·feer·*mar*
connection conexión ⓕ ko·nek·*syon*
conservative conservador(a) ⓜ/ⓕ kon·ser·va·*dor*/kon·ser·va·*do*·ra
constipation estreñimiento ⓜ es·tre·nyee·*myen*·to
consulate consulado ⓜ kon·soo·*la*·do
contact lenses lentes ⓕ pl de contacto *len*·tes de kon·*tak*·to
contemporary contemporáneo/a ⓜ/ⓕ kon·tem·po·*ra*·ne·o/a
contraceptive anticonceptivo ⓜ an·tee·kon·sep·*tee*·vo
contract contrato ⓜ kon·*tra*·to
convenience store tienda ⓕ de artículos básicos *tyen*·da de ar·*tee*·koo·los *ba*·see·kos
convent convento ⓜ kon·*ven*·to
cook cocinero/a ⓜ/ⓕ ko·see·*ne*·ro/a
cook cocinar ko·see·*nar*
cookie galleta ⓕ ga·*ye*·ta
corkscrew sacacorchos ⓜ sa·ka·*kor*·chos
corn maíz ⓜ ma·*ees*
cornflakes copos ⓜ pl de maíz *ko*·pos de ma·*ees*
corner esquina ⓕ es·*kee*·na
corrupt corrupto/a ⓜ/ⓕ ko·*roop*·to/a
cost ⓜ coste ⓜ *kos*·te
cost costar kos·*tar*
Costa Rica Costa Rica ⓕ *kos*·ta *ree*·ka
cottage cheese requesón ⓜ re·ke·*son*
cotton algodón ⓜ al·go·*don*
cotton balls bolas ⓕ pl de algodón *bo*·las de al·go·*don*
cough tos ⓕ tos
cough medicine jarabe ⓜ kha·*ra*·be
count contar kon·*tar*
counter (shop) mostrador ⓜ mos·tra·*dor*
country (nation) país ⓜ pa·*ees*
countryside campo ⓜ *kam*·po
courgette calabacín ⓜ ka·la·ba·*seen*
court (legal) tribunal ⓜ tree·boo·*nal*
court (tennis) cancha ⓕ *kan*·cha
cousin primo/a ⓜ/ⓕ *pree*·mo/a
cover charge (restaurant) precio ⓜ del cubierto *pre*·syo del koo·*byer*·to
cover charge (venue) precio ⓜ de entrada *pre*·syo de en·*tra*·da
cow vaca ⓕ *va*·ka
craft market mercado ⓜ de artesanía mer·*ka*·do de ar·te·sa·*nee*·a
craft artesanía ⓕ ar·te·sa·*nee*·a
crash (accident) choque ⓜ *cho*·ke
crazy loco/a ⓜ/ⓕ *lo*·ko/a
cream crema ⓕ *kre*·ma
cream cheese queso ⓜ cremoso *ke*·so kre·*mo*·so
creche guardería ⓕ gwar·de·*ree*·a
credit card tarjeta ⓕ de crédito tar·*khe*·ta de *kre*·dee·to
crocodile cocodrilo ⓜ ko·ko·*dree*·lo
crop cosecha ⓕ ko·*se*·cha
crowded abarrotado/a ⓜ/ⓕ a·ba·ro·*ta*·do/a
Cuba Cuba ⓕ *koo*·ba
cucumber pepino ⓜ pe·*pee*·no
cup taza ⓕ *ta*·sa
cupboard armario ⓜ ar·*ma*·ryo
currency exchange cambio ⓜ (de dinero) *kam*·byo (de dee·*ne*·ro)

current corriente Ⓕ ko·*ryen*·te
current affairs informativo Ⓜ een·for·ma·*tee*·vo
curry powder curry Ⓜ en polvo *koo*·ree en *pol*·vo
customs aduana Ⓕ a·*dwa*·na
cut cortar kor·*tar*
cutlery cubiertos Ⓜ pl koo·*byer*·tos
CV historial Ⓜ profesional ees·to·*ryal* pro·fe·syo·*nal*
cycle andar en bicicleta an·*dar* en bee·see·*kle*·ta
cycling ciclismo Ⓜ see·*klees*·mo
cyclist ciclista Ⓜ&Ⓕ see·*klees*·ta

D

dad papá Ⓜ pa·*pa*
daily diariamente dya·rya·*men*·te
dance baile Ⓕ *bai*·le
dance bailar bai·*lar*
dangerous peligroso/a Ⓜ/Ⓕ pe·lee·*gro*·so/a
dark oscuro/a Ⓜ/Ⓕ os·*koo*·ro/a
date (appointment) cita Ⓕ *see*·ta
date (day) fecha Ⓕ *fe*·cha
date (a person) salir con sa·*leer* kon
date of birth fecha Ⓕ de nacimiento *fe*·cha de na·see·*myen*·to
daughter hija Ⓕ *ee*·kha
dawn alba Ⓕ *al*·ba
day día Ⓜ *dee*·a
day after tomorrow pasado mañana pa·*sa*·do ma·*nya*·na
day before yesterday anteayer an·te·a·*yer*
dead muerto/a Ⓜ/Ⓕ *mwer*·to/a
deaf sordo/a Ⓜ/Ⓕ *sor*·do/a
decide decidir de·see·*deer*
deep profundo/a Ⓜ/Ⓕ pro·*foon*·do/a
deforestation deforestación Ⓕ de·fo·res·ta·*syon*
delay demora Ⓕ de·*mo*·ra
deliver entregar en·tre·*gar*
democracy democracia Ⓕ de·mo·*kra*·see·a
demonstration (protest) manifestación Ⓕ ma·nee·fes·ta·*syon*
dengue fever fiebre Ⓕ del dengue *fye*·bre del *den*·ge
dental floss hilo Ⓜ dental *ee*·lo den·*tal*
dentist dentista Ⓜ&Ⓕ den·*tees*·ta
deodorant desodorante Ⓜ de·so·do·*ran*·te
depart (person) partir par·*teer*
depart (plane etc) salir sa·*leer*
department store grande almacén Ⓜ *gran*·de al·ma·*sen*
departure (person) partida Ⓕ par·*tee*·da
departure (plane etc) salida Ⓕ sa·*lee*·da
deposit (bank) depósito Ⓜ de·*po*·see·to
descendant descendiente Ⓜ de·sen·*dyen*·te
desert desierto Ⓜ de·*syer*·to
design diseño Ⓜ dee·*se*·nyo
destination destino Ⓜ des·*tee*·no
detail detalle Ⓜ de·*ta*·ye
detective novel novela Ⓕ negra no·ve·la *ne*·gra
diabetes diabetes Ⓕ dya·*be*·tes
dial tone tono Ⓜ *to*·no
diaper pañal Ⓜ pa·*nyal*
diaphragm diafragma Ⓜ dya·*frag*·ma
diarrhoea diarrea Ⓕ dya·*re*·a
diary agenda Ⓕ a·*khen*·da
dictionary diccionario Ⓜ deek·syo·*na*·ryo
die morir mo·*reer*
diet (customary food) dieta Ⓕ *dye*·ta
diet (slimming) régimen Ⓜ *re*·khee·men
different diferente dee·fe·*ren*·te
difficult difícil dee·*fee*·seel
dining car vagón Ⓜ restaurante va·*gon* res·tow·*ran*·te
digital camera cámara Ⓕ digital *ka*·ma·ra dee·khee·*tal*

dinner cena Ⓕ *se*·na
direct directo/a Ⓜ/Ⓕ dee·*rek*·to/a
direct-dial servicio Ⓜ telefónico automático ser·*vee*·syo te·le·*fo*·nee·ko ow·to·*ma*·tee·ko
director director(a) Ⓜ/Ⓕ dee·rek·*tor*/dee·rek·*to*·ra
dirty sucio/a Ⓜ/Ⓕ *soo*·syo/a
disabled minusválido/a Ⓜ/Ⓕ mee·noos·*va*·lee·do/a
disco discoteca Ⓕ dees·ko·*te*·ka
discount descuento Ⓜ des·*kwen*·to
discover descubrir des·koo·*breer*
discrimination discriminación Ⓕ dees·kree·mee·na·*syon*
disease enfermedad Ⓕ en·fer·mee·*da*
disk disco Ⓜ *dees*·ko
disposable camera cámara Ⓕ descartable *ka*·ma·ra des·kar·*ta*·ble
diving submarinismo Ⓜ soob·ma·ree·*nees*·mo
diving equipment equipo Ⓜ de inmersión e·*kee*·po de een·mer·*syon*
dizzy mareado/a Ⓜ/Ⓕ ma·re·*a*·do/a
do hacer a·*ser*
doctor médico/a Ⓜ/Ⓕ *me*·dee·ko/a
dog perro/a Ⓜ/Ⓕ *pe*·ro/a
dole subsidio Ⓜ de desempleo soob·*see*·dyo de des·em·*ple*·o
doll muñeca Ⓕ moo·*nye*·ka
domestic (country) nacional na·syo·*nal*
domestic flight vuelo Ⓜ doméstico *vwe*·lo do·*mes*·tee·ko
Dominican Republic República Ⓕ Dominicana re·*poo*·blee·ka do·mee·nee·*ka*·na
donkey burro Ⓜ *boo*·ro
door puerta Ⓕ *pwer*·ta
dope droga Ⓕ *dro*·ga
double doble *do*·ble
double bed cama Ⓕ de matrimonio *ka*·ma de ma·tree·*mo*·nyo
double copies (photos) dos copias Ⓕ pl dos *ko*·pyas
double room habitación Ⓕ doble a·bee·ta·*syon* *do*·ble
down hacia abajo a·*see*·a a·*ba*·kho
downhill cuesta abajo *kwes*·ta a·*ba*·kho
dozen docena Ⓕ do·*se*·na
draw dibujar dee·boo·*khar*
dream soñar so·*nyar*
dress vestido Ⓜ ves·*tee*·do
drink copa Ⓕ *ko*·pa
drink tomar to·*mar*
drinkable potable po·*ta*·ble
drive conducir kon·doo·*seer*
drivers licence carnet Ⓜ kar·*net*
drug (medicinal) medicina Ⓕ me·dee·*see*·na
drug addiction drogadicción Ⓕ dro·ga·deek·*syon*
drug dealer traficante Ⓜ de drogas tra·fee·*kan*·te de *dro*·gas
drugs (illegal) drogas Ⓕ pl *dro*·gas
drums batería Ⓕ ba·te·*ree*·a
drunk borracho/a Ⓜ/Ⓕ bo·*ra*·cho/a
dry seco/a Ⓜ/Ⓕ *se*·ko/a
dry secar se·*kar*
duck pato Ⓜ *pa*·to
dummy (pacifier) chupete Ⓜ choo·*pe*·te
during durante doo·*ran*·te
DVD DVD Ⓜ de *oo*·ve *de*
dysentry disentería Ⓕ dee·sen·te·*ree*·a

E

each cada *ka*·da
ear oreja Ⓕ o·*re*·kha
early temprano tem·*pra*·no
earn ganar ga·*nar*
earplugs tapones Ⓜ pl para los oídos ta·*po*·nes *pa*·ra los o·*ee*·dos
earrings aretes Ⓜ pl a·*re*·tes
Earth Tierra Ⓕ *tye*·ra
earthquake terremoto Ⓜ te·re·*mo*·to
east este Ⓜ *es*·te
Easter Pascua Ⓕ *pas*·kwa
easy fácil *fa*·seel

eat comer ko·*mer*
economy class clase ⓕ turística *kla*·se too·*rees*·tee·ka
Ecuador Ecuador ⓜ e·kwa·*dor*
education educación ⓕ e·doo·ka·*syon*
egg huevo ⓜ *we*·vo
eggplant berenjena ⓕ be·ren·*khe*·na
elections elecciones ⓕ pl e·lek·*syo*·nes
electrician electricista ⓜ&ⓕ e·lek·tree·*sees*·ta
electricity electricidad ⓕ e·lek·tree·see·*da*
elevator ascensor ⓜ a·sen·*sor*
El Salvador El Salvador ⓜ el sal·va·*dor*
embarrassed avergonzado/a ⓜ/ⓕ a·ver·gon·*sa*·do/a
embassy embajada ⓕ em·ba·*kha*·da
emergency emergencia ⓕ e·mer·*khen*·sya
emotional emocional e·mo·syo·*nal*
employee empleado/a ⓜ/ⓕ em·ple·*a*·do/a
employer patrón/patrona ⓜ/ⓕ pa·*tron*/pa·*tro*·na
empty vacío/a ⓜ/ⓕ va·*see*·o/a
end fin ⓜ feen
end acabar a·ka·*bar*
endangered species especies ⓕ pl en peligro de extinción es·*pe*·syes en pe·*lee*·gro de ek·steen·*syon*
engagement (marriage) compromiso ⓜ kom·pro·*mee*·so
engine motor ⓜ mo·*tor*
engineer ingeniero/a ⓜ/ⓕ een·khe·*nye*·ro/a
engineering ingeniería ⓕ een·khe·nye·*ree*·a
England ⓕ Inglaterra een·gla·*te*·ra
English (language) inglés ⓜ een·*gles*
English inglés/inglesa ⓜ/ⓕ een·*gles*/een·*gle*·sa
enjoy (oneself) divertirse dee·ver·*teer*·se
enough suficiente soo·fee·*syen*·te
enter entrar en·*trar*
entertainment guide guía ⓕ de los espectáculos *gee*·a de los es·pek·*ta*·koo·los
envelope sobre ⓜ *so*·bre
environment medio ⓜ ambiente *me*·dyo am·*byen*·te
epilepsy epilepsia ⓕ e·pee·*lep*·sya
equality igualdad ⓕ ee·gwal·*da*
equipment equipo ⓜ e·*kee*·po
escalator escalera ⓕ mecánica es·ka·*le*·ra me·*ka*·nee·ka
euthanasia eutanasia ⓕ e·oo·ta·*na*·sya
evening noche ⓕ *no*·che
everything todo *to*·do
example ejemplo ⓜ e·*khem*·plo
excellent excelente ek·se·*len*·te
excess baggage exceso ⓜ de equipage ek·*se*·so de e·kee·*pa*·khe
exchange cambio ⓜ de dinero *kam*·byo de dee·*ne*·ro
exchange cambiar kam·*byar*
exchange rate tipo ⓜ de cambio *tee*·po de *kam*·byo
excluded no incluido/a ⓜ/ⓕ no een·kloo·*ee*·do/a
exhaust (car) escape ⓜ es·*ka*·pe
exhibition exposición ⓕ ek·spo·see·*syon*
exit salida ⓕ sa·*lee*·da
expensive caro/a ⓜ/ⓕ *ka*·ro/a
experience experiencia ⓕ ek·spe·*ryen*·sya
exploitation explotación ⓕ ek·splo·ta·*syon*
express expreso/a ⓜ/ⓕ ek·*spre*·so/a
express mail correo ⓜ urgente ko·*re*·o oor·*khen*·te
extension (visa) prolongación ⓕ pro·lon·ga·*syon*
eye ojo ⓜ *o*·kho
eye drops gotas ⓕ pl para los ojos *go*·tas *pa*·ra los *o*·khos

F

F

fabric tela ⓕ *te*·la
face cara ⓕ *ka*·ra
factory fábrica ⓕ *fa*·bree·ka
factory worker obrero/a ⓜ/ⓕ o·*bre*·ro/a
fall (tumble) caída ⓕ ka·*ee*·da
fall (season) otoño ⓜ o·*to*·nyo
family familia ⓕ fa·*mee*·lya
family name apellido ⓜ a·pe·*yee*·do
famous conocido/a ⓜ/ⓕ ko·no·*see*·do/a
fan (person) hincha ⓜ&ⓕ *een*·cha
fan (machine) ventilador ⓜ ven·tee·la·*dor*
fan belt correa ⓕ del ventilador ko·*re*·a del ven·tee·la·*dor*
fantasy fantasía ⓕ fan·ta·*see*·a
far lejos *le*·khos
farm granja ⓕ *gran*·kha
farmer agricultor(a) ⓜ/ⓕ a·gree·kool·*tor*/a·gree·kool·*to*·ra
fast rápido/a ⓜ/ⓕ *ra*·pee·do/a
fat gordo/a ⓜ/ⓕ *gor*·do/a
father padre ⓜ *pa*·dre
father-in-law suegro ⓜ *swe*·gro
faucet grifo ⓜ *gree*·fo
fault (someone's) culpa ⓕ *kool*·pa
faulty defectuoso/a ⓜ/ⓕ de·fek·*two*·so/a
feel sentir sen·*teer*
feelings sentimientos ⓜ pl sen·tee·*myen*·tos
fence cerca ⓕ *ser*·ka
fencing (sport) esgrima ⓕ es·*gree*·ma
fever fiebre ⓕ *fye*·bre
few pocos/as ⓜ/ⓕ pl *po*·kos/as
fiance(e) prometido/a ⓜ/ⓕ pro·me·*tee*·do/a
fiction (literature) (literatura de) ficción ⓕ(lee·te·ra·*too*·ra de) feek·*syon*
fig higo ⓜ *ee*·go
fight pelea ⓕ pe·*le*·a
film (roll for camera) película ⓕ pe·*lee*·koo·la
film speed sensibilidad ⓕ sen·see·bee·lee·*da*
filtered con filtro kon *feel*·tro
find encontrar en·kon·*trar*
fine multa ⓕ *mool*·ta
finger dedo ⓜ *de*·do
finish terminar ter·mee·*nar*
fire fuego ⓜ *fwe*·go
firewood leña ⓕ *le*·nya
first primero/a ⓜ/ⓕ pree·*me*·ro/a
first class primera clase ⓕ pree·*me*·ra *kla*·se
first-aid kit maletín ⓜ de primeros auxilios ma·le·*teen* de pree·*me*·ros ow·*ksee*·lyos
fish pez ⓜ pes
fish (as food) pescado ⓜ pes·*ka*·do
fish shop pescadería ⓕ pes·ka·de·*ree*·a
fishing pesca ⓕ *pes*·ka
flag bandera ⓕ ban·*de*·ra
flamingo flamenco ⓜ fla·*men*·ko
flashlight (torch) linterna ⓕ leen·*ter*·na
flannel (wash cloth) toallita ⓕ to·a·*yee*·ta
flat llano/a ⓜ/ⓕ *ya*·no/a
flea pulga ⓕ *pool*·ga
flood inundación ⓕ ee·noon·da·*syon*
floor (ground) suelo ⓜ *swe*·lo
floor (storey) piso ⓜ *pee*·so
florist florista ⓜ&ⓕ flo·*rees*·ta
flour harina ⓕ a·*ree*·na
flower flor ⓕ flor
flu gripe ⓕ *gree*·pe
fly mosca ⓕ *mos*·ka
fly volar vo·*lar*
foggy brumoso/a ⓜ/ⓕ broo·*mo*·so/a
follow seguir se·*geer*
food comida ⓕ ko·*mee*·da
food poisoning intoxicación ⓕ alimenticia een·tok·see·ka·*syon* a·lee·men·*tee*·sya

food supplies víveres ⓜ pl *vee*·ve·res
foot pie ⓜ pye
football (soccer) fútbol ⓜ *foot*·bol
footpath acera ⓕ a·*se*·ra
footpath (CAm) andén ⓜ an·*den*
footpath (SAm) vereda ⓕ ve·*re*·da
foreign extranjero/a ⓜ/ⓕ ek·stran·*khe*·ro/a
foreigner extranjero/a ⓜ/ⓕ ek·stran·*khe*·ro/a
forest bosque ⓜ *bos*·ke
forever para siempre *pa*·ra *syem*·pre
forget olvidar ol·vee·*dar*
forgive perdonar per·do·*nar*
fork tenedor ⓜ te·ne·*dor*
fortnight quincena ⓕ keen·*se*·na
foyer vestíbulo ⓜ ves·*tee*·boo·lo
fragile frágil *fra*·kheel
France Francia ⓕ *fran*·sya
free (gratis) gratis *gra*·tees
free (not bound) libre *lee*·bre
freeze congelar kon·khe·*lar*
fridge refrigeradora ⓕ re·free·khe·ra·*do*·ra
friend amigo/a ⓜ/ⓕ a·*mee*·go/a
frog rana ⓕ *ra*·na
frost escarcha ⓕ es·*kar*·cha
frostbite congelación ⓕ kon·khe·la·*syon*
frozen foods productos ⓜ pl congelados pro·*dook*·tos kon·khe·*la*·dos
fruit fruta ⓕ *froo*·ta
fruit picking recolección ⓕ de fruta re·ko·lek·*syon* de *froo*·ta
fry freír fre·*eer*
frying pan sartén ⓕ sar·*ten*
full lleno/a ⓜ/ⓕ *ye*·no/a
full-time a tiempo completo a *tyem*·po kom·*ple*·to
fun diversión ⓕ dee·ver·*syon*
funeral funeral ⓜ foo·ne·*ral*
funny gracioso/a ⓜ/ⓕ gra·*syo*·so/a
furniture muebles ⓜ pl *mwe*·bles
future futuro ⓜ foo·*too*·ro

G

game (play) juego ⓜ *khwe*·go
game (sport) partido ⓜ par·*tee*·do
garage (car repair) taller ⓜ ta·*yer*
garage (car shelter) garage ⓜ ga·*ra*·khe
garden jardín ⓜ khar·*deen*
gardening jardinería ⓕ khar·dee·ne·*ree*·a
garlic ajo ⓜ *a*·kho
gas (petrol) gasolina ⓕ ga·so·*lee*·na
gas cartridge cartucho ⓜ de gas kar·*too*·cho de gas
gate verja ⓕ *ver*·kha
gears marchas ⓕ pl *mar*·chas
general general khe·ne·*ral*
Germany ⓕ Alemania a·le·*ma*·nya
gift regalo ⓜ re·*ga*·lo
gig actuación ⓕ ak·twa·*syon*
ginger jengibre ⓜ khen·*khee*·bre
girl chica ⓕ *chee*·ka
girlfriend novia ⓕ *no*·vya
give dar dar
glandular fever fiebre ⓕ glandular *fye*·bre glan·doo·*lar*
glass (drinking) vaso ⓜ *va*·so
glass (material) vidrio ⓜ *vee*·dryo
glasses anteojos ⓕ pl an·te·*o*·khos
glossy brillante bree·*yan*·te
gloves guantes ⓜ pl *gwan*·tes
go ir eer
go out with salir con sa·*leer* kon
goat cabra ⓕ *ka*·bra
god dios dyos
goggles anteojos ⓜ pl an·te·*o*·khos
gold oro ⓜ *o*·ro
golf ball pelota ⓕ de golf pe·*lo*·ta de golf
golf course cancha ⓕ de golf *kan*·cha de golf
good bueno/a ⓜ/ⓕ *bwe*·no/a
government gobierno ⓜ go·*byer*·no
grams gramos ⓜ pl *gra*·mos
grandchild nieto/a ⓜ/ⓕ *nye*·to/a
grandfather abuelo ⓜ a·*bwe*·lo

grandmother abuela Ⓕ a·*bwe*·la
grapefruit pomelo Ⓜ po·*me*·lo
grapes uvas Ⓕ pl *oo*·vas
grass hierba Ⓕ *yer*·ba
grave tumba Ⓕ *toom*·ba
great fantástico/a Ⓜ/Ⓕ fan·*tas*·tee·ko/a
green verde *ver*·de
greengrocer verdulero/a Ⓜ/Ⓕ ver·doo·*le*·ro/a
grey gris grees
grocery almacén Ⓜ al·ma·*sen*
groundnut maní Ⓜ ma·*nee*
group grupo Ⓜ *groo*·po
grow crecer kre·*ser*
Guatemala Guatemala Ⓕ gwa·te·*ma*·la
guess adivinar a·dee·vee·*nar*
guide (audio) guía Ⓕ audio *gee*·a *ow*·dyo
guide (person) guía Ⓜ&Ⓕ *gee*·a
guide dog perro Ⓜ guía *pe*·ro *gee*·a
guidebook guía Ⓕ *gee*·a
guided tour recorrido Ⓜ guiado re·ko·*ree*·do gee·*a*·do
guilty culpable kool·*pa*·ble
guinea pig cuy Ⓜ kooy
guitar guitarra Ⓕ gee·*ta*·ra
gum (chewing) chicle Ⓜ *chee*·kle
gum (mouth) encía Ⓕ en·*see*·a
gymnastics gimnasia Ⓕ kheem·*na*·sya
gynaecologist ginecólogo/a Ⓜ/Ⓕ khee·ne·*ko*·lo·go/a

H

hail granizo Ⓜ gra·*nee*·so
hair pelo Ⓜ *pe*·lo
haircut corte Ⓜ de pelo *kor*·te de *pe*·lo
hairdresser peluquero/a Ⓜ/Ⓕ pe·loo·*ke*·ro/a
half medio/a Ⓜ/Ⓕ *me*·dyo/a
hallucinate alucinar a·loo·see·*nar*
ham jamón Ⓜ kha·*mon*
hammer martillo Ⓜ mar·*tee*·yo
hammock hamaca Ⓕ a·*ma*·ka
hand mano Ⓕ *ma*·no
handbag bolso Ⓜ *bol*·so
handicraft artesanía Ⓕ ar·te·sa·*nee*·a
handkerchief pañuelo Ⓜ pa·*nywe*·lo
handlebar manillar Ⓜ ma·nee·*yar*
handmade hecho/a Ⓜ/Ⓕ a mano *e*·cho/a a *ma*·no
handsome buen mozo/a Ⓜ/Ⓕ bwen *mo*·so/a
happy feliz fe·*lees*
harassment acoso Ⓜ a·*ko*·so
harbour puerto Ⓜ *pwer*·to
hard (not easy) difícil dee·*fee*·seel
hard (not soft) duro/a Ⓜ/Ⓕ *doo*·ro/a
hardware store ferretería Ⓕ fe·re·te·*ree*·a
hash hachís Ⓜ a·*chees*
hat sombrero Ⓜ som·*bre*·ro
have tener te·*ner*
hay fever alergia Ⓕ de polén a·*ler*·khya de po·*len*
he él el
head cabeza Ⓕ ka·*be*·sa
headache dolor Ⓜ de cabeza do·*lor* de ka·*be*·sa
headlights faros Ⓜ pl *fa*·ros
health salud Ⓕ sa·*loo*
hear oír o·*eer*
hearing aid audífono Ⓜ ow·*dee*·fo·no
heart corazón Ⓜ ko·ra·*son*
heart condition condición Ⓕ cardíaca kon·dee·*syon* kar·*dee*·a·ka
heat calor Ⓜ ka·*lor*
heater estufa Ⓕ es·*too*·fa
heating calefacción Ⓕ ka·le·fak·*syon*
heavy pesado/a Ⓜ/Ⓕ pe·*sa*·do/a
helmet casco Ⓜ *kas*·ko
help ayudar a·yoo·*dar*
her su soo
herbalist herborista Ⓜ&Ⓕ er·bo·*rees*·ta
herbs hierbas Ⓕ pl *yer*·bas

here aquí a·*kee*
heroin heroína ⓕ e·ro·*ee*·na
herring arenque ⓜ a·*ren*·ke
high alto/a ⓜ/ⓕ *al*·to/a
high school instituto ⓜ een·stee·*too*·to
hike ir de excursión eer de ek·skoor·*syon*
hiking excursionismo ⓜ ek·skoor·syo·*nees*·mo
hiking boots botas ⓕ pl de montaña *bo*·tas de mon·*ta*·nya
hiking route camino ⓜ rural ka·*mee*·no roo·*ral*
hill colina ⓕ ko·*lee*·na
Hindu hindú ⓜ&ⓕ een·*doo*
hire alquilar al·kee·*lar*
his su soo
historical histórico/a ⓜ/ⓕ ees·*to*·ree·ko/a
hitchhike hacer dedo a·*ser de*·do
HIV positive seropositivo/a ⓜ/ⓕ se·ro·po·see·*tee*·vo/a
holiday día ⓜ festivo *dee*·a fes·*tee*·vo
holidays vacaciones ⓕ pl va·ka·*syo*·nes
home casa ⓕ *ka*·sa
homeless sin techo seen *te*·cho
homemaker ama ⓕ de casa *a*·ma de *ka*·sa
Honduras Honduras ⓕ on·*doo*·ras
honey miel ⓕ myel
honeymoon luna ⓕ de miel *loo*·na de myel
horoscope horóscopo ⓜ o·*ros*·ko·po
horse caballo ⓜ ka·*ba*·yo
horse riding equitación ⓕ e·kee·ta·*syon*
horseradish rábano ⓜ picante *ra*·ba·no pee·*kan*·te
hospital hospital ⓜ os·pee·*tal*
hospitality hospitalidad ⓕ os·pee·ta·lee·*da*
hot caliente ka·*lyen*·te
hot water agua ⓕ caliente *a*·gwa ka·*lyen*·te
hotel hotel ⓜ o·*tel*
house casa ⓕ *ka*·sa
how como *ko*·mo
how much cuanto *kwan*·to
hug abrazo ⓜ a·*bra*·so
huge enorme e·*nor*·me
human rights derechos ⓜ pl humanos de·*re*·chos oo·*ma*·nos
hummingbird colibrí ⓜ ko·lee·*bree*
(be) hungry tener hambre te·*ner am*·bre
hunting caza ⓕ *ka*·sa
(be in a) hurry tener prisa te·*ner pree*·sa
hurt dañar da·*nyar*
husband esposo ⓜ es·*po*·so
hut cabaña ⓕ ka·*ba*·nya

I

I yo yo
ice hielo ⓜ *ye*·lo
ice axe piolet ⓜ pyo·*let*
ice cream helado ⓜ e·*la*·do
ice-cream parlour heladería ⓕ e·la·de·*ree*·a
ice hockey hockey ⓜ sobre hielo *kho*·kee *so*·bre *ye*·lo
identification identificación ⓕ ee·den·tee·fee·ka·*syon*
identification card (ID) cédula ⓜ de identidad *se*·doo·la de ee·den·tee·*da*
idiot idiota ⓜ&ⓕ ee·*dyo*·ta
if si see
ill enfermo/a ⓜ/ⓕ en·*fer*·mo/a
illegal ilegal ee·le·*gal*
immigration inmigración ⓕ een·mee·gra·*syon*
important importante eem·por·*tan*·te
impossible imposible eem·po·*see*·ble
included incluido/a ⓜ/ⓕ een·kloo·*ee*·do/a
income tax impuesto ⓜ sobre la renta eem·*pwes*·to *so*·bre la *ren*·ta

indicators (car) direccionales ⓜ pl dee·rek·syo·*na*·les
indigestion indigestion ⓕ een·dee·khes·*tyon*
industry industria ⓕ een·*doos*·trya
infection infección ⓕ een·fek·*syon*
inflammation inflamación ⓕ een·fla·ma·*syon*
information información ⓕ een·for·ma·*syon*
influenza gripe ⓕ *gree*·pe
ingredient ingrediente ⓜ een·gre·*dyen*·te
inhaler inhalador ⓜ ee·na·la·*dor*
inject inyectarse een·yek·*tar*·se
injection inyección ⓕ een·yek·*syon*
injury herida ⓕ e·*ree*·da
innocent inocente ee·no·*sen*·te
inside adentro a·*den*·tro
instructor instructor(a) ⓜ/ⓕ een·strook·*tor*/een·strook·*to*·ra
instructor (skiing) monitor(a) ⓜ/ⓕ mo·nee·*tor*/mo·nee·*to*·ra
insurance seguro ⓜ se·*goo*·ro
interesting interesante een·te·re·*san*·te
intermission descanso ⓜ des·*kan*·so
international internacional een·ter·na·syo·*nal*
internet cafe cibercafé ⓜ see·ber·ka·*fe*
interpreter intérprete ⓜ&ⓕ een·*ter*·pre·te
interview entrevista ⓕ en·tre·*vees*·ta
invite invitar een·vee·*tar*
iron (clothes) plancha ⓕ *plan*·cha
island isla ⓕ *ees*·la
IT informática ⓕ een·for·*ma*·tee·ka
itch picazón ⓜ pee·ka·*son*
itemised detallado/a ⓜ/ⓕ de·ta·*ya*·do/a
itinerary itinerario ⓜ ee·tee·ne·*ra*·ryo
IUD (contraceptive device) DIU ⓜ de ee oo

J

jacket chaqueta ⓕ cha·*ke*·ta
jaguar jaguar ⓜ kha·*gwar*
jail cárcel ⓕ *kar*·sel
jam mermelada ⓕ mer·me·*la*·da
Japan Japón ⓜ kha·*pon*
jar jarra ⓕ *kha*·ra
jaw mandíbula ⓕ man·*dee*·boo·la
jealous celoso/a ⓜ/ⓕ se·*lo*·so/a
jeep yip ⓜ yeep
jewellery joyería ⓕ kho·ye·*ree*·a
Jewish judío/a ⓜ/ⓕ khoo·*dee*·o/a
job trabajo ⓜ tra·*ba*·kho
jogging footing ⓜ foo·*teen*
joke broma ⓕ *bro*·ma
journalist periodista ⓜ&ⓕ pe·ryo·*dees*·ta
judge juez ⓜ&ⓕ khwes
juice jugo ⓜ *khoo*·go
jump saltar sal·*tar*
jumper (sweater) chompa ⓜ *chom*·pa
jumper leads cables ⓜ pl de arranque *ka*·bles de a·*ran*·ke

K

ketchup salsa ⓕ de tomate *sal*·sa de to·*ma*·te
key llave ⓕ *ya*·ve
keyboard teclado ⓜ te·*kla*·do
kick patada ⓕ pa·*ta*·da
kick dar una patada dar *oo*·na pa·*ta*·da
kill matar ma·*tar*
kilogram kilo ⓜ *kee*·lo
kilometre kilómetro ⓜ kee·*lo*·me·tro
kind amable a·*ma*·ble
kindergarten jardín ⓜ de infancia • kinder ⓜ khar·*deen* de een·*fan*·sya • *keen*·der
king rey ⓜ ray
kiss beso ⓜ *be*·so
kiss besar be·*sar*
kitchen cocina ⓕ ko·*see*·na
kitten gatito/a ⓜ/ⓕ ga·*tee*·to/a

knapsack mochila ⓕ mo·*chee*·la
knee rodilla ⓕ ro·*dee*·ya
knife cuchillo ⓜ koo·*chee*·yo
know (someone) conocer ko·no·*ser*
know (something) saber sa·*ber*

L

labourer obrero/a ⓜ/ⓕ o·*bre*·ro/a
lace encaje ⓜ en·*ka*·khe
lager cerveza ⓕ rubia ser·*ve*·sa *roo*·bya
lake lago ⓜ *la*·go
lamb cordero ⓜ kor·*de*·ro
land tierra ⓕ *tye*·ra
landlady propietaria ⓕ pro·pye·*ta*·rya
landlord propietario ⓜ pro·pye·*ta*·ryo
language idioma ⓜ ee·*dyo*·ma
laptop computadora ⓕ portátil kom·poo·ta·*do*·ra por·*ta*·teel
lard manteca ⓕ de cerdo man·*te*·ka de *ser*·do
large grande *gran*·de
laser pointer puntero ⓜ láser poon·*te*·ro *la*·ser
late tarde *tar*·de
Latin America Latinoamérica ⓕ la·tee·no·a·*me*·ree·ka
Latin American latinoamericano/a ⓜ/ⓕ la·tee·no·a·me·ree·*ka*·no/a
laugh reírse re·*eer*·se
laundrette lavandería ⓕ la·van·de·*ree*·a
laundry lavandería ⓕ la·van·de·*ree*·a
law ley ⓕ lay
lawyer abogado/a ⓜ/ⓕ a·bo·*ga*·do/a
laxatives laxantes ⓜ pl lak·*san*·tes
lazy perezoso/a ⓜ/ⓕ pe·re·*so*·so/a
leader jefe/a ⓜ/ⓕ *khe*·fe/a
leaf hoja ⓕ *o*·kha
learn aprender a·pren·*der*
leather cuero ⓜ *kwe*·ro
leave partir par·*teer*
lecturer profesor(a) ⓜ/ⓕ pro·fe·*sor*/pro·fe·*so*·ra
leek puerro ⓜ *pwe*·ro
left (direction) izquierda ⓕ ees·*kyer*·da
left-luggage office consigna ⓕ kon·*seeg*·na
left-wing izquierdista ees·kyer·*dees*·ta
leg (body) pierna ⓕ *pyer*·na
legal legal le·*gal*
legislation legislación ⓕ le·khees·la·*syon*
lemon limón ⓜ lee·*mon*
lemonade limonada ⓕ lee·mo·*na*·da
lens objetivo ⓜ ob·khe·*tee*·vo
lentils lentejas ⓕ pl len·*te*·khas
lesbian lesbiana ⓕ les·*bya*·na
less de menos de *me*·nos
letter carta ⓕ *kar*·ta
lettuce lechuga ⓕ le·*choo*·ga
liar mentiroso/a ⓜ/ⓕ men·tee·*ro*·so/a
library biblioteca ⓕ bee·blyo·*te*·ka
lice piojos ⓜ pl *pyo*·khos
license plate number matrícula ⓕ ma·*tree*·koo·la
lie (not stand) tumbarse toom·*bar*·se
life vida ⓕ *vee*·da
lifejacket chaleco ⓜ salvavidas cha·*le*·ko sal·va·*vee*·das
lift (elevator) ascensor ⓜ a·sen·*sor*
lift levantar le·van·*tar*
light luz ⓕ loos
light (colour) claro/a ⓜ/ⓕ *kla*·ro/a
light (not heavy) ligero/a ⓜ/ⓕ lee·*khe*·ro/a
light bulb bombilla ⓕ bom·*bee*·ya
light meter fotómetro ⓜ fo·*to*·me·tro
lighter encendedor ⓜ en·sen·de·*dor*
lights (on car) faros ⓜ pl *fa*·ros
like (affection) gustar(le) goos·*tar*(·le)
lime lima ⓕ *lee*·ma

line línea ⓕ *lee*·ne·a
lip balm bálsamo ⓜ de labios *bal*·sa·mo de *la*·byos
lips labios ⓜ pl *la*·byos
lipstick lápiz ⓜ de labios *la*·pees de *la*·byos
liquor store bodega ⓕ bo·*de*·ga
listen escuchar es·koo·*char*
live vivir vee·*veer*
liver hígado ⓜ *ee*·ga·do
lizard lagartija ⓕ la·gar·*tee*·kha
local local lo·*kal*
lock (door) cerradura ⓕ se·ra·*doo*·ra
lock cerrar se·*rar*
locked cerrado/a ⓜ/ⓕ con llave se·*ra*·do/a kon *ya*·ve
lollies caramelos ⓜ pl ka·ra·*me*·los
long largo/a ⓜ/ⓕ *lar*·go/a
long-distance larga distancia *lar*·ga dees·*tan*·sya
look mirar mee·*rar*
look after cuidar de kwee·*dar* de
look for buscar boos·*kar*
lookout mirador ⓜ mee·ra·*dor*
loose change monedas ⓕ pl sueltas mo·*ne*·das *swel*·tas
lose perder per·*der*
lost perdido/a ⓜ/ⓕ per·*dee*·do/a
lost-property office oficina ⓕ de objetos perdidos o·fee·*see*·na de ob·*khe*·tos per·*dee*·dos
loud ruidoso/a ⓜ/ⓕ rwee·*do*·so/a
love querer ke·*rer*
lover amante ⓜ&ⓕ a·*man*·te
low bajo/a ⓜ/ⓕ *ba*·kho/a
lubricant lubricante ⓜ loo·bree·*kan*·te
luck suerte ⓕ *swer*·te
lucky afortunado/a ⓜ/ⓕ a·for·too·*na*·do/a
luggage equipaje ⓜ e·kee·*pa*·khe
luggage lockers consigna ⓕ automática kon·*seeg*·na ow·to·*ma*·tee·ka
luggage tag etiqueta ⓕ de equipaje e·tee·*ke*·ta de e·kee·*pa*·khe
lump bulto ⓜ *bool*·to
lunch almuerzo ⓜ al·*mwer*·so
lungs pulmones ⓜ pl pool·*mo*·nes
luxurious de lujo de *loo*·kho

M

macaw papagayo ⓜ pa·pa·*ga*·yo
machine máquina ⓕ *ma*·kee·na
made of (cotton) hecho/a ⓜ/ⓕ de (algodón) *e*·cho/a de (al·go·*don*)
magazine revista ⓕ re·*vees*·ta
magician mago/a ⓜ/ⓕ *ma*·go/a
mail correo ⓜ ko·*re*·o
mailbox buzón ⓜ boo·*son*
main principal preen·see·*pal*
make hacer a·*ser*
make-up maquillaje ⓜ ma·kee·*ya*·khe
malaria malaria ⓕ ma·*la*·rya
mallet mazo ⓜ *ma*·so
mammogram mamograma ⓜ ma·mo·*gra*·ma
man hombre ⓜ *om*·bre
manager director(a) ⓜ/ⓕ dee·rek·*tor*/dee·rek·*to*·ra
mandarin mandarina ⓕ man·da·*ree*·na
manual manual ma·*nwal*
many muchos/as ⓜ/ⓕ pl *moo*·chos/as
map mapa ⓜ *ma*·pa
margarine margarina ⓕ mar·ga·*ree*·na
marital status estado ⓜ civil es·*ta*·do see·*veel*
market mercado ⓜ mer·*ka*·do
marmalade mermelada ⓕ mer·me·*la*·da
marriage matrimonio ⓜ ma·tree·*mo*·nyo
married casado/a ⓜ/ⓕ ka·*sa*·do/a
marry casarse ka·*sar*·se
martial arts artes ⓜ pl marciales *ar*·tes mar·*sya*·les
mass (Catholic) misa ⓕ *mee*·sa
massage masaje ⓜ ma·*sa*·khe

masseur/masseuse masajista ⓜ&ⓕ ma·sa·*khees*·ta
mat esterilla ⓕ es·te·*ree*·ya
match (sport) partido ⓜ par·*tee*·do
matches fósforos ⓜ pl *fos*·fo·ros
mattress colchón ⓜ kol·*chon*
maybe quizás kee·*sas*
mayonnaise mayonesa ⓕ ma·yo·*ne*·sa
mayor alcalde ⓜ&ⓕ al·*kal*·de
measles sarampión ⓜ sa·ram·*pyon*
meat carne ⓕ *kar*·ne
mechanic mecánico/a ⓜ/ⓕ me·*ka*·nee·ko/a
media medios ⓜ pl de comunicación *me*·dyos de ko·moo·nee·ka·*syon*
medicine medicina ⓕ me·dee·*see*·na
meditation meditación ⓕ me·dee·ta·*syon*
meet encontrar en·kon·*trar*
melon melón ⓜ me·*lon*
member miembro ⓜ&ⓕ *myem*·bro
menstruation menstruación ⓕ mens·trwa·*syon*
menu menú ⓜ me·*noo*
message mensaje ⓜ men·*sa*·khe
metre (distance) metro ⓜ *me*·tro
metro subteráneo ⓜ soob·te·*ra*·ne·o
metro station estación ⓕ de subterráneo es·ta·*syon* de soob·te·*ra*·ne·o
Mexico México ⓜ *me*·khee·ko
microwave oven microondas ⓜ mee·kro·*on*·das
midnight medianoche ⓕ me·dya·*no*·che
migraine migraña ⓕ mee·*gra*·nya
military militares ⓜ pl mee·lee·*ta*·res
military service servicio ⓜ militar ser·*vee*·syo mee·lee·*tar*
milk leche ⓕ *le*·che
millimetre milímetro ⓜ mee·*lee*·me·tro
million millón ⓜ mee·*yon*
mince (meat) carne ⓕ molida *kar*·ne mo·*lee*·da
mind (look after) cuidar kwee·*dar*
mineral water agua ⓜ mineral *a*·gwa mee·ne·*ral*
mints pastillas ⓕ pl de menta pas·*tee*·yas de *men*·ta
minute minuto ⓜ mee·*noo*·to
mirror espejo ⓜ es·*pe*·kho
miscarriage aborto ⓜ natural a·*bor*·to na·too·*ral*
miss (feel absence of) extrañar ek·stra·*nyar*
mistake error ⓜ e·*ror*
mix mezclar mes·*klar*
mobile phone teléfono ⓜ móvil/celular te·*le*·fo·no *mo*·veel/se·loo·*lar*
moisturiser crema ⓕ hidratante *kre*·ma ee·dra·*tan*·te
monastery monasterio ⓜ mo·nas·*te*·ryo
money dinero ⓜ dee·*ne*·ro
month mes ⓜ mes
monument monumento ⓜ mo·noo·*men*·to
moon luna ⓕ *loo*·na
more más mas
morning mañana ⓕ ma·*nya*·na
morning sickness náuseas ⓕ pl del embarazo *now*·se·as del em·ba·*ra*·so
mosque mezquita ⓕ mes·*kee*·ta
mosquito mosquito ⓜ mos·*kee*·to
mosquito coil espiral ⓜ repelente contra mosquitos es·pee·*ral* re·pe·*len*·te *kon*·tra mos·*kee*·tos
mosquito net mosquitera ⓕ mos·kee·*te*·ra
mother madre ⓕ *ma*·dre
mother-in-law suegra ⓕ *swe*·gra
motorboat motora ⓕ mo·*to*·ra
motorcycle motocicleta ⓕ mo·to·see·*kle*·ta
motorway autopista ⓕ ow·to·*pees*·ta
mountain montaña ⓕ mon·*ta*·nya

mountain bike bicicleta ⓕ de montaña bee·see·*kle*·ta de mon·*ta*·nya
mountain path sendero ⓜ sen·*de*·ro
mountain range cordillera ⓕ kor·dee·*ye*·ra
mountaineering alpinismo ⓜ al·pee·*nees*·mo
mouse ratón ⓜ ra·*ton*
mouth boca ⓕ *bo*·ka
movie película ⓕ pe·*lee*·koo·la
mp3 player reproductor ⓜ de mp3 re·pro·dook·*tor* de *e*·me pe tres
mud lodo ⓜ *lo*·do
mum mamá ⓕ ma·*ma*
muscle músculo ⓜ *moos*·koo·lo
museum museo ⓜ moo·*se*·o
mushroom champiñón ⓜ cham·pee·*nyon*
music música ⓕ *moo*·see·ka
musician músico/a ⓜ/ⓕ *moo*·see·ko/a
Muslim musulmán/musulmana ⓜ/ⓕ moo·sool·*man*/moo·sool·*ma*·na
mussels mejillones ⓜ pl me·khee·*yo*·nes
mustard mostaza ⓕ mos·*ta*·sa
mute mudo/a ⓜ/ⓕ *moo*·do/a
my mi mee

N

nail clippers cortauñas ⓜ kor·ta·*oo*·nyas
name nombre ⓜ *nom*·bre
napkin servilleta ⓕ ser·vee·*ye*·ta
nappy pañal ⓜ pa·*nyal*
nappy rash irritación ⓕ de pañal ee·ree·ta·*syon* de pa·*nyal*
national nacional na·syo·*nal*
national park parque ⓜ nacional *par*·ke na·syo·*nal*
nationality nacionalidad ⓕ na·syo·na·lee·*da*
nature naturaleza ⓕ na·too·ra·*le*·sa
naturopathy naturopatia ⓕ na·too·ro·*pa*·tya
nausea náusea ⓕ *now*·se·a
near (to) cerca (de) *ser*·ka (de)
nearby cerca *ser*·ka
nearest más cercano/a ⓜ/ⓕ mas ser·*ka*·no/a
necessary necesario/a ⓜ/ⓕ ne·se·*sa*·ryo/a
neck cuello ⓜ *kwe*·yo
need necesitar ne·se·see·*tar*
needle (sewing) aguja ⓕ a·*goo*·kha
needle (syringe) jeringuilla ⓕ khe·reen·*gee*·ya
neither tampoco tam·*po*·ko
net red ⓕ re
Netherlands Holanda ⓕ o·*lan*·da
never nunca *noon*·ka
new nuevo/a ⓜ/ⓕ *nwe*·vo/a
New Year Año ⓜ Nuevo *a*·nyo *nwe*·vo
New Zealand Nueva Zelanda ⓕ *nwe*·va se·*lan*·da
news noticias ⓕ pl no·*tee*·syas
newsagency quiosco ⓜ kee·*os*·ko
newspaper periódico ⓜ pe·*ryo*·dee·ko
next próximo/a ⓜ/ⓕ *prok*·see·mo/a
next to al lado de al *la*·do de
Nicaragua Nicaragua ⓕ nee·ka·*ra*·gwa
nice (object) bueno/a ⓜ/ⓕ *bwe*·no/a
nice (person) simpático/a ⓜ/ⓕ seem·*pa*·tee·ko/a
nickname apodo ⓜ a·*po*·do
night noche ⓕ *no*·che
night life vida ⓕ nocturna *vee*·da nok·*toor*·na
noisy ruidoso/a ⓜ/ⓕ rwee·*do*·so/a
non-direct indirecto/a een·dee·*rek*·to/a
none nada *na*·da
nonfiction literatura ⓕ no novelesca lee·te·ra·*too*·ra no no·ve·*les*·ka
nonsmoking no fumadores no foo·ma·*do*·res
noodles fideos ⓜ pl fee·*de*·os

noon mediodía Ⓜ me·dyo·*dee*·a
north norte Ⓜ *nor*·te
nose nariz Ⓕ na·*rees*
notebook cuaderno Ⓜ kwa·*der*·no
nothing nada *na*·da
novel novela Ⓕ no·*ve*·la
now ahora a·*o*·ra
nuclear energy energía Ⓕ nuclear e·ner·*khee*·a noo·kle·*ar*
nuclear testing pruebas Ⓕ pl nucleares *prwe*·bas noo·kle·*a*·res
nuclear waste desperdicios Ⓜ pl nucleares des·per·*dee*·syos noo·kle·*a*·res
number número Ⓜ *noo*·me·ro
nun monja Ⓕ *mon*·kha
nurse enfermero/a Ⓜ/Ⓕ en·fer·*me*·ro/a
nut nuez Ⓕ nwes

O

oats avena Ⓕ a·*ve*·na
ocean océano Ⓜ o·se·a·no
off (spoiled) pasado/a Ⓜ/Ⓕ pa·*sa*·do/a
office oficina Ⓕ o·fee·*see*·na
office worker oficinista Ⓜ&Ⓕ o·fee·see·*nees*·ta
often a menudo a me·*noo*·do
oil aceite Ⓜ a·*say*·te
old viejo/a Ⓜ/Ⓕ *vye*·kho/a
olive aceituna Ⓕ a·say·*too*·na
olive oil aceite Ⓜ de oliva a·*say*·te de o·*lee*·va
on en en
once una vez *oo*·na ves
one-way ticket boleto Ⓜ sencillo bo·*le*·to sen·*see*·yo
onion cebolla Ⓕ se·*bo*·ya
only sólo *so*·lo
open abierto/a Ⓜ/Ⓕ a·*byer*·to/a
open abrir a·*breer*
opening hours horas Ⓕ pl de apertura *o*·ras de a·per·*too*·ra
opera house teatro Ⓜ de la ópera te·*a*·tro de la *o*·pe·ra
operation (medical) operación Ⓕ o·pe·ra·*syon*
operator operador(a) Ⓜ/Ⓕ o·pe·ra·*dor*/o·pe·ra·*do*·ra
opinion opinión Ⓕ o·pee·*nyon*
opposite frente a *fren*·te a
or o o
orange (fruit) naranja Ⓕ na·*ran*·kha
orange (colour) naranjo/a Ⓜ/Ⓕ na·*ran*·kho/a
orange juice jugo Ⓜ de naranja *khoo*·go de na·*ran*·kha
orchestra orquesta Ⓕ or·*kes*·ta
orchid orquídea Ⓕ or·*kee*·de·a
order (command) orden Ⓕ *or*·den
order (placement) orden Ⓜ *or*·den
order ordenar or·de·*nar*
ordinary corriente ko·*ryen*·te
orgasm orgasmo Ⓜ or·*gas*·mo
original original o·ree·khee·*nal*
other otro/a Ⓜ/Ⓕ *o*·tro/a
our nuestro/a Ⓜ/Ⓕ *nwes*·tro/a
outside afuera a·*fwe*·ra
ovarian cyst quiste Ⓜ ovárico *kees*·te o·*va*·ree·ko
oven horno Ⓜ *or*·no
over (above) sobre *so*·bre
overcoat abrigo Ⓜ a·*bree*·go
overdose sobredosis Ⓕ so·bre·*do*·sees
owner dueño/a Ⓜ/Ⓕ *dwe*·nyo/a
oxygen oxígeno Ⓜ ok·*see*·khe·no
oyster ostra Ⓕ *os*·tra
ozone layer capa Ⓕ de ozono *ka*·pa de o·*so*·no

P

pacemaker marcapasos Ⓜ mar·ka·*pa*·sos
pacifier chupete Ⓜ choo·*pe*·te
package paquete Ⓜ pa·*ke*·te
packet paquete Ⓜ pa·*ke*·te
padlock candado Ⓜ kan·*da*·do
page página Ⓕ *pa*·khee·na
pain dolor Ⓜ do·*lor*

painful doloroso/a ⓜ/ⓕ do·lo·*ro*·so/a
painkillers analgésicos ⓜ pl a·nal·*khe*·see·kos
paint pintar peen·*tar*
painter pintor(a) ⓜ/ⓕ peen·*tor*/peen·*to*·ra
painting (art) pintura ⓕ peen·*too*·ra
painting (canvas) cuadro ⓜ *kwa*·dro
pair (couple) pareja ⓕ pa·*re*·kha
palace palacio ⓜ pa·*la*·syo
pan olla ⓕ *o*·ya
panoramic panorámico/a ⓜ/ⓕ pa·no·*ra*·mee·ko/a
Panama Panamá ⓕ pa·na·*ma*
panther pantera ⓕ pan·*te*·ra
pants pantalones ⓜ pl pan·ta·*lo*·nes
panty liners salvaeslips ⓜ pl *sal*·va·e·sleeps
pantyhose medias ⓕ pl *me*·dyas
pap smear citología ⓕ see·to·lo·*khee*·a
paper papel ⓜ pa·*pel*
paperwork trabajo ⓜ administrativo tra·*ba*·kho ad·mee·nees·tra·*tee*·vo
Paraguay Paraguay ⓜ pa·ra·*gway*
parcel paquete ⓜ pa·*ke*·te
parents padres ⓜ pl *pa*·dres
park parque ⓜ *par*·ke
park (car) estacionar es·ta·syo·*nar*
parliament parlamento ⓜ par·la·*men*·to
parrot loro ⓜ *lo*·ro
part parte ⓕ *par*·te
partner (relationship) pareja ⓜ&ⓕ pa·*re*·kha
part-time a tiempo parcial a *tyem*·po par·*syal*
party (celebration) fiesta ⓕ *fyes*·ta
party (politics) partido ⓜ par·*tee*·do
pass (mountain) paso ⓜ *pa*·so
pass (permit) pase ⓜ *pa*·se
passenger pasajero/a ⓜ/ⓕ pa·sa·*khe*·ro/a
passport pasaporte ⓜ pa·sa·*por*·te
passport number número ⓜ de pasaporte *noo*·me·ro de pa·sa·*por*·te
past pasado ⓜ pa·*sa*·do
path sendero ⓜ sen·*de*·ro
pay pagar pa·*gar*
payment pago ⓜ *pa*·go
pea guisante ⓕ gee·*san*·te
peace paz ⓕ pas
peach durazno ⓜ doo·*ras*·no
peak cumbre ⓕ *koom*·bre
peanut maní ⓜ ma·*nee*
pear pera ⓕ *pe*·ra
pedestrian peatón ⓜ&ⓕ pe·a·*ton*
pegs (tent) estacas ⓕ pl es·*ta*·kas
pen (ballpoint) bolígrafo ⓜ bo·*lee*·gra·fo
pencil lápiz ⓜ *la*·pees
penis pene ⓜ *pe*·ne
penicillin penicilina ⓕ pe·nee·see·*lee*·na
penknife navaja ⓕ na·*va*·kha
pensioner pensionado/a ⓜ/ⓕ pen·syo·*na*·do/a
people gente ⓕ *khen*·te
pepper (spice) pimienta ⓕ pee·*myen*·ta
per (day) por (día) por (*dee*·a)
percent por ciento por *syen*·to
performance actuación ⓕ ak·twa·*syon*
perfume perfume ⓜ per·*foo*·me
period pain dolor ⓜ menstrual do·*lor* mens·*trwal*
permission permiso ⓜ per·*mee*·so
permit permiso ⓜ per·*mee*·so
permit permitir per·mee·*teer*
person persona ⓕ per·*so*·na
perspire sudar soo·*dar*
Peru Perú ⓜ pe·*roo*
petition petición ⓕ pe·tee·*syon*
petrol gasolina ⓕ ga·so·*lee*·na
pharmacy farmacia ⓕ far·*ma*·sya
pharmacist farmacéutico/a ⓜ/ⓕ far·ma·*see*·oo·tee·ko/a
phone book guía ⓕ telefónica *gee*·a te·le·*fo*·nee·ka

phone box cabina ⓕ telefónica ka·*bee*·na te·le·*fo*·nee·ka
phone card tarjeta ⓕ de teléfono tar·*khe*·ta de te·*le*·fo·no
photo fotografía ⓕ fo·to·gra·*fee*·a
photocopier fotocopiadora ⓕ fo·to·ko·pya·*do*·ra
photographer fotógrafo/a ⓜ/ⓕ fo·*to*·gra·fo/a
photography fotografía ⓕ fo·to·gra·*fee*·a
phrasebook libro ⓜ de frases *lee*·bro de *fra*·ses
pick (up) levantar le·van·*tar*
pickaxe piqueta ⓕ pee·*ke*·ta
pickles pepinillos ⓜ pl pe·pee·*nee*·yos
pie empanada ⓕ em·pa·*na*·da
piece pedazo ⓜ pe·*da*·so
pig cerdo ⓜ *ser*·do
pill pastilla ⓕ pas·*tee*·ya
the Pill la píldora ⓕ la *peel*·do·ra
pillow almohada ⓕ al·mo·*a*·da
pillowcase funda ⓕ de almohada *foon*·da de al·mo·*a*·da
pineapple ananá(s) ⓜ a·na·*na(s)*
pink rosa *ro*·sa
pistachio pistacho ⓜ pees·*ta*·cho
place lugar ⓜ loo·*gar*
place of birth lugar ⓜ de nacimiento loo·*gar* de na·see·*myen*·to
plane avión ⓜ a·*vyon*
planet planeta ⓜ pla·*ne*·ta
plant planta ⓕ *plan*·ta
plant sembrar sem·*brar*
plastic plástico ⓜ *plas*·tee·ko
plate plato ⓜ *pla*·to
plateau meseta ⓕ me·*se*·ta
platform plataforma ⓕ pla·ta·*for*·ma
play obra ⓕ *o*·bra
play (a game) jugar khoo·*gar*
play (the guitar) tocar (la guitarra) to·*kar* (la gee·*ta*·ra)
play (tennis) jugar (al tenis) khoo·*gar* (al *te*·nees)
plug (bath) tapón ⓜ ta·*pon*
plug (electricity) enchufe ⓜ en·*choo*·fe
plum ciruela ⓕ see·*rwe*·la
pocket bolsillo ⓜ bol·*see*·yo
poetry poesía ⓕ po·e·*see*·a
point punto ⓜ *poon*·to
point apuntar a·poon·*tar*
poisonous venenoso/a ⓜ/ⓕ ve·ne·*no*·so/a
police policía ⓕ po·lee·*see*·a
police station comisaría ⓕ ko·mee·sa·*ree*·a
policy política ⓕ po·*lee*·tee·ka
policy (insurance) póliza ⓕ *po*·lee·sa
politician político/a ⓜ/ⓕ po·*lee*·tee·ko/a
politics política ⓕ po·*lee*·tee·ka
polls sondeos ⓜ pl son·*de*·os
pollution contaminación ⓕ kon·ta·mee·na·*syon*
pony potro ⓜ *po*·tro
pool (game) billar ⓜ bee·*yar*
pool (swimming) piscina ⓕ pee·*see*·na
poor pobre *po*·bre
popular popular po·poo·*lar*
pork cerdo ⓜ *ser*·do
port puerto ⓜ *pwer*·to
port (wine) oporto ⓜ o·*por*·to
portable CD player reproductor ⓜ de compacts portátil re·pro·dook·*tor* de *kom*·paks por·*ta*·teel
possible posible po·*see*·ble
post code código ⓜ postal *ko*·dee·go pos·*tal*
post office correos ⓜ pl ko·*re*·os
postage franqueo ⓜ fran·*ke*·o
postcard postal ⓕ pos·*tal*
pot (ceramic) cacharro ⓜ ka·*cha*·ro
pot (kitchen) olla ⓕ *o*·ya
pot (dope) chocolate ⓜ cho·ko·*la*·te
potato papa ⓕ *pa*·pa
pottery alfarería ⓕ al·fa·re·*ree*·a
pound (money) libra ⓕ *lee*·bra
poverty pobreza ⓕ po·*bre*·sa

power poder ⓜ po·*der*
prawn langostino ⓜ lan·gos·*tee*·no
prayer oración ⓕ o·ra·*syon*
prefer preferir pre·fe·*reer*
pregnancy test kit prueba ⓕ del embarazo *prwe*·ba del em·ba·*ra*·so
pregnant embarazada ⓕ em·ba·ra·*sa*·da
premenstrual tension tensión ⓕ premenstrual ten·*syon* pre·mens·*trwal*
prepare preparar pre·pa·*rar*
present (gift) regalo ⓜ re·*ga*·lo
presentation presentación ⓕ pre·sen·ta·*syon*
president presidente/a ⓜ/ⓕ pre·see·*den*·te/a
pressure presión ⓕ pre·*syon*
pretty bonito/a ⓜ/ⓕ bo·*nee*·to/a
prevent prevenir pre·ve·*neer*
price precio ⓜ *pre*·syo
priest sacerdote ⓜ sa·ser·*do*·te
prime minister (man) primer ministro ⓜ pree·*mer* mee·*nees*·tro
prime minister (woman) primera ministra ⓕ pree·*me*·ra mee·*nees*·tra
prison cárcel ⓕ *kar*·sel
prisoner prisionero/a ⓜ/ⓕ pree·syo·*ne*·ro/a
private privado/a ⓜ/ⓕ pree·*va*·do/a
produce producir pro·doo·*seer*
profit beneficio ⓜ be·ne·*fee*·syo
programme programa ⓜ pro·*gra*·ma
projector proyector ⓜ pro·yek·*tor*
promise promesa ⓕ pro·*me*·sa
proposal propuesta ⓕ pro·*pwes*·ta
protect proteger pro·te·*kher*
protected protegido/a ⓜ/ⓕ pro·te·*khee*·do/a
protest protesta ⓕ pro·*tes*·ta
protest protestar pro·tes·*tar*
provisions provisiones ⓕ pl pro·vee·*syo*·nes
prune ciruela ⓕ pasa see·*rwe*·la *pa*·sa
public telephone teléfono ⓜ público te·*le*·fo·no *poo*·blee·ko
public toilet baños ⓜ pl *ba*·nyos
Puerto Rico Puerto ⓜ Rico *pwer*·to *ree*·ko
pull jalar kha·*lar*
pump bomba ⓕ *bom*·ba
pumpkin calabaza ⓕ ka·la·*ba*·sa
puncture pinchar peen·*char*
punish castigar kas·tee·*gar*
puppy cachorro ⓜ ka·*cho*·ro
pure puro/a ⓜ/ⓕ *poo*·ro/a
purple morado/a ⓜ/ⓕ mo·*ra*·do/a
push empujar em·poo·*khar*
put poner po·*ner*

Q

qualifications cualificaciones ⓕ pl kwa·lee·fee·ka·*syo*·nes
quality calidad ⓕ ka·lee·*da*
quarantine cuarentena ⓕ kwa·ren·*te*·na
quarrel pelea ⓕ pe·*le*·a
quarter cuarto ⓜ *kwar*·to
queen reina ⓕ *ray*·na
question pregunta ⓕ pre·*goon*·ta
queue cola ⓕ *ko*·la
quick rápido/a ⓜ/ⓕ *ra*·pee·do/a
quiet tranquilo/a ⓜ/ⓕ tran·*kee*·lo/a

R

rabbit conejo ⓜ ko·*ne*·kho
race (people) raza ⓕ *ra*·sa
race (sport) carrera ⓕ ka·*re*·ra
racetrack (sport) pista ⓕ *pees*·ta
racing bike bicicleta ⓕ de carreras bee·see·*kle*·ta de ka·*re*·ras
racquet raqueta ⓕ ra·*ke*·ta
radiator radiador ⓜ ra·dya·*dor*
radish rábano ⓜ *ra*·ba·no
railway ferrocarril ⓜ fe·ro·ka·*reel*
railway station estación ⓕ de tren es·ta·*syon* de tren
rain lluvia ⓕ *yoo*·vya
raincoat impermeable ⓜ eem·per·me·*a*·ble
raisin pasa ⓕ de uva *pa*·sa de *oo*·va

rape violar vyo·*lar*
rare raro/a ⓜ/ⓕ *ra*·ro/a
rash irritación ⓕ ee·ree·ta·*syon*
raspberry frambuesa ⓕ fram·*bwe*·sa
rat rata ⓕ *ra*·ta
raw crudo/a ⓜ/ⓕ *kroo*·do/a
razor afeitadora ⓕ a·fay·ta·*do*·ra
razor blade hoja ⓕ de afeitar o·kha de a·fay·*tar*
read leer le·*er*
ready listo/a ⓜ/ⓕ *lees*·to/a
real estate agent agente ⓜ inmobiliario a·*khen*·te een·mo·bee·*lya*·ryo
realistic realista re·a·*lees*·ta
reason razón ⓕ ra·*son*
receipt recibo ⓜ re·*see*·bo
receive recibir re·see·*beer*
recently recientemente re·syen·te·*men*·te
recognise reconocer re·ko·no·*ser*
recommend recomendar re·ko·men·*dar*
recording grabación ⓕ gra·ba·*syon*
recyclable reciclable re·see·*kla*·ble
recycle reciclar re·see·*klar*
red rojo/a ⓜ/ⓕ *ro*·kho/a
referee árbitro ⓜ *ar*·bee·tro
references (work) referencias ⓕ pl re·fe·*ren*·syas
refrigerator refrigeradora ⓕ re·free·khe·ra·*do*·ra
refugee refugiado/a ⓜ/ⓕ re·foo·*khya*·do/a
refund reembolso ⓜ re·em·*bol*·so
refuse negar(se) ne·*gar*(·se)
registered mail correo ⓜ certificado ko·*re*·o ser·tee·fee·*ka*·do
relationship relación ⓕ re·la·*syon*
relax relajarse re·la·*khar*·se
relic reliquia ⓕ re·*lee*·kya
religion religión ⓕ re·lee·*khyon*
religious religioso/a ⓜ/ⓕ re·lee·*khyo*·so/a
remote remoto/a ⓜ/ⓕ re·*mo*·to/a
remote control mando ⓜ a distancia *man*·do a dees·*tan*·sya
rent alquiler ⓜ al·kee·*ler*
rent alquilar al·kee·*lar*
repair reparar re·pa·*rar*
republic república ⓕ re·*poo*·blee·ka
reservation reserva ⓕ re·*ser*·va
reserve hacer una reserva a·*ser* *oo*·na re·*ser*·va
rest descansar des·kan·*sar*
restaurant restaurante ⓜ res·tow·*ran*·te
resume currículum ⓜ koo·*ree*·koo·loom
retired jubilado/a ⓜ/ⓕ khoo·bee·*la*·do/a
return volver vol·*ver*
return ticket boleto ⓜ de ida y vuelta (bo·*le*·to) de *ee*·da ee *vwel*·ta
reverse charge call llamada ⓕ a cobro revertido ya·*ma*·da a *ko*·bro re·ver·*tee*·do
review crítica ⓕ *kree*·tee·ka
rhythm ritmo ⓜ *reet*·mo
rice arroz ⓜ a·*ros*
rich rico/a ⓜ/ⓕ *ree*·ko/a
ride paseo ⓜ pa·*se*·o
ride montar mon·*tar*
right (correct) correcto/a ⓜ/ⓕ ko·*rek*·to/a
right (direction) derecha de·*re*·cha
right-wing derechista de·re·*chees*·ta
ring (on finger) anillo ⓜ a·*nee*·yo
ring (by phone) llamar por teléfono ya·*mar* por te·*le*·fo·no
rip-off estafa ⓕ es·*ta*·fa
risk riesgo ⓜ *ryes*·go
river río ⓜ *ree*·o
road calle ⓕ *ka*·ye
rob robar ro·*bar*
rock (stone) roca ⓕ *ro*·ka
rock climbing escalada ⓕ es·ka·*la*·da
rock group grupo ⓜ de rock *groo*·po de rok
roll (bread) bollo ⓜ *bo*·yo

romance novel novela ⓕ rosa no·*ve*·la *ro*·sa
romantic romántico/a ⓜ/ⓕ ro·*man*·tee·ko/a
roof techo ⓜ *te*·cho
room habitación ⓕ a·bee·ta·*syon*
room number número ⓜ de habitación *noo*·me·ro de a·bee·ta·*syon*
rope cuerda ⓕ *kwer*·da
round redondo/a ⓜ/ⓕ re·*don*·do/a
roundabout glorieta ⓕ glo·*rye*·ta
route ruta ⓕ *roo*·ta
rowing remo ⓜ *re*·mo
rubbish basura ⓕ ba·*soo*·ra
rug alfombra ⓕ al·*fom*·bra
ruins ruinas ⓕ pl *rwee*·nas
rules reglas ⓕ pl *re*·glas
rum ron ⓜ ron
running (sport) footing ⓜ foo·*teen*

S

sad triste *trees*·te
saddle sillín ⓜ see·*yeen*
safe caja ⓕ fuerte *ka*·kha *fwer*·te
safe seguro/a ⓜ/ⓕ se·*goo*·ro/a
safe sex sexo ⓜ seguro *sek*·so se·*goo*·ro
sail vela ⓕ *ve*·la
sailing boat barco ⓜ de vela *bar*·ko de *ve*·la
saint santo/a ⓜ/ⓕ *san*·to/a
salad ensalada ⓕ en·sa·*la*·da
salary salario ⓜ sa·*la*·ryo
sales tax IVA ⓜ ee·va
salt sal ⓕ sal
same igual ee·*gwal*
sand arena ⓕ a·*re*·na
sandals sandalias ⓕ pl san·*da*·lyas
sanitary napkins compresas ⓕ pl kom·*pre*·sas
saucepan olla ⓕ o·ya
sauna sauna ⓕ *sow*·na
sausage salchicha ⓕ sal·*chee*·cha
say decir de·*seer*
scale (climb) trepar tre·*par*
scarf bufanda ⓕ boo·*fan*·da
school escuela ⓕ es·*kwe*·la
science ciencia ⓕ *syen*·sya
science fiction ciencia ⓕ ficción *syen*·sya feek·*syon*
scientist científico/a ⓜ/ⓕ syen·*tee*·fee·ko/a
scissors tijeras ⓕ pl tee·*khe*·ras
score marcar mar·*kar*
scoreboard marcador ⓜ mar·ka·*dor*
screen pantalla ⓕ pan·*ta*·ya
sea mar ⓜ mar
seasickness mareo ⓜ ma·*re*·o
seaside orilla ⓕ del mar o·*ree*·ya del mar
season estación ⓕ es·ta·*syon*
seat asiento ⓜ a·*syen*·to
seatbelt cinturón ⓜ de seguridad seen·too·*ron* de se·goo·ree·*da*
second segundo ⓜ se·*goon*·do
second segundo/a ⓜ/ⓕ se·*goon*·do/a
second-hand de segunda mano de se·*goon*·da *ma*·no
secretary secretario/a ⓜ/ⓕ se·kre·*ta*·ryo/a
see ver ver
selfish egoista ⓜ&ⓕ e·go·*ees*·ta
self-service autoservicio ⓜ ow·to·ser·*vee*·syo
sell vender ven·*der*
send enviar en·*vyar*
sensible juicioso/a ⓜ/ⓕ khwee·*syo*·so/a
sensual sensual sen·*swal*
separate separado/a ⓜ/ⓕ se·pa·*ra*·do/a
separate separar se·pa·*rar*
series serie ⓕ *se*·rye
serious serio/a ⓜ/ⓕ *se*·ryo/a
service charge servicio ⓜ ser·*vee*·syo
service station gasolinera ⓕ ga·so·lee·*ne*·ra
several varios/as ⓜ/ⓕ *va*·ryos/as
sew coser ko·*ser*

sex sexo ⓜ *sek*·so
sexism sexismo ⓜ sek·*sees*·mo
shade sombra ⓕ *som*·bra
shadow sombra ⓕ *som*·bra
shampoo champú ⓜ cham·*poo*
shape forma ⓕ *for*·ma
share (with) compartir kom·par·*teer*
shave afeitarse a·fay·*tar*·se
shaving cream espuma ⓕ de afeitar es·*poo*·ma de a·fay·*tar*
she ella *e*·ya
sheep oveja ⓕ o·*ve*·kha
sheet (bed) sábana ⓕ *sa*·ba·na
ship barco ⓜ *bar*·ko
shirt camisa ⓕ ka·*mee*·sa
shoe shop zapatería ⓕ sa·pa·te·*ree*·a
shoes zapatos ⓜ pl sa·*pa*·tos
shoot disparar dees·pa·*rar*
shop tienda ⓕ *tyen*·da
shoplifting hurto en tiendas *oor*·to en *tyen*·das
(go) shopping ir de compras eer de *kom*·pras
shopping centre centro ⓜ comercial *sen*·tro ko·mer·*syal*
short (height) bajo/a ⓜ/ⓕ *ba*·kho/a
short (length) corto/a ⓜ/ⓕ *kor*·to/a
shortage escasez ⓕ es·ka·*ses*
shorts pantalones ⓜ pl cortos pan·ta·*lo*·nes *kor*·tos
short stories cuentos ⓜ pl *kwen*·tos
shoulders hombros ⓜ pl *om*·bros
shout gritar gree·*tar*
show espectáculo ⓜ es·pek·*ta*·koo·lo
show mostrar mos·*trar*
shower ducha ⓕ *doo*·cha
shrine capilla ⓕ ka·*pee*·ya
shut cerrado/a ⓜ/ⓕ se·*ra*·do/a
shy tímido/a ⓜ/ⓕ *tee*·mee·do/a
sick enfermo/a ⓜ/ⓕ en·*fer*·mo/a
side lado ⓜ *la*·do
sign señal ⓕ se·*nyal*
signature firma ⓕ *feer*·ma
silk seda ⓕ *se*·da
silver plata ⓕ *pla*·ta
SIM card tarjeta ⓕ SIM tar·*khe*·ta seem
simple sencillo/a ⓜ/ⓕ sen·*see*·yo/a
since (time) desde *des*·de
sing cantar kan·*tar*
singer cantante ⓜ&ⓕ kan·*tan*·te
single (unmarried) soltero/a ⓜ/ⓕ sol·*te*·ro/a
single room habitación ⓕ individual a·bee·ta·*syon* een·dee·vee·*dwal*
singlet camiseta ⓕ ka·mee·*se*·ta
sister hermana ⓕ er·*ma*·na
sit sentarse sen·*tar*·se
size (clothes) talla ⓕ *ta*·ya
size (general) tamaño ta·*ma*·nyo
skateboarding monopatinaje ⓜ mo·no·pa·tee·*na*·khe
ski esquiar es·*kyar*
skiing esquí ⓜ es·*kee*
ski lift telesquí ⓜ te·le·*skee*
skis esquís ⓜ pl es·*kees*
skimmed milk leche ⓕ desnatada *le*·che des·na·*ta*·da
skin piel ⓕ pyel
skirt falda ⓕ *fal*·da
sky cielo ⓜ *sye*·lo
sleep dormir dor·*meer*
sleeping bag saco ⓜ de dormir *sa*·ko de dor·*meer*
sleeping car coche ⓜ cama *ko*·che *ka*·ma
sleeping pills pastillas ⓕ pl para dormir pas·*tee*·yas *pa*·ra dor·*meer*
(be) sleepy tener sueño te·*ner* *swe*·nyo
slide (film) diapositiva ⓕ dya·po·see·*tee*·va
slow lento/a ⓜ/ⓕ *len*·to/a
slowly despacio des·*pa*·syo
small pequeño/a ⓜ/ⓕ pe·*ke*·nyo/a
smell olor ⓜ o·*lor*
smile sonreír son·re·*eer*
smoke fumar foo·*mar*
snack tentempié ⓜ ten·tem·*pye*
snail caracol ⓜ ka·ra·*kol*

snake serpiente Ⓕ ser·*pyen*·te
snorkelling buceo Ⓜ boo·*se*·o
snow nieve Ⓕ *nye*·ve
snowboarding surf Ⓜ sobre la nieve soorf *so*·bre la *nye*·ve
soap jabón Ⓜ kha·*bon*
soap opera telenovela Ⓕ te·le·no·*ve*·la
soccer fútbol Ⓜ *foot*·bol
social welfare asistencia Ⓕ social a·sees·*ten*·sya so·*syal*
socialist socialista so·sya·*lees*·ta
socks calcetines Ⓜ pl kal·se·*tee*·nes
soft drink gaseosa Ⓕ ga·se·*o*·sa
soldier soldado Ⓜ sol·*da*·do
some algunos/as Ⓜ/Ⓕ pl al·*goo*·nos/as
someone alguien *al*·gyen
something algo *al*·go
sometimes de vez en cuando de ves en *kwan*·do
son hijo Ⓜ *ee*·kho
song canción Ⓕ kan·*syon*
soon pronto *pron*·to
sore dolorido/a Ⓜ/Ⓕ do·lo·*ree*·do/a
soup sopa Ⓕ *so*·pa
sour cream crema Ⓕ agria *kre*·ma *a*·grya
south sur Ⓜ soor
South America Sudamérica Ⓕ soo·da·*me*·ree·ka
South American sudamericano/a Ⓜ/Ⓕ soo·da·me·ree·*ka*·no/a
souvenir recuerdo Ⓜ re·*kwer*·do
souvenir shop tienda Ⓕ de recuerdos *tyen*·da de re·*kwer*·dos
soy milk leche Ⓕ de soya *le*·che de *so*·ya
soy sauce salsa Ⓕ de soya *sal*·sa de *so*·ya
space espacio Ⓜ es·*pa*·syo
spade pala Ⓕ *pa*·la
Spain España Ⓕ es·*pa*·nya
speak hablar a·*blar*
special especial es·pe·*syal*
specialist especialista Ⓜ&Ⓕ es·pe·sya·*lees*·ta
speed velocidad Ⓕ ve·lo·see·*da*
speed limit límite Ⓜ de velocidad *lee*·mee·te de ve·lo·see·*da*
speedometer velocímetro Ⓜ ve·lo·*see*·me·tro
spermicide espermicida Ⓕ es·per·mee·*see*·da
spider araña Ⓕ a·*ra*·nya
spinach espinacas Ⓕ pl es·pee·*na*·kas
spoon cuchara Ⓕ koo·*cha*·ra
sport deportes Ⓜ pl de·*por*·tes
sports store tienda Ⓕ deportiva *tyen*·da de·por·*tee*·va
sportsperson deportista Ⓜ&Ⓕ de·por·*tees*·ta
sprain torcedura Ⓕ tor·se·*doo*·ra
spring (mechanical) muelle Ⓜ *mwe*·ye
spring (season) primavera Ⓕ pree·ma·*ve*·ra
square (shape) cuadrado Ⓜ kwa·*dra*·do
square (town) plaza Ⓕ *pla*·sa
stadium estadio Ⓜ es·*ta*·dyo
stage escenario Ⓜ e·se·*na*·ryo
stairway escalera Ⓕ es·ka·*le*·ra
stamp sello Ⓜ *se*·yo
standby ticket boleto Ⓜ de lista de espera bo·*le*·to de *lees*·ta de es·*pe*·ra
stars estrellas Ⓕ pl es·*tre*·yas
start comenzar ko·men·*sar*
station estación Ⓕ es·ta·*syon*
statue estatua Ⓕ es·*ta*·twa
stay (at a hotel) alojarse a·lo·*khar*·se
stay (remain) quedarse ke·*dar*·se
STD (sexually transmitted disease) enfermedad Ⓕ de transmisión sexual en·fer·mee·*da* de trans·mee·*syon* sek·*swal*
steak (beef) bistec Ⓜ bees·*tek*
steal robar ro·*bar*

steep escarpado/a Ⓜ/Ⓕ es·kar·*pa*·do/a
step paso Ⓜ *pa*·so
stereo equipo Ⓜ estereofónico e·*kee*·po es·te·re·o·*fo*·nee·ko
stingy tacaño/a Ⓜ/Ⓕ ta·*ka*·nyo/a
stockings medias Ⓕ pl *me*·dyas
stomach estómago Ⓜ es·*to*·ma·go
stomachache dolor Ⓜ de estómago do·*lor* de es·*to*·ma·go
stone piedra Ⓕ *pye*·dra
stoned (drugged) volado/a Ⓜ/Ⓕ vo·*la*·do/a
stop parada Ⓕ pa·*ra*·da
stop parar pa·*rar*
storm tormenta Ⓕ tor·*men*·ta
story cuento Ⓜ *kwen*·to
stove estufa Ⓕ es·*too*·fa
straight recto/a Ⓜ/Ⓕ *rek*·to/a
strange extraño/a Ⓜ/Ⓕ ek·*stra*·nyo/a
stranger extraño/a Ⓜ/Ⓕ ek·*stra*·nyo/a
strawberry frutilla Ⓕ froo·*tee*·ya
stream arroyo Ⓜ a·*ro*·yo
street calle Ⓕ *ka*·ye
street market feria Ⓕ *fe*·rya
string cuerda Ⓕ *kwer*·da
strong fuerte *fwer*·te
stubborn testarudo/a Ⓜ/Ⓕ tes·ta·*roo*·do/a
student estudiante Ⓜ&Ⓕ es·too·*dyan*·te
studio estudio Ⓜ es·*too*·dyo
stupid estúpido/a Ⓜ/Ⓕ es·*too*·pee·do/a
style estilo Ⓜ es·*tee*·lo
subtitles subtítulos Ⓜ pl soob·*tee*·too·los
suburb barrio Ⓜ *ba*·ryo
subway subteráneo soob·te·*ra*·ne·o
sugar azúcar Ⓜ a·*soo*·kar
sugar cane caña Ⓕ de azúcar *ka*·nya de a·*soo*·kar
suit traje Ⓜ *tra*·khe
suitcase maleta Ⓕ ma·*le*·ta
summer verano Ⓜ ve·*ra*·no
sun sol Ⓜ sol
sunblock crema Ⓕ solar *kre*·ma so·*lar*
sunburn quemadura Ⓕ de sol ke·ma·*doo*·ra de sol
sunglasses anteojos Ⓕ pl de sol an·te·o·khos de sol
sunny soleado/a Ⓜ/Ⓕ so·le·*a*·do/a
sunrise amanecer Ⓜ a·ma·ne·*ser*
sunset puesta Ⓕ del sol *pwes*·ta del sol
sunstroke insolación Ⓕ een·so·la·*syon*
supermarket supermercado Ⓜ soo·per·mer·*ka*·do
superstition superstición Ⓕ soo·per·stee·*syon*
supporters hinchas Ⓜ&Ⓕ pl *een*·chas
surf hacer surf a·*ser* soorf
surface mail por vía terrestre por *vee*·a te·*res*·tre
surf hacer surfing Ⓜ a·*ser soorf*·een
surfboard tabla Ⓕ de surf *ta*·bla de soorf
surname apellido Ⓜ a·pe·*yee*·do
surprise sorpresa Ⓕ sor·*pre*·sa
sweater (jumper) jersey Ⓜ kher·*say*
sweet dulce *dool*·se
swim nadar na·*dar*
swimming pool piscina Ⓕ pee·*see*·na
swimsuit traje Ⓜ de baño *tra*·khe de *ba*·nyo
synagogue sinagoga Ⓕ see·na·*go*·ga
synthetic sintético/a Ⓜ/Ⓕ seen·*te*·tee·ko/a
syringe jeringa Ⓕ khe·*reen*·ga

T

table mesa Ⓕ *me*·sa
table tennis ping pong Ⓜ peen pon
tablecloth mantel Ⓜ man·*tel*
tail rabo Ⓜ *ra*·bo
tailor sastre Ⓜ *sas*·tre

T

take tomar to·*mar*
talk hablar a·*blar*
tall alto/a Ⓜ/Ⓕ *al*·to/a
tampons tampones Ⓜ pl tam·*po*·nes
tanning lotion bronceador Ⓜ bron·se·a·*dor*
tap (faucet) grifo Ⓜ *gree*·fo
tapir danta Ⓕ *dan*·ta
tasty sabroso/a Ⓜ/Ⓕ sa·*bro*·so/a
tax impuesto Ⓜ eem·*pwes*·to
taxi stand parada Ⓕ de taxis pa·*ra*·da de *tak*·sees
tea té Ⓜ te
teacher profesor(a) Ⓜ/Ⓕ pro·fe·*sor*/pro·fe·*so*·ra
team equipo Ⓜ e·*kee*·po
teaspoon cucharita Ⓕ koo·cha·*ree*·ta
teeth dientes Ⓜ pl *dyen*·tes
telegram telegrama Ⓜ te·le·*gra*·ma
telephone teléfono Ⓜ te·*le*·fo·no
telephone llamar (por teléfono) ya·*mar* (por te·*le*·fo·no)
telephone centre central Ⓕ telefónica sen·*tral* te·le·*fo*·nee·ka
telephoto lens teleobjetivo Ⓜ te·le·ob·khe·*tee*·vo
television televisión Ⓕ te·le·vee·*syon*
tell decir de·*seer*
temperature (fever) fiebre Ⓕ *fye*·bre
temperature (weather) temperatura Ⓕ tem·pe·ra·*too*·ra
temple templo Ⓜ *tem*·plo
tennis court cancha Ⓕ de tenis *kan*·cha de *te*·nees
tent carpa Ⓕ *kar*·pa
tent pegs estacas Ⓕ de carpa es·*ta*·kas de *kar*·pa
terrible terible te·*ree*·ble
test prueba Ⓕ *prwe*·ba
testimonial literature literatura Ⓕ testimonial lee·te·ra·*too*·ra tes·tee·mo·*nyal*
thank dar gracias dar *gra*·syas
the Pill píldora Ⓕ *peel*·do·ra
theatre teatro Ⓜ te·*a*·tro
their su soo
they ellos/ellas Ⓜ/Ⓕ pl e·yos/e·yas
thief ladrón/ladrona Ⓜ/Ⓕ la·*dron*/la·*dro*·na
thin delgado/a Ⓜ/Ⓕ del·*ga*·do/a
think pensar pen·*sar*
third tercio Ⓜ *ter*·syo
thirst sed Ⓕ se
(be) thirsty tener sed Ⓕ te·*ner* se
this éste/a Ⓜ/Ⓕ *es*·te/a
throat garganta Ⓕ gar·*gan*·ta
thrush (medical) aftas Ⓜ pl *af*·tas
ticket boleto Ⓜ bo·*le*·to
ticket collector revisor(a) Ⓜ/Ⓕ re·vee·*sor*/re·vee·*so*·ra
ticket machine máquina Ⓕ de boletos *ma*·kee·na de bo·*le*·tos
ticket office (theatre, cinema) taquilla Ⓕ ta·*kee*·ya
ticket office (general) boletería Ⓕ bo·le·te·*ree*·a
tide marea Ⓕ ma·*re*·a
tight apretado/a Ⓜ/Ⓕ a·pre·*ta*·do/a
time (hour) hora Ⓕ *o*·ra
time (period) tiempo Ⓜ *tyem*·po
time difference diferencia Ⓕ de horas dee·fe·*ren*·sya de *o*·ras
timetable horario Ⓜ o·*ra*·ryo
tin (can) lata Ⓕ *la*·ta
tin opener abrelatas Ⓜ a·bre·*la*·tas
tiny pequeñito/a Ⓜ/Ⓕ pe·ke·*nyee*·to/a
tip (gratuity) propina Ⓕ pro·*pee*·na
tired cansado/a Ⓜ/Ⓕ kan·*sa*·do/a
tissues pañuelos Ⓜ pl de papel pa·*nywe*·los de pa·*pel*
toast tostada Ⓕ tos·*ta*·da
toaster tostadora Ⓕ tos·ta·*do*·ra
tobacco tabaco Ⓜ ta·*ba*·ko
tobacconist estanquero Ⓜ es·tan·*ke*·ro
tobogganing ir en tobogán eer en to·bo·*gan*
today hoy oy
toe dedo Ⓜ del pie *de*·do del pye

DICTIONARY

together juntos/as Ⓜ/Ⓕ pl *khoon*·tos/as
toilet baño Ⓜ • servicio Ⓜ *ba*·nyo • ser·*vee*·syo
toilet paper papel Ⓜ higiénico pa·*pel* ee·*khye*·nee·ko
tomato tomate Ⓜ to·*ma*·te
tomato sauce salsa Ⓕ de tomate sal·*sa* de to·*ma*·te
tomorrow mañana Ⓕ ma·*nya*·na
tonight esta noche *es*·ta *no*·che
too (expensive) demasiado (caro/a) Ⓜ/Ⓕ de·ma·*sya*·do (*ka*·ro/a)
tooth (back) muela Ⓕ *mwe*·la
toothache dolor Ⓜ de muelas do·*lor* de *mwe*·las
toothbrush cepillo Ⓜ de dientes se·*pee*·yo de *dyen*·tes
toothpaste pasta Ⓕ dentífrica *pas*·ta den·*tee*·free·ka
toothpick palillo Ⓜ pa·*lee*·yo
torch (flashlight) linterna Ⓕ leen·*ter*·na
touch tocar to·*kar*
tour excursión Ⓕ ek·skoor·*syon*
tourist turista Ⓜ&Ⓕ too·*rees*·ta
tourist office oficina Ⓕ de turismo o·fee·*see*·na de too·*rees*·mo
towards hacia *a*·sya
towel toalla Ⓕ to·*a*·ya
tower torre Ⓕ *to*·re
toxic waste residuos Ⓜ pl tóxicos re·*see*·dwos *tok*·see·kos
toy shop juguetería Ⓕ khoo·ge·te·*ree*·a
track (path) camino Ⓜ ka·*mee*·no
track (sports) pista Ⓕ *pees*·ta
trade comercio Ⓜ ko·*mer*·syo
traffic tráfico Ⓜ *tra*·fee·ko
traffic lights semáforos Ⓜ pl se·*ma*·fo·ros
trail camino Ⓜ ka·*mee*·no
train tren Ⓜ tren
train station estación Ⓕ de tren es·ta·*syon* de tren
tram tranvía Ⓜ tran·*vee*·a
transit lounge sala Ⓕ de tránsito *sa*·la de *tran*·see·to
translate traducir tra·doo·*seer*
transport transporte Ⓜ trans·*por*·te
travel viajar vya·*khar*
travel agency agencia Ⓕ de viajes a·*khen*·sya de *vya*·khes
travel books libros Ⓜ pl de viajes *lee*·bros de *vya*·khes
travel sickness mareo Ⓜ ma·*re*·o
travellers cheque cheque Ⓜ de viajero *che*·ke de vya·*khe*·ro
tree árbol Ⓜ *ar*·bol
trip viaje Ⓜ *vya*·khe
trousers pantalones Ⓜ pl pan·ta·*lo*·nes
truck camión Ⓜ ka·*myon*
trust confianza Ⓕ kon·*fyan*·sa
trust confiar kon·*fyar*
try (attempt) probar pro·*bar*
T-shirt camiseta Ⓕ ka·mee·*se*·ta
tube (tyre) cámara Ⓕ de aire *ka*·ma·ra de *ai*·re
tuna atún Ⓜ a·*toon*
tune melodía Ⓕ me·lo·*dee*·a
turkey pavo Ⓜ *pa*·vo
turn doblar do·*blar*
TV tele Ⓕ *te*·le
tweezers pinzas Ⓕ pl *peen*·sas
twice dos veces dos *ve*·ses
twin beds dos camas Ⓕ pl dos *ka*·mas
twins gemelos/as Ⓜ/Ⓕ pl khe·*me*·los/as
type tipo Ⓜ *tee*·po
typical típico/a Ⓜ/Ⓕ *tee*·pee·ko/a
tyre llanta Ⓕ *yan*·ta

U

ultrasound ecografía Ⓕ e·ko·gra·*fee*·a
umbrella paraguas Ⓜ pa·*ra*·gwas
umpire árbitro/a Ⓜ/Ⓕ ar·*bee*·tro/a
uncle tío Ⓜ *tee*·o
uncomfortable incómodo/a Ⓜ/Ⓕ een·*ko*·mo·do/a

underpants (men) calzoncillos ⓜ pl kal·son·*see*·yos
underpants (women) bragas ⓕ pl *bra*·gas
understand entender en·ten·*der*
underwater camera cámara ⓕ submarina *ka*·ma·ra soob·ma·*ree*·na
underwear ropa ⓕ interior *ro*·pa een·te·*ryor*
unemployed desempleado/a ⓜ/ⓕ des·em·ple·*a*·do/a
unfair injusto/a ⓜ/ⓕ een·*khoos*·to/a
uniform uniforme ⓜ oo·nee·*for*·me
universe universo ⓜ oo·nee·*ver*·so
university universidad ⓕ oo·nee·ver·see·*da*
unleaded sin plomo seen *plo*·mo
unsafe inseguro/a ⓜ/ⓕ een·se·*goo*·ro/a
until hasta *as*·ta
unusual extraño/a ⓜ/ⓕ ek·*stra*·nyo/a
up arriba a·*ree*·ba
uphill cuesta arriba *kwes*·ta a·*ree*·ba
urgent urgente oor·*khen*·te
Uruguay Uruguay ⓜ oo·roo·*gway*
USA Los Estados ⓜ pl Unidos los es·*ta*·dos oo·*nee*·dos
useful útil *oo*·teel

V

vacant vacante va·*kan*·te
vacation vacaciones ⓕ pl va·ka·*syo*·nes
vaccination vacuna ⓕ va·*koo*·na
vagina vagina ⓕ va·*khee*·na
vaginal discharge flujo ⓜ vaginal *floo*·kho va·khee·*nal*
validate validar va·lee·*dar*
valley valle ⓜ *va*·ye
valuable valioso/a ⓜ/ⓕ va·*lyo*·so/a
value valor ⓜ va·*lor*
van caravana ⓕ ka·ra·*va*·na
veal ternera ⓕ ter·*ne*·ra
vegan vegetariano/a estricto/a ⓜ/ⓕ ve·khe·ta·*rya*·no/a es·*treek*·to/a
vegetable verdura ⓕ ver·*doo*·ra
vegetable garden huerta ⓕ *wer*·ta
vegetarian vegetariano/a ⓜ/ⓕ ve·khe·ta·*rya*·no/a
vein vena ⓕ *ve*·na
venereal disease enfermedad ⓕ venérea en·fer·me·*da* ve·*ne*·re·a
Venezuela Venezuela ⓕ ve·ne·*swe*·la
venue local ⓜ lo·*kal*
very muy mooy
video tape cinta ⓕ de vídeo *seen*·ta de *vee*·de·o
view vista ⓕ *vees*·ta
village pueblo ⓜ *pwe*·blo
vinegar vinagre ⓜ vee·*na*·gre
vineyard viñedo ⓜ vee·*nye*·do
virus virus ⓜ *vee*·roos
visa visado ⓜ vee·*sa*·do
visit visitar vee·see·*tar*
vitamins vitaminas ⓕ pl vee·ta·*mee*·nas
voice voz ⓕ vos
vote votar vo·*tar*
vulture buitre ⓜ *bwee*·tre

W

wage sueldo ⓜ *swel*·do
wait esperar es·pe·*rar*
waiter camarero/a ⓜ/ⓕ ka·ma·*re*·ro/a
waiting room sala ⓕ de espera *sa*·la de es·*pe*·ra
wake up despertarse des·per·*tar*·se
walk caminar ka·mee·*nar*
wall (inside) pared ⓕ pa·*re*
wallet cartera ⓕ kar·*te*·ra
want querer ke·*rer*
war guerra ⓕ *ge*·ra
wardrobe vestuario ⓜ ves·*twa*·ryo
warm templado/a ⓜ/ⓕ tem·*pla*·do/a
warn advertir ad·ver·*teer*
wash (oneself) lavarse la·*var*·se
wash (something) lavar la·*var*
wash cloth (flannel) toallita ⓕ to·a·*yee*·ta

washing machine lavadora ⓕ la·va·*do*·ra
watch reloj ⓜ de pulsera re·*lokh* de pool·*se*·ra
watch mirar mee·*rar*
water agua ⓕ *a*·gwa
boiled water agua ⓕ hervida *a*·gwa er·*vee*·da
still water agua ⓕ sin gas *a*·gwa seen gas
tap water agua ⓕ del grifo *a*·gwa del *gree*·fo
water bottle cantimplora ⓕ kan·teem·*plo*·ra
waterfall cascada ⓕ kas·*ka*·da
watermelon sandía ⓕ san·*dee*·a
waterproof impermeable eem·per·me·*a*·ble
waterskiing esquí ⓜ acuático es·*kee* a·*kwa*·tee·ko
water skis esquís ⓜ pl acuáticos es·*kees* a·*kwa*·tee·kos
wave ola ⓕ *o*·la
way camino ⓜ ka·*mee*·no
we nosotros/as ⓜ/ⓕ no·*so*·tros/as
weak débil *de*·beel
wealthy rico/a ⓜ/ⓕ *ree*·ko/a
wear llevar ye·*var*
weather tiempo ⓜ *tyem*·po
wedding boda ⓕ *bo*·da
wedding cake tarta ⓕ nupcial *tar*·ta noop·*syal*
wedding present regalo ⓜ de bodas re·*ga*·lo de *bo*·das
week semana ⓕ se·*ma*·na
weekend fin ⓜ de semana feen de se·*ma*·na
weight peso ⓜ *pe*·so
welcome dar la bienvenida dar la byen·ve·*nee*·da
welfare bienestar ⓜ byen·es·*tar*
well bien byen
well (water) pozo ⓜ *po*·so
west oeste ⓜ o·*es*·te
wet mojado/a ⓜ/ⓕ mo·*kha*·do/a
what que ke
wheel rueda ⓕ *rwe*·da
wheelchair silla ⓕ de ruedas *see*·ya de *rwe*·das
when cuando *kwan*·do
where donde *don*·de
white blanco/a ⓜ/ⓕ *blan*·ko/a
whiteboard pizarra ⓕ blanca pee·*sa*·ra *blan*·ka
who quien kyen
why por qué por ke
wide ancho/a ⓜ/ⓕ *an*·cho/a
widow viuda ⓕ *vyoo*·da
widower viudo ⓜ *vyoo*·do
wife esposa ⓕ es·*po*·sa
win ganar ga·*nar*
wind viento ⓜ *vyen*·to
window ventana ⓕ ven·*ta*·na
window-shopping mirar escaparates mee·*rar* es·ka·pa·*ra*·tes
windscreen parabrisas ⓜ pa·ra·*bree*·sas
windsurfing hacer windsurfing a·*ser* *gween*·soorf·een
wine vino ⓜ *vee*·no
red wine vino ⓜ tinto *vee*·no *teen*·to
sparkling wine vino ⓜ espumoso *vee*·no es·poo·*mo*·so
white wine vino ⓜ blanco *vee*·no *blan*·ko
winery bodega ⓕ bo·*de*·ga
wings alas ⓕ pl *a*·las
winner ganador(a) ⓜ/ⓕ ga·na·*dor*/ ga·na·*do*·ra
winter invierno ⓜ een·*vyer*·no
wire alambre ⓜ a·*lam*·bre
wish desear de·se·*ar*
with con kon
within (an hour) dentro de (una hora) *den*·tro de (*oo*·na *o*·ra)
without sin seen
woman mujer ⓕ moo·*kher*
wonderful maravilloso/a ⓜ/ⓕ ma·ra·vee·*yo*·so/a
wood madera ⓕ ma·*de*·ra
wool lana ⓕ *la*·na
word palabra ⓕ pa·*la*·bra

Y

work (occupation) trabajo ⓜ tra·*ba*·kho
work (of art) obra ⓕ *o*·bra
work trabajar tra·ba·*khar*
work experience experiencia ⓕ laboral ek·spe·*ryen*·sya la·bo·*ral*
work permit permiso ⓜ de trabajo per·*mee*·so de tra·*ba*·kho
workout entreno ⓜ en·*tre*·no
workshop taller ⓜ ta·*yer*
world mundo ⓜ *moon*·do
World Cup La Copa ⓕ Mundial la *ko*·pa moon·*dyal*
worried preocupado/a ⓜ/ⓕ pre·o·koo·*pa*·do/a
worship (pray) rezar re·*sar*
wrist muñeca ⓕ moo·*nye*·ka
write escribir es·kree·*beer*
writer escritor(a) ⓜ/ⓕ es·kree·*tor*/ es·kree·*to*·ra
wrong equivocado/a ⓜ/ⓕ e·kee·vo·*ka*·do/a
(this) year (este) año *(es*·te) *a*·nyo

Y

yellow amarillo/a ⓜ/ⓕ a·ma·*ree*·yo/a
yellow fever fiebre ⓕ amarilla *fye*·bre a·ma·*ree*·ya
yes sí see
(not) yet todavía (no) to·da·*vee*·a (no)
yesterday ayer a·*yer*
yogurt yogur ⓜ yo·*goor*
you sg inf tú too
you sg pol Usted oos·*te*
you pl Ustedes oos·*te*·des
young joven *kho*·ven
youth hostel albergue ⓜ juvenil al·*ber*·ge khoo·ve·*neel*

Z

zodiac zodíaco ⓜ so·*dee*·a·ko
zoo zoológico ⓜ so·o·*lo*·khee·ko

Dictionary

SPANISH *to* ENGLISH

español – inglés

Nouns in the dictionary have their gender indicated by ⓜ or ⓕ. If it's a plural noun, you'll also see pl. When a word that could be either a noun or a verb has no gender indicated, it's a verb. For food terms, see the **menu decoder**.

A

a bordo a *bor*·do aboard
a larga distancia a *lar*·ga dees·*tan*·sya long-distance
a menudo a me·*noo*·do often
a tiempo a *tyem*·po on time
a través a tra·*ves* across
abajo a·*ba*·kho below
abarrotado/a ⓜ/ⓕ a·ba·ro·*ta*·do/a crowded
abeja ⓕ a·*be*·kha bee
abierto/a ⓜ/ⓕ a·*byer*·to/a open
abogado/a ⓜ/ⓕ a·bo·*ga*·do/a lawyer
aborto ⓜ a·*bor*·to abortion
— natural na·too·*ral* miscarriage
abrazo ⓜ a·*bra*·so hug
abrebotellas ⓜ a·bre·bo·*te*·yas bottle opener
abrelatas ⓜ a·bre·*la*·tas can opener • tin opener
abrigo ⓜ a·*bree*·go overcoat
abrir a·*breer* open
abuela ⓕ a·*bwe*·la grandmother
abuelo ⓜ a·*bwe*·lo grandfather
aburrido/a ⓜ/ⓕ a·boo·*ree*·do/a boring
acabar a·ka·*bar* end
acampar a·kam·*par* camp
acantilado ⓜ a·kan·tee·*la*·do cliff
accidente ⓜ ak·see·*den*·te accident
aceptar a·sep·*tar* accept
acera ⓕ a·*se*·ra footpath
acondicionador ⓜ a·kon·dee·syo·na·*dor* conditioner
aconsejar a·kon·se·*khar* advise
acoso ⓜ a·*ko*·so harassment
activista ⓜ&ⓕ ak·tee·*vees*·ta activist
actuación ⓕ ak·twa·*syon* gig • performance
acupuntura ⓕ a·koo·poon·*too*·ra acupuncture
adaptador ⓜ a·dap·ta·*dor* adaptor
addicto/a ⓜ/ⓕ a·*deek*·to/a addicted
adentro a·*den*·tro inside
adivinar a·dee·vee·*nar* guess
administración ⓕ ad·mee·nees·tra·*syon* administration
admitir ad·mee·*teer* accept • acknowledge • admit
aduana ⓕ a·*dwa*·na customs
adulto/a ⓜ/ⓕ a·*dool*·to/a adult
advertir ad·ver·*teer* warn
aerolínea ⓕ a·e·ro·*lee*·ne·a airline

aeropuerto ⓜ a·e·ro·*pwer*·to airport
afeitadora ⓕ a·fay·ta·*do*·ra razor
afeitarse a·fay·*tar*·se shave
afortunado/a ⓜ/ⓕ a·for·too·*na*·do/a lucky
agencia ⓕ **de viajes** a·*khen*·sya de *vya*·khes travel agency
agenda ⓕ a·*khen*·da diary
agresivo/a ⓜ/ⓕ a·gre·*see*·vo/a aggressive
agricultor(a) ⓜ/ⓕ a·gree·kool·*tor*/ a·gree·kool·*to*·ra farmer
agricultura ⓕ a·gree·kool·*too*·ra agriculture
aguja ⓕ a·*goo*·kha needle (sewing)
ahora a·o·ra now
aire ⓜ *ai*·re air
— acondicionado a·kon·dee·syo·*na*·do air-conditioning
ajedrez ⓜ a·khe·*dres* chess
al fondo de al *fon*·do de at the bottom
al lado de al *la*·do de next to
alambre ⓜ a·*lam*·bre wire
alas ⓕ pl *a*·las wings
albergue ⓜ **juvenil** al·*ber*·ge khoo·ve·*neel* youth hostel
alcalde ⓜ&ⓕ al·*kal*·de mayor
Alemania a·le·*ma*·nya Germany
alergia ⓕ a·*ler*·khya allergy
alfarería ⓕ al·fa·re·*ree*·a pottery
alfombra ⓕ al·*fom*·bra rug
algo *al*·go something
algodón ⓜ al·go·*don* cotton
alguien *al*·gyen someone
algún al·*goon* some
alguno/a ⓜ/ⓕ sg al·*goo*·no/a any
algunos/as ⓜ/ⓕ pl al·*goo*·nos/as any
almacén ⓜ al·ma·*sen* general store
almohada ⓕ al·mo·*a*·da pillow
almuerzo ⓜ al·*mwer*·so lunch
alojamiento ⓜ a·lo·kha·*myen*·to accommodation
alojarse a·lo·*khar*·se stay (at a hotel)
alpinismo ⓜ al·pee·*nees*·mo mountaineering
alquilar al·kee·*lar* hire • rent
— un carro oon *ka*·ro hire a car
alquiler ⓜ al·kee·*ler* hire • rental
altar ⓜ al·*tar* altar
alto/a ⓜ/ⓕ *al*·to/a high • tall
altura ⓕ al·*too*·ra altitude
alucinar a·loo·see·*nar* hallucinate
ama ⓕ **de casa** *a*·ma de *ka*·sa homemaker
amable a·*ma*·ble kind
amanecer ⓜ a·ma·ne·*ser* sunrise
amante ⓜ&ⓕ a·*man*·te lover
amarillo/a ⓜ/ⓕ a·ma·*ree*·yo/a yellow
ambulancia ⓕ am·boo·*lan*·sya ambulance
amigo/a ⓜ/ⓕ a·*mee*·go/a friend
ampolla ⓕ am·*po*·ya blister
analgésicos ⓜ pl a·nal·*khe*·see·kos painkillers
análisis ⓜ **de sangre** a·*na*·lee·sees de *san*·gre blood test
anaranjado/a ⓜ/ⓕ a·na·ran·*kha*·do/a orange (colour)
anarquista ⓜ&ⓕ a·nar·*kees*·ta anarchist
ancho/a ⓜ/ⓕ *an*·cho/a wide
andar an·*dar* walk
— en bicicleta en bee·see·*kle*·ta cycle
anillo ⓜ a·*nee*·yo ring (on finger)
año *a*·nyo year
Año Nuevo ⓜ *a*·nyo *nwe*·vo New Year
anteayer an·te·a·*yer* day before yesterday
anteojos ⓜ pl an·te·*o*·khos glasses • goggles
— de sol de sol sunglasses
antes *an*·tes before
antibióticos ⓜ pl an·tee·*byo*·tee·kos antibiotics
anticonceptivo ⓜ an·tee·kon·sep·*tee*·vo contraceptive

antigüedad ⓕ an·tee·gwe·*da* antique
antiguo/a ⓜ/ⓕ an·*tee*·gwo/a ancient
antihistaminicos ⓜ pl an·tee·ees·ta·*mee*·nee·kos antihistamines
antiséptico ⓜ an·tee·*sep*·tee·ko antiseptic
anuncio ⓜ a·*noon*·syo advertisement
apellido ⓜ a·pe·*yee*·do family name • surname
apéndice ⓜ a·*pen*·dee·se appendix
apodo ⓜ a·*po*·do nickname
aprender a·pren·*der* learn
apretado/a ⓜ/ⓕ a·pre·*ta*·do/a tight
apuesta ⓕ a·*pwes*·ta bet
apuntar a·poon·*tar* point
aquí a·*kee* here
araña ⓕ a·*ra*·nya spider
árbitro ⓜ *ar*·bee·tro referee
árbol ⓜ *ar*·bol tree
arena ⓕ a·*re*·na sand
arenque ⓜ a·*ren*·ke herring
aretes ⓜ pl a·*re*·tes earrings
armadillo ⓜ ar·ma·*dee*·yo armadillo
armario ⓜ ar·*ma*·ryo cupboard
arqueológico/a ⓜ/ⓕ ar·ke·o·*lo*·khee·ko/a archaeological
arquitecto/a ⓜ/ⓕ ar·kee·*tek*·to/a architect
arquitectura ⓕ ar·kee·tek·*too*·ra architecture
arrendar a·ren·*dar* hire • rent
arriba a·*ree*·ba above • up
arroyo ⓜ a·*ro*·yo stream
arte ⓜ *ar*·te art
artes ⓜ pl **marciales** *ar*·tes mar·*sya*·les martial arts
artesanía ⓕ ar·te·sa·*nee*·a craft • handicraft
artista ⓜ&ⓕ ar·*tees*·ta artist
— callejero/a ⓜ/ⓕ ka·ye·*khe*·ro/a busker
ascensor ⓜ a·sen·*sor* elevator • lift
asiento ⓜ a·*syen*·to seat
asistencia ⓕ **social** a·sees·*ten*·sya so·*syal* social welfare
asma ⓜ *as*·ma asthma
aspirina ⓕ as·pee·*ree*·na aspirin
atascado/a ⓜ/ⓕ a·tas·*ka*·do/a blocked
atletismo ⓜ at·le·*tees*·mo athletics
atmósfera ⓕ at·*mos*·fe·ra atmosphere
audífono ⓜ ow·*dee*·fo·no hearing aid
auto ⓜ *ow*·to car
autobús ⓜ ow·to·*boos* bus (city)
automatico/a ⓜ/ⓕ ow·to·*ma*·tee·ko/a automatíc
autopista ⓕ ow·to·*pees*·ta motorway
autoservicio ⓜ ow·to·ser·*vee*·syo self-service
avenida ⓕ a·ve·*nee*·da avenue
avergonzado/a ⓜ/ⓕ a·ver·gon·*sa*·do/a embarrassed
averiado/a ⓜ/ⓕ a·ve·*rya*·do/a broken down (machine)
avión ⓜ a·*vyon* plane
ayer a·*yer* yesterday
ayudar a·yoo·*dar* help
azul a·*sool* blue

B

baile ⓜ *bai*·le dance
bailar bai·*lar* dance
bajo/a ⓜ/ⓕ *ba*·kho/a low • short (height)
balcón ⓜ bal·*kon* balcony
balde ⓜ *bal*·de bucket
bálsamo ⓜ **de labios** *bal*·sa·mo de *la*·byos lip balm
banco ⓜ *ban*·ko bank (money)
bandera ⓕ ban·*de*·ra flag
baño ⓜ *ba*·nyo bath • bathroom • toilet
baños ⓜ pl *ba*·nyos toilets
barato/a ⓜ/ⓕ ba·*ra*·to/a cheap
barbero ⓜ bar·*be*·ro barber

barco ⓜ *bar*·ko boat • ship
— de vela de *ve*·la sailing boat
barrio ⓜ *ba*·ryo suburb
basquetbol ⓜ *bas*·ket·bol basketball
basura ⓕ ba·*soo*·ra rubbish
batería ⓕ ba·te·*ree*·a battery (car) • drums
bautizo ⓜ bow·*tee*·so baptism
bebé ⓜ&ⓕ be·*be* baby
bello/a ⓜ/ⓕ *be*·yo/a beautiful
beneficio ⓜ be·ne·*fee*·syo profit
besar be·*sar* kiss
beso ⓜ *be*·so kiss
biblia ⓕ *bee*·blya bible
biblioteca ⓕ bee·blyo·*te*·ka library
bicho ⓜ *bee*·cho bug
bici ⓕ *bee*·see bike
bicicleta ⓕ bee·see·*kle*·ta bicycle
— de carreras de ka·*re*·ras racing bike
— de montaña de mon·*ta*·nya mountain bike
bien byen well
bienestar ⓜ byen·es·*tar* welfare
billar ⓜ bee·*yar* pool (game)
billetes ⓜ pl **de banco** bee·*ye*·tes de *ban*·ko banknotes
biografía ⓕ byo·gra·*fee*·a biography
birome ⓕ bee·*ro*·me ballpoint pen
blanco y negro *blan*·ko ee *ne*·gro B&W (film)
blanco/a ⓜ/ⓕ *blan*·ko/a white
boca ⓕ *bo*·ka mouth
boda ⓕ *bo*·da wedding
bodega ⓕ bo·*de*·ga liquor store • winery
bol ⓜ bol bowl
bolas ⓕ pl **de algodón** *bo*·las de al·go·*don* cotton balls
boletería ⓕ bo·le·te·*ree*·a ticket office
boleto ⓜ bo·*le*·to ticket
— de ida y vuelta de *ee*·da ee *vwel*·ta return ticket
— de lista de espera de *lees*·ta de es·*pe*·ra standby ticket
— sencillo sen·*see*·yo one-way ticket
bolígrafo ⓜ bo·*lee*·gra·fo pen (ballpoint)
bolsa ⓕ **de compras** *bol*·sa de *kom*·pras shopping bag
bolsillo ⓜ bol·*see*·yo pocket
bolso ⓜ *bol*·so bag (general) • handbag
bomba ⓕ *bom*·ba bomb • pump
bombillo ⓜ bom·*bee*·yo light bulb
bondadoso/a ⓜ/ⓕ bon·da·*do*·so/a caring
bonito/a ⓜ/ⓕ bo·*nee*·to/a pretty
bosque ⓜ *bos*·ke forest
botas ⓕ pl *bo*·tas boots
— de montaña de mon·*ta*·nya hiking boots
botella ⓕ bo·*te*·ya bottle
botón ⓜ bo·*ton* button
boxeo ⓜ bok·*se*·o boxing
bragas ⓕ pl *bra*·gas underpants (women)
brazo ⓜ *bra*·so arm
briliante bree·*lyan*·te brilliant • glossy
broma ⓕ *bro*·ma joke
bronceador ⓜ bron·se·a·*dor* tanning lotion
bronquitis ⓜ bron·*kee*·tees bronchitis
brújula ⓕ *broo*·khoo·la compass
brumoso/a ⓜ/ⓕ broo·*mo*·so/a foggy
buceo ⓜ boo·*se*·o snorkelling
budista ⓜ&ⓕ boo·*dees*·ta Buddhist
bueno/a ⓜ/ⓕ *bwe*·no/a good • nice
bufanda ⓕ boo·*fan*·da scarf
bulto ⓜ *bool*·to lump
burro ⓜ *boo*·ro donkey
buscar boos·*kar* look for
buzón ⓜ boo·*son* mailbox

C

caballo ⓜ ka·*ba*·yo horse
cabaña ⓕ ka·*ba*·nya hut
cabeza ⓕ ka·*be*·sa head

cabina ⓕ **telefónica** ka·*bee*·na te·le·*fo*·nee·ka phone box
cable ⓜ *ka*·ble cable
cables ⓜ pl **de arranque** *ka*·bles de a·*ran*·ke jumper leads
cabra ⓕ *ka*·bra goat
cacharro ⓜ ka·*cha*·ro pot (ceramic)
cachorro ⓜ ka·*cho*·ro puppy
cacto ⓜ *kak*·to cactus
cada *ka*·da each
cadena ⓕ ka·*de*·na chain
— de bici de *bee*·see bike chain
cafetería ⓕ ka·fe·te·*ree*·a cafe
caída ⓕ ka·*ee*·da fall (tumble)
caja ⓕ *ka*·kha box
— fuerte *fwer*·te safe
— registradora re·khees·tra·*do*·ra cash register
cajero ⓜ **automático** ka·*khe*·ro ow·to·*ma*·tee·ko ATM
cajero/a ⓜ/ⓕ ka·*khe*·ro/a cashier
cajón ⓜ **con llave** ka·*khon* kon *ya*·ve locker
calcetines ⓜ pl kal·se·*tee*·nes socks
calculadora ⓕ kal·koo·la·*do*·ra calculator
calefacción ⓕ ka·le·fak·*syon* heating
— central sen·*tral* central heating
calendario ⓜ ka·len·*da*·ryo calendar
calidad ⓕ ka·lee·*da* quality
caliente ka·*lyen*·te hot
calle ⓕ *ka*·ye road
calor ⓜ ka·*lor* heat
calzoncillos ⓜ pl kal·son·*see*·yos underpants (men)
cama ⓕ *ka*·ma bed
— de matrimonio de ma·tree·*mo*·nyo double bed
cámara ⓕ **(fotográfica)** *ka*·ma·ra (fo·to·*gra*·fee·ka) camera
— de aire de *ai*·re tube (tyre)
— descartable des·kar·*ta*·ble disposable camera
— digital de·khee·*tal* digital camera
— submarina soob·ma·*ree*·na underwater camera
camarero/a ⓜ/ⓕ ka·ma·*re*·ro/a waiter
cambiar kam·*byar* change • exchange
cambio ⓜ *kam*·byo change (coins) • exchange
— de dinero de dee·*ne*·ro currency exchange
caminar ka·mee·*nar* walk
camino ⓜ ka·*mee*·no track • trail • way
— de bici de *bee*·see bike path
— rural roo·*ral* hiking route
camión ⓜ ka·*myon* truck
camisa ⓕ ka·*mee*·sa shirt
camiseta ⓕ ka·mee·*se*·ta singlet • T-shirt
cámping ⓜ *kam*·peen campsite
campo ⓜ *kam*·po countryside
caña ⓕ **de azúcar** *ka*·nya de a·*soo*·kar sugar cane
canasta ⓕ ka·*nas*·ta basket
cancelar kan·se·*lar* cancel
cáncer ⓜ *kan*·ser cancer
cancha ⓕ **de golf** *kan*·cha de golf golf course
cancha ⓕ **de tenis** *kan*·cha de *te*·nees tennis court
canción ⓕ kan·*syon* song
candado ⓜ kan·*da*·do padlock
candidiasis ⓜ kan·dee·*dya*·sees thrush (medical)
cansado/a ⓜ/ⓕ kan·*sa*·do/a tired
cantante ⓜ&ⓕ kan·*tan*·te singer
cantar kan·*tar* sing
cantidad ⓕ kan·tee·*da* amount
cantimplora ⓕ kan·teem·*plo*·ra water bottle
capa ⓕ **de ozono** *ka*·pa de o·*so*·no ozone layer
capacidad ⓕ **de SMS** ka·pa·see·*da* de e·se *em*·e e·se SMS capability
capilla ⓕ ka·*pee*·ya shrine
capote ⓜ ka·*po*·te cloak
cara ⓕ *ka*·ra face
caramelos ⓜ pl ka·ra·*me*·los lollies

C

caravana Ⓕ ka·ra·*va*·na caravan • van
cárcel Ⓕ *kar*·sel jail • prison
caries Ⓕ *ka*·ryes cavity (tooth)
carnet Ⓜ kar·*net* drivers licence
carnicería Ⓕ kar·nee·se·*ree*·a butcher's shop
caro/a Ⓜ/Ⓕ *ka*·ro/a expensive
carpa Ⓕ *kar*·pa tent
carpintero Ⓜ kar·peen·*te*·ro carpenter
carrera Ⓕ ka·*re*·ra race (sport)
carro Ⓜ *ka*·ro car
carta Ⓕ *kar*·ta letter
cartas Ⓕ pl *kar*·tas cards
cartera Ⓕ kar·*te*·ra wallet
cartucho Ⓜ **de gas** kar·*too*·cho de gas gas cartridge
casa Ⓕ *ka*·sa home • house
casado/a Ⓜ/Ⓕ ka·*sa*·do/a married
casarse ka·*sar*·se marry
cascada Ⓕ kas·*ka*·da waterfall
casco Ⓜ *kas*·ko helmet
casi *ka*·see almost
castigar kas·tee·*gar* punish
castillo Ⓜ kas·*tee*·yo castle
catedral Ⓕ ka·te·*dral* cathedral
católico/a Ⓜ/Ⓕ ka·*to*·lee·ko/a Catholic
caza Ⓕ *ka*·sa hunting
cédula Ⓜ **de identidad** *se*·doo·la de ee·den·tee·*da* identification card (ID)
celebración Ⓕ se·le·bra·*syon* celebration
celoso/a Ⓜ/Ⓕ se·*lo*·so/a jealous
cementerio Ⓜ se·men·*te*·ryo cemetery
cena Ⓕ *se*·na dinner
cenicero Ⓜ se·nee·*se*·ro ashtray
centavo Ⓜ sen·*ta*·vo cent
centímetro Ⓜ sen·*tee*·me·tro centimetre
central Ⓕ **telefónica** sen·*tral* te·le·*fo*·nee·ka telephone centre
centro Ⓜ *sen*·tro centre
— comercial ko·mer·*syal* shopping centre
— de la ciudad de la syoo·*da* city centre
Centroamérica Ⓕ sen·tro·a·*me*·ree·ka Central America
centroamericano/a Ⓜ/Ⓕ sen·tro·a·me·ree·*ka*·no/a Central American
cepillo Ⓜ **de dientes** se·*pee*·yo de *dyen*·tes toothbrush
cerámica Ⓕ se·*ra*·mee·ka ceramic
cerca Ⓕ *ser*·ka fence
cerca *ser*·ka near • nearby
cerrado/a Ⓜ/Ⓕ se·*ra*·do/a closed • locked • shut
— con llave kon *ya*·ve locked
cerradura Ⓕ se·ra·*doo*·ra lock (door)
cerrar se·*rar* close • lock • shut
certificado Ⓜ ser·tee·fee·*ka*·do certificate
chaleco Ⓜ **salvavidas** cha·*le*·ko sal·va·*vee*·das life jacket
champú Ⓜ cham·*poo* shampoo
chaqueta Ⓕ cha·*ke*·ta jacket
cheque Ⓜ *che*·ke cheque
— de viajero de vya·*khe*·ro travellers cheque
chica Ⓕ *chee*·ka girl
chicle Ⓜ *chee*·kle chewing gum
chico Ⓜ *chee*·ko boy
choque Ⓜ *cho*·ke crash (accident)
chupete Ⓜ choo·*pe*·te dummy • pacifier
cibercafé Ⓜ see·ber·ka·*fe* internet cafe
ciclismo Ⓜ see·*klees*·mo cycling
ciclista Ⓜ&Ⓕ see·*klees*·ta cyclist
ciego/a Ⓜ/Ⓕ *sye*·go/a blind
cielo Ⓜ *sye*·lo sky
ciencia Ⓕ *syen*·sya science
— ficción feek·*syon* science fiction
científico/a Ⓜ/Ⓕ syen·*tee*·fee·ko/a scientist
cigarillo Ⓜ see·ga·*ree*·yo cigarette

DICTIONARY

cigarro ⓜ see·*ga*·ro cigar
cine ⓜ *see*·ne cinema
cinta ⓕ **de vídeo** *seen*·ta de *vee*·de·o video tape
cinturón ⓜ **de seguridad** seen·too·*ron* de se·goo·ree·*da* seatbelt
circo ⓜ *seer*·ko circus
cita ⓕ *see*·ta appointment • date
citología ⓕ see·to·lo·*khee*·a pap smear
ciudad ⓕ syoo·*da* city
ciudadanía ⓕ syoo·da·da·*nee*·a citizenship
claro/a ⓜ/ⓕ *kla*·ro/a light (colour)
clase ⓕ *kla*·se class
— preferente pre·fe·*ren*·te business class
— turística too·*rees*·tee·ka economy class
clásico/a ⓜ/ⓕ *kla*·see·ko/a classical
cliente/a ⓜ/ⓕ *klyen*·te/a client
cobrar (un cheque) ko·*brar* (oon *che*·ke) cash (a cheque)
coca ⓕ *ko*·ka coca plant • coke (drug)
cocaína ⓕ ko·ka·*ee*·na cocaine
coche ⓜ **cama** *ko*·che *ka*·ma sleeping car
cocina ⓕ ko·*see*·na cuisine • kitchen
cocinar ko·see·*nar* cook
cocinero/a ⓜ/ⓕ ko·see·*ne*·ro/a chef • cook
cocodrilo ⓜ ko·ko·*dree*·lo crocodile
codeína ⓕ ko·de·*ee*·na codeine
código ⓜ **postal** *ko*·dee·go pos·*tal* post code
coima ⓕ *koy*·ma bribe
coimear koy·me·*ar* bribe
cola ⓕ *ko*·la queue
colchón ⓜ kol·*chon* mattress
colega ⓜ&ⓕ ko·*le*·ga colleague
cólera ⓕ *ko*·le·ra cholera
colibrí ⓜ ko·lee·*bree* hummingbird
colina ⓕ ko·*lee*·na hill

color ⓜ ko·*lor* colour
comedia ⓕ ko·*me*·dya comedy
comenzar ko·men·*sar* begin • start
comer ko·*mer* eat
comerciante ⓜ&ⓕ ko·mer·*syan*·te business person
comercio ⓜ ko·*mer*·syo trade
comida ⓕ ko·*mee*·da food
— de bebé de be·*be* baby food
comisaría ⓕ ko·mee·sa·*ree*·a police station
como *ko*·mo how
cómodo/a ⓜ/ⓕ *ko*·mo·do/a comfortable
cómpact ⓜ *kom*·pak CD
compañero/a ⓜ/ⓕ kom·pa·*nye*·ro/a companion
compañía ⓕ kom·pa·*nyee*·a company
compartir kom·par·*teer* share (with)
comprar kom·*prar* buy
compresas ⓕ pl kom·*pre*·sas sanitary napkins
compromiso ⓜ kom·pro·*mee*·so engagement (marriage)
computadora ⓕ kom·poo·ta·*do*·ra computer
— portátil por·*ta*·teel laptop
comunión ⓕ ko·moo·*nyon* communion
comunista ⓜ&ⓕ ko·moo·*nees*·ta communist
con kon with
— filtro *feel*·tro filtered
concierto ⓜ kon·*syer*·to concert
condición ⓕ **cardíaca** kon·dee·*syon* kar·*dee*·a·ka heart condition
condón ⓜ kon·*don* condom
conducir kon·doo·*seer* drive
conejo ⓜ ko·*ne*·kho rabbit
conexión ⓕ ko·nek·*syon* connection
confesión ⓕ kon·fe·*syon* confession
confianza ⓕ kon·*fyan*·sa trust
confiar kon·*fyar* trust
confirmar kon·feer·*mar* confirm

C

congelación ⓕ kon·khe·la·*syon* frostbite
conocer ko·no·*ser* know (a person)
conocido/a ⓜ/ⓕ ko·no·*see*·do/a famous
consejo ⓜ kon·*se*·kho advice
conservador(a) ⓜ/ⓕ kon·ser·va·*dor*/kon·ser·va·*do*·ra conservative
consigna ⓕ kon·*see*·nya left-luggage office
— automática ow·to·*ma*·tee·ka luggage lockers
construir kon·stroo·*eer* build
consulado ⓜ kon·soo·*la*·do consulate
contaminación ⓕ kon·ta·mee·na·*syon* pollution
contar kon·*tar* count
contemporáneo/a ⓜ/ⓕ kon·tem·po·*ra*·ne·o/a contemporary
contrato ⓜ kon·*tra*·to contract
control ⓜ kon·*trol* checkpoint
convento ⓜ kon·*ven*·to convent
copa ⓕ *ko*·pa drink
corazón ⓜ ko·ra·*son* heart
cordillera ⓕ kor·dee·*ye*·ra mountain range
corpiño ⓜ kor·*pee*·nyo bra
correcto/a ⓜ/ⓕ ko·*rek*·to/a right (correct)
correo ⓜ ko·*re*·o mail
— aéreo a·e·re·o airmail
— certificado ser·tee·fee·*ka*·do registered mail
— urgente oor·*khen*·te express mail
correos ⓜ pl ko·*re*·os post office
corrida ⓕ ko·*ree*·da bullfight
corriente ⓕ ko·*ryen*·te current
corriente ko·*ryen*·te ordinary
corrupto/a ⓜ/ⓕ ko·*roop*·to/a corrupt
cortar kor·*tar* cut
cortauñas ⓜ kor·ta·*oo*·nyas nail clippers
corte ⓜ **de pelo** *kor*·te de *pe*·lo haircut

corto/a ⓜ/ⓕ *kor*·to/a short (length)
cosecha ⓕ ko·*se*·cha crop • harvest
coser ko·*ser* sew
costa ⓕ *kos*·ta coast
costar kos·*tar* cost
crecer kre·*ser* grow
crema ⓕ *kre*·ma cream
— agria *a*·grya sour cream
— hidratante ee·dra·*tan*·te moisturiser
— solar so·*lar* sunblock
cristiano/a ⓜ/ⓕ krees·*tya*·no/a Christian
crítica ⓕ *kree*·tee·ka review
crudo/a ⓜ/ⓕ *kroo*·do/a raw
cuaderno ⓜ kwa·*der*·no notebook
cuadrado ⓜ kwa·*dra*·do square (place)
cuadro ⓜ *kwa*·dro painting (canvas)
cualificaciones ⓕ pl kwa·lee·fee·ka·*syo*·nes qualifications
cuando *kwan*·do when
cuanto *kwan*·to how much
cuarentena ⓕ kwa·ren·*te*·na quarantine
cuarto ⓜ *kwar*·to quarter
cubiertos ⓜ pl koo·*byer*·tos cutlery
cucaracha ⓕ koo·ka·*ra*·cha cockroach
cuchara ⓕ koo·*cha*·ra spoon
cucharita ⓕ koo·cha·*ree*·ta teaspoon
cuchillo ⓜ koo·*chee*·yo knife
cuenta ⓕ *kwen*·ta bill • check
— bancaria ban·*ka*·rya bank account
cuento ⓜ *kwen*·to short story • story
cuerda ⓕ *kwer*·da rope • string
— para tender la ropa *pa*·ra ten·*der* la *ro*·pa clothes line
cuero ⓜ *kwe*·ro leather
cuerpo ⓜ *kwer*·po body
cuervo ⓜ *kwer*·vo vulture
cuesta abajo *kwes*·ta a·*ba*·kho downhill
cuesta arriba *kwes*·ta a·*ree*·ba uphill

cueva Ⓕ *kwe*·va cave
cuidar kwee·*dar* care for • mind (an object)
culo Ⓜ *koo*·lo bum (body)
culpa Ⓕ *kool*·pa (someone's) fault
culpable kool·*pa*·ble guilty
cumbre Ⓕ *koom*·bre peak
cumpleaños Ⓜ koom·ple·*a*·nyos birthday
cupón Ⓜ koo·*pon* coupon
curitas Ⓕ pl koo·*ree*·tas Band-Aids
currículum Ⓜ koo·*ree*·koo·loom resume

D

dañar da·*nyar* hurt
danta Ⓕ *dan*·ta tapir
dar dar give
— gracias *gra*·syas thank
— la bienvenida la byen·ve·*nee*·da welcome
— una patada *oo*·na pa·*ta*·da kick
de de from
— cercanías ser·ka·*nee*·as local
— (cuatro) estrellas (*kwa*·tro) es·*tre*·yas (four-)star
— derecha de·*re*·cha right-wing
— izquierda ees·*kyer*·da left-wing
— lujo *loo*·kho luxurious
— menos *me*·nos less
— segunda mano se·*goon*·da *ma*·no second-hand
— vez en cuando ves en *kwan*·do sometimes
débil *de*·beel weak
decidir de·see·*deer* decide
decir de·*seer* say • tell
dedo Ⓜ *de*·do finger
— del pie del pye toe
defectuoso/a Ⓜ/Ⓕ de·fek·*two*·so/a faulty
deforestación Ⓕ de·fo·res·ta·*syon* deforestation
dejar entrar de·*khar* en·*trar* admit (allow to enter)
delgado/a Ⓜ/Ⓕ del·*ga*·do/a thin
demasiado (caro/a) Ⓜ/Ⓕ de·ma·*sya*·do (*ka*·ro/a) too (expensive)
democracia Ⓕ de·mo·*kra*·see·a democracy
demora Ⓕ de·*mo*·ra delay
dentista Ⓜ&Ⓕ den·*tees*·ta dentist
dentro de (una hora) *den*·tro de (*oo*·na *o*·ra) within (an hour)
deportes Ⓜ pl de·*por*·tes sport
deportista Ⓜ&Ⓕ de·por·*tees*·ta sportsperson
depósito Ⓜ de·*po*·see·to deposit (bank)
derecha de·*re*·cha right (direction)
derechista de·re·*chees*·ta right-wing
derechos Ⓜ pl de·*re*·chos rights
— civiles see·*vee*·les civil rights
— de animales de a·nee·*ma*·les animal rights
— humanos oo·*ma*·nos human rights
desayuno Ⓜ de·sa·*yoo*·no breakfast
descansar des·kan·*sar* rest
descanso Ⓜ des·*kan*·so intermission
descendiente Ⓜ de·sen·*dyen*·te descendant
descomponerse des·kom·po·*ner*·se break down
descubrir des·koo·*breer* discover
descuento Ⓜ des·*kwen*·to discount
desde *des*·de since (time)
desear de·se·*ar* wish
desempleado/a Ⓜ/Ⓕ des·em·ple·*a*·do/a unemployed
desierto Ⓜ de·*syer*·to desert
desodorante Ⓜ de·so·do·*ran*·te deodorant
despacio des·*pa*·syo slowly
despertador Ⓜ des·per·ta·*dor* alarm clock
despertarse des·per·*tar*·se wake up
después de des·*pwes* de after
destino Ⓜ des·*tee*·no destination
detallado/a Ⓜ/Ⓕ de·ta·*ya*·do/a itemised
detalle Ⓜ de·*ta*·ye detail

detener de·te·*ner* arrest
detrás de de·*tras* de behind
día ⓜ *dee*·a day
— festivo fes·*tee*·vo holiday
diafragma ⓜ dya·*frag*·ma diaphragm
diapositiva ⓕ dya·po·see·*tee*·va slide (film)
diariamente dya·rya·*men*·te daily
diarrea ⓕ dya·*re*·a diarrhoea
dibujar dee·boo·*khar* draw
diccionario ⓜ deek·syo·*na*·ryo dictionary
dientes ⓜ pl *dyen*·tes teeth
diferencia ⓕ **de horas** dee·fe·*ren*·sya de *o*·ras time difference
diferente dee·fe·*ren*·te different
difícil dee·*fee*·seel difficult
dinero ⓜ dee·*ne*·ro money
— en efectivo en e·fek·*tee*·vo cash
dios dyos god (general)
dirección ⓕ dee·rek·*syon* address
direccionales ⓜ pl dee·rek·syo·*na*·les indicators (car)
directo/a ⓜ/ⓕ dee·*rek*·to/a direct
director(a) ⓜ/ⓕ dee·rek·*tor*/dee·rek·*to*·ra director
disco ⓜ *dees*·ko disk
discoteca ⓕ dees·ko·*te*·ka disco
discriminación ⓕ dees·kree·mee·na·*syon* discrimination
discutir dees·koo·*teer* argue
diseño ⓜ dee·*se*·nyo design
disentería ⓕ dee·sen·te·*ree*·a dysentry
disparar dees·pa·*rar* shoot
DIU ⓜ de·ee·*oo* IUD (contraceptive device)
diversión ⓕ dee·ver·*syon* fun
divertirse dee·ver·*teer*·se enjoy (oneself)
doblar do·*blar* turn
doble *do*·ble double
docena ⓕ do·*se*·na dozen
dolor ⓜ do·*lor* pain
— de cabeza de ka·*be*·sa headache
— de estómago de es·*to*·ma·go stomachache
— de muelas de *mwe*·las toothache
— menstrual mens·*trwal* period pain
dolorido/a ⓜ/ⓕ do·lo·*ree*·do/a sore
doloroso/a ⓜ/ⓕ do·lo·*ro*·so/a painful
donde *don*·de where
dormir dor·*meer* sleep
dos ⓜ/ⓕ dos two
— camas ⓕ pl *ka*·mas twin beds
— copias ⓕ pl *ko*·pyas double copies (photos)
— veces *ve*·ses twice
droga ⓕ *dro*·ga drug (illegal)
drogadicción ⓕ dro·ga·deek·*syon* drug addiction
drogas ⓕ pl *dro*·gas drugs (illegal)
ducha ⓕ *doo*·cha shower
dueño/a ⓜ/ⓕ *dwe*·nyo/a owner
dulce ⓜ *dool*·se candy • sweet
durante doo·*ran*·te during
duro/a ⓜ/ⓕ *doo*·ro/a hard (not soft)

E

ecografía ⓕ e·ko·gra·*fee*·a ultrasound
edad ⓕ e·*da* age
edificio ⓜ e·dee·*fee*·syo building
educación ⓕ e·doo·ka·*syon* education
egoista ⓜ&ⓕ e·go·*ees*·ta selfish
ejemplo ⓜ e·*khem*·plo example
ejército ⓜ e·*kher*·see·to army
él el he
elecciones ⓕ pl e·lek·*syo*·nes elections
electricidad ⓕ e·lek·tree·see·*da* electricity
electricista ⓜ&ⓕ e·lek·tree·*sees*·ta electrician
ella *e*·ya she

ellos/ellas ⓜ/ⓕ pl e·yos/e·yas they
embajada ⓕ em·ba·*kha*·da embassy
embajador(a) ⓜ/ⓕ em·ba·kha·*dor*/em·ba·kha·*do*·ra ambassador
embarazada ⓕ em·ba·ra·*sa*·da pregnant
embarcarse em·bar·*kar*·se board (plane, ship)
emborrachado/a ⓜ/ⓕ em·bo·ra·*cha*·do/a drunk
embrague ⓜ em·*bra*·ge clutch
emergencia ⓕ e·mer·*khen*·sya emergency
emocional e·mo·syo·*nal* emotional
empleado/a ⓜ/ⓕ em·ple·*a*·do/a employee
empujar em·poo·*khar* push
en en in • on
— el extranjero el ek·stran·*khe*·ro abroad
encaje ⓜ en·*ka*·khe lace
encantador(a) ⓜ/ⓕ en·kan·ta·*dor*/en·kan·ta·*do*·ra charming
encendedor ⓜ en·sen·de·*dor* lighter
enchufe ⓜ en·*choo*·fe plug (electricity)
encía ⓕ en·*see*·a gum (mouth)
encontrar en·kon·*trar* meet • find
energía ⓕ **nuclear** e·ner·*khee*·a noo·kle·*ar* nuclear energy
enfadado/a ⓜ/ⓕ en·fa·*da*·do/a angry
enfermedad ⓕ en·fer·mee·*da* disease
— venérea ve·*ne*·re·a venereal disease
enfermero/a ⓜ/ⓕ en·fer·*me*·ro/a nurse
enfermo/a ⓜ/ⓕ en·*fer*·mo/a sick
enorme e·*nor*·me huge
entender en·ten·*der* understand
entrar en·*trar* enter
entre *en*·tre among • between
entregar en·tre·*gar* deliver
entrenador(a) ⓜ/ⓕ en·tre·na·*dor*/en·tren·na·*do*·ra coach
entreno ⓜ en·*tre*·no workout
entrevista ⓕ en·tre·*vees*·ta interview
enviar en·*vyar* send
epilepsia ⓕ e·pee·*lep*·sya epilepsy
equipaje ⓜ e·kee·*pa*·khe luggage
equipo ⓜ e·*kee*·po equipment • team
— de inmersión de een·mer·*syon* diving equipment
— estereofónico es·te·re·o·*fo*·nee·ko stereo
equitación ⓕ e·kee·ta·*syon* horse riding
equivocado/a ⓜ/ⓕ e·kee·vo·*ka*·do/a wrong
error ⓜ e·*ror* mistake
escalada ⓕ es·ka·*la*·da rock climbing
escalera ⓕ es·ka·*le*·ra stairway
— electrica e·*lek*·tree·ka escalator
escape ⓜ es·*ka*·pe exhaust (car)
escarcha ⓕ es·*kar*·cha frost
escarpado/a ⓜ/ⓕ es·kar·*pa*·do/a steep
escasez ⓕ es·ka·*ses* shortage
escenario ⓜ e·se·*na*·ryo stage
escoger es·ko·*kher* choose
escribir es·kree·*beer* write
escritor(a) ⓜ/ⓕ es·kree·*tor*/es·kree·*to*·ra writer
escuchar es·koo·*char* listen
escuela ⓕ es·*kwe*·la school
esgrima ⓕ es·*gree*·ma fencing (sport)
espacio ⓜ es·*pa*·syo space
espalda ⓕ es·*pal*·da back (body)
España es·*pa*·nya Spain
especial es·pe·*syal* special
especialista ⓜ&ⓕ es·pe·sya·*lees*·ta specialist
espectáculo ⓜ es·pek·*ta*·koo·lo show
espejo ⓜ es·*pe*·kho mirror
esperar es·pe·*rar* wait
espermicida ⓕ es·per·mee·*see*·da spermicide

esposa ⓕ es·*po*·sa wife
esposo ⓜ es·*po*·so husband
espuma ⓕ **de afeitar** es·*poo*·ma de a·fay·*tar* shaving cream
esquí ⓜ es·*kee* skiing
— acuático a·*kwa*·tee·ko waterskiing
esquiar es·*kyar* ski
esquina ⓕ es·*kee*·na corner
esquís ⓜ pl es·*kees* skis
— acuáticos a·*kwa*·tee·kos water skis
esta noche es·ta *no*·che tonight
estacas ⓕ pl es·*ta*·kas pegs (tent)
estación ⓕ es·ta·*syon* season • station
— de tren de tren railway station
— de autobuses de ow·to·*boo*·ses bus station (city)
— de ómnibuses de *om*·nee·boo·ses bus station (intercity)
— de subterráneo de soob·te·*ra*·ne·o metro station
estacionamiento ⓜ es·ta·syo·na·*myen*·to car park
estacionar es·ta·syo·*nar* park (car)
estadio ⓜ es·*ta*·dyo stadium
estado ⓜ **civil** es·*ta*·do see·*veel* marital status
estafa ⓕ es·*ta*·fa rip-off
estanquero ⓜ es·tan·*ke*·ro tobacconist
estar es·*tar* be
— aburrido/a ⓜ/ⓕ a·boo·*ree*·do/a be bored
— de acuerdo de a·*kwer*·do agree
estatua ⓕ es·*ta*·twa statue
este ⓜ *es*·te east
éste/a ⓜ/ⓕ *es*·te/a this
esterilla ⓕ es·te·*ree*·ya mat
esteticista ⓜ&ⓕ es·te·tee·*sees*·ta beautician
estilo ⓜ es·*tee*·lo style
estómago ⓜ es·*to*·ma·go stomach
estrellas ⓕ pl es·*tre*·yas stars
estreñimiento ⓜ es·tre·nyee·*myen*·to constipation
estudiante ⓜ&ⓕ es·too·*dyan*·te student
estudio ⓜ es·*too*·dyo studio
estufa ⓕ es·*too*·fa heater • stove
estúpido/a ⓜ/ⓕ es·*too*·pee·do/a stupid
etiqueta ⓕ **de equipaje** e·tee·*ke*·ta de e·kee·*pa*·khe luggage tag
exceso ⓜ **de equipaje** ek·*se*·so de e·kee·*pa*·khe excess baggage
excursión ⓕ ek·skoor·*syon* tour
excursionismo ⓜ ek·skoor·syo·*nees*·mo hiking
experiencia ⓕ ek·spe·*ryen*·sya experience
— laboral la·bo·*ral* work experience
explotación ⓕ ek·splo·ta·*syon* exploitation
exposición ⓕ ek·spo·see·*syon* exhibition
expreso/a ⓜ/ⓕ ek·*spre*·so/a express
exterior ⓜ ek·ste·*ryor* outside
extrañar ek·stra·*nyar* miss (feel absence of)
extranjero/a ⓜ/ⓕ ek·stran·*khe*·ro/a foreign • foreigner
extraño/a ⓜ/ⓕ ek·*stra*·nyo/a strange • stranger • unusual

F

fábrica ⓕ *fa*·bree·ka factory
fácil *fa*·seel easy
facturación ⓕ fak·too·ra·*syon* check-in (airport)
— de equipaje de e·kee·*pa*·khe check-in (luggage)
falda ⓕ *fal*·da skirt
familia ⓕ fa·*mee*·lya family
fantástico/a ⓜ/ⓕ fan·*tas*·tee·ko/a fantastic • great
farmacia ⓕ far·*ma*·sya chemist • pharmacy
faros ⓜ pl *fa*·ros headlights
fastidiado/a ⓜ/ⓕ fas·tee·*dya*·do/a annoyed

fecha ⓕ *fe*·cha date (day)
— de nacimiento de na·see·*myen*·to date of birth
feliz fe·*lees* happy
feria ⓕ *fe*·rya street market
ferretería ⓕ fe·re·te·*ree*·a hardware store
ficción ⓕ feek·*syon* fiction
fiebre ⓕ *fye*·bre fever
— amarilla a·ma·*ree*·ya yellow fever
— del dengue del *den*·ge dengue fever
— del heno del *e*·no hay fever
— glandular glan·doo·*lar* glandular fever
fiesta ⓕ *fyes*·ta party (celebration)
fin ⓜ feen end
— de semana de se·*ma*·na weekend
firma ⓕ *feer*·ma signature
flamenco ⓜ fla·*men*·ko flamenco (dance) • flamingo
flor ⓕ flor flower
florista ⓜ&ⓕ flo·*rees*·ta florist
flujo ⓜ **vaginal** *floo*·kho va·khee·*nal* vaginal discharge
foco ⓜ *fo*·ko lightbulb
footing foo·*teen* jogging
forma ⓕ *for*·ma shape
fósforos ⓜ pl *fos*·fo·ros matches
fotocopiadora ⓕ fo·to·ko·pee·a·*do*·ra photocopier
fotografía ⓕ fo·to·gra·*fee*·a photo • photography
fotógrafo/a ⓜ/ⓕ fo·*to*·gra·fo/a photographer
fotómetro ⓜ fo·*to*·me·tro light meter
frágil *fra*·kheel fragile
franqueo ⓜ fran·*ke*·o postage
frazada ⓕ fra·*sa*·da blanket
freír fre·*eer* fry
freno ⓜ pl *fre*·no brake
frente a *fren*·te a opposite
frigorífico ⓜ free·go·*ree*·fee·ko fridge
frío/a ⓜ/ⓕ *free*·o/a cold
frontera ⓕ fron·*te*·ra border (frontier)
fuego ⓜ *fwe*·go fire
fuerte *fwer*·te strong
fumar foo·*mar* smoke
funda ⓕ **de almohada** *foon*·da de al·mo·*a*·da pillowcase
funeral ⓜ foo·ne·*ral* funeral
fútbol ⓜ *foot*·bol football • soccer
futuro ⓜ foo·*too*·ro future

G

ganador(a) ⓜ/ⓕ ga·na·*dor*/ ga·na·*do*·ra winner
ganar ga·*nar* earn • win
garage ⓜ ga·*ra*·khe garage (car shelter)
garganta ⓕ gar·*gan*·ta throat
gas ⓜ gas gas (for cooking)
gasolina ⓕ ga·so·*lee*·na gas • petrol
gasolinera ⓕ ga·so·lee·*ne*·ra service station
gatito/a ⓜ/ⓕ ga·*tee*·to/a kitten
gato/a ⓜ/ⓕ *ga*·to/a cat
gemelos/as ⓜ/ⓕ pl khe·*me*·los/as twins
general khe·ne·*ral* general
gente ⓕ *khen*·te people
gimnasia ⓕ kheem·*na*·sya gymnastics
ginecólogo/a ⓜ/ⓕ khee·ne·*ko*·lo·go/a gynaecologist
glorieta ⓕ glo·*rye*·ta roundabout
gobierno ⓜ go·*byer*·no government
goma ⓕ *go*·ma gum (chewing)
gordo/a ⓜ/ⓕ *gor*·do/a fat
gotas ⓕ pl **para los ojos** *go*·tas *pa*·ra los *o*·khos eye drops
grabación ⓕ gra·ba·*syon* recording
gracioso/a ⓜ/ⓕ gra·*syo*·so/a funny
gramos ⓜ pl *gra*·mos grams
grande *gran*·de big

grandes almacenes ⓜ pl *gran*·des al·ma·*se*·nes department store
granizo ⓜ gra·*nee*·so hail
granja ⓕ *gran*·kha farm
grifo ⓜ *gree*·fo faucet • tap
gripe ⓕ *gree*·pe influenza
gris grees grey
gritar gree·*tar* shout
grupo ⓜ *groo*·po band (music) • group
— de rock de rok rock group
— sanguíneo san·*gwee*·ne·o blood group
guantes ⓜ pl *gwan*·tes gloves
guardarropa ⓜ gwar·da·*ro*·pa cloakroom
guardería ⓕ gwar·de·*ree*·a child-minding service • creche
guerra ⓕ *ge*·ra war
guía ⓕ *gee*·a guidebook
— audio *ow*·dyo audio guide
— de espectaculos de es·pek·*ta*·koo·los entertainment guide
— telefónica te·le·*fo*·nee·ka phone book
guía ⓜ&ⓕ *gee*·a guide (person)
guitarra ⓕ gee·*ta*·ra guitar
gustar(le) goos·*tar*(le) like

H

habitación a·bee·ta·*syon* bedroom • room
— doble *do*·ble double room
— individual een·dee·vee·*dwal* single room
hablar a·*blar* speak • talk
hacer a·*ser* do • make
— dedo *de*·do hitchhike
— surf soorf surf
— windsurf *gween*·soorf windsurfing
hachís ⓜ a·*chees* hash
hacia *a*·sya towards
— abajo a·*ba*·kho down
hamaca ⓕ a·*ma*·ka hammock
hasta *as*·ta until
hecho/a ⓜ/ⓕ *e*·cho/a made
— a mano a *ma*·no handmade
— de (algodón) de (al·go·*don*) made of (cotton)
heladería ⓕ e·la·de·*ree*·a ice-cream parlour
helar e·*lar* freeze
herborista ⓜ&ⓕ er·bo·*rees*·ta herbalist
herida ⓕ e·*ree*·da injury
hermana ⓕ er·*ma*·na sister
hermano ⓜ er·*ma*·no brother
hermoso/a ⓜ/ⓕ er·*mo*·so/a handsome
heroína ⓕ e·ro·*ee*·na heroin
hielo ⓜ *ye*·lo ice
hierba ⓕ *yer*·ba grass
hígado ⓜ *ee*·ga·do liver
hija ⓕ *ee*·kha daughter
hijo ⓜ *ee*·kho son
hilo ⓜ *ee*·lo thread
— dental den·*tal* dental floss
hinchas ⓜ&ⓕ pl *een*·chas fans (supporters)
hindú ⓜ&ⓕ een·*doo* Hindu
historial ⓜ **profesional** ees·to·*ryal* pro·fe·syo·*nal* CV
histórico/a ⓜ/ⓕ ees·*to*·ree·ko/a historical
hoja ⓕ *o*·kha leaf
— de afeitar de a·fay·*tar* razor blade
Holanda ⓕ o·*lan*·da Netherlands
hombre ⓜ *om*·bre man
hombros ⓜ pl *om*·bros shoulders
hora ⓕ *o*·ra time
horario ⓜ o·*ra*·ryo timetable
horas ⓕ pl **de abrir** o·ras de a·*breer* opening hours
hormiga ⓕ or·*mee*·ga ant
horno ⓜ *or*·no oven
horóscopo ⓜ o·*ros*·ko·po horoscope
hospital ⓜ os·pee·*tal* hospital
hosteleria ⓕ os·te·le·*ree*·a hospitality
hotel ⓜ o·*tel* hotel
hoy oy today

huerta ⓕ *wer*·ta vegetable garden
hueso ⓜ *we*·so bone
hurto ⓜ **en tiendas** *oor*·to en *tyen*·das shoplifting

I

identificación ⓕ ee·den·tee·fee·ka·*syon* identification
idioma ⓜ ee·*dyo*·ma language
idiota ⓜ&ⓕ ee·*dyo*·ta idiot
iglesia ⓕ ee·*gle*·sya church
igual ee·*gwal* same
igualdad ⓕ ee·gwal·*da* equality
ilegal ee·le·*gal* illegal
impermeable ⓜ eem·per·me·*a*·ble raincoat
impermeable eem·per·me·*a*·ble waterproof
importante eem·por·*tan*·te important
imposible eem·po·*see*·ble impossible
impuesto ⓜ eem·*pwes*·to tax
— sobre la renta *so*·bre la *ren*·ta income tax
incluido/a ⓜ/ⓕ een·kloo·*ee*·do/a included
incómodo/a ⓜ/ⓕ een·*ko*·mo·do/a uncomfortable
indigestion ⓕ een·dee·khes·*tyon* indigestion
industria ⓕ een·*doos*·trya industry
infección ⓕ een·fek·*syon* infection
inflamación ⓕ een·fla·ma·*syon* inflammation
información ⓕ een·for·ma·*syon* information
informática ⓕ een·for·*ma*·tee·ka IT
informativo ⓜ een·for·ma·*tee*·vo current affairs
ingeniería ⓕ een·khe·nye·*ree*·a engineering
ingeniero/a ⓜ/ⓕ een·khe·*nye*·ro/a engineer
Inglaterra ⓕ een·gla·*te*·ra England
inglés ⓜ een·*gles* English (language)
inglés/inglesa ⓜ/ⓕ een·*gles*/een·*gle*·sa English
ingrediente ⓜ een·gre·*dyen*·te ingredient
inhalador ⓜ een·a·la·*dor* inhaler
injusto/a ⓜ/ⓕ een·*khoos*·to/a unfair
inmigración ⓕ een·mee·gra·*syon* immigration
inocente ee·no·*sen*·te innocent
inseguro/a ⓜ/ⓕ een·se·*goo*·ro/a unsafe
insolación ⓕ een·so·la·*syon* sunstroke
instituto ⓜ een·stee·*too*·to high school
instructor(a) ⓜ/ⓕ een·strook·*tor*/een·strook·*to*·ra instructor
interesante een·te·re·*san*·te interesting
internacional een·ter·na·syo·*nal* international
intérprete ⓜ&ⓕ een·*ter*·pre·te interpreter
intoxicación ⓕ **alimenticia** een·tok·see·ka·*syon* a·lee·men·*tee*·sya food poisoning
inundación ⓕ ee·noon·da·*syon* flood
invierno ⓜ een·*vyer*·no winter
invitar een·vee·*tar* invite
inyección ⓕ een·yek·*syon* injection
inyectarse een·yek·*tar*·se inject
ir eer go
— de compras de *kom*·pras shop
— de excursión de ek·skoor·*syon* hike
— en tobogán en to·bo·*gan* tobogganing
irritación ⓕ ee·ree·ta·*syon* irritation • rash
— de pañal de pa·*nyal* nappy rash
isla ⓕ *ees*·la island
itinerario ⓜ ee·tee·ne·*ra*·ryo itinerary
IVA ⓜ *ee*·va sales tax
izquierda ⓕ ees·*kyer*·da left (direction)

J

jabón ⓜ kha·*bon* soap
jaguar ⓜ kha·*gwar* jaguar
jalar kha·*lar* pull
Japón ⓜ kha·*pon* Japan
jarabe ⓜ kha·*ra*·be cough medicine
jardín ⓜ khar·*deen* garden
— botánico bo·*ta*·nee·ko botanic garden
— de infantes de een·*fan*·tes kindergarten
jardinería ⓕ khar·dee·ne·*ree*·a gardening
jarra ⓕ *kha*·ra jar
jefe/a ⓜ/ⓕ *khe*·fe/a boss • leader • manager
jeringa ⓕ khe·*reen*·ga syringe
jersey ⓜ kher·*say* jumper • sweater
jockey ⓜ kho·*kay* jockey
joven *kho*·ven young
joyería ⓕ kho·ye·*ree*·a jewellery
jubilado/a ⓜ/ⓕ khoo·bee·*la*·do/a retired
judío/a ⓜ/ⓕ khoo·*dee*·o/a Jewish
juego ⓜ *khwe*·go game (play)
— de computadora de kom·poo·ta·*do*·ra computer game
juegos ⓜ pl **olímpicos** *khwe*·gos o·*leem*·pee·kos Olympic Games
juez ⓜ&ⓕ khwes judge
jugar khoo·*gar* play (a game)
— al tenis al *te*·nees play tennis
juguetería ⓕ khoo·ge·te·*ree*·a toy shop
juicioso/a ⓜ/ⓕ khwee·*syo*·so/a sensible
juntos/as ⓜ/ⓕ pl *khoon*·tos/as together

L

la píldora ⓕ la *peel*·do·ra the Pill
labios ⓜ pl *la*·byos lips
lado ⓜ *la*·do side
ladrón/ladrona ⓜ/ⓕ la·*dron*/la·*dro*·na thief
lagartija ⓕ la·gar·*tee*·kha lizard
lago ⓜ *la*·go lake
lana ⓕ *la*·na wool
lápiz ⓜ *la*·pees pencil
— de labios de *la*·byos lipstick
largo/a ⓜ/ⓕ *lar*·go/a long
lata ⓕ *la*·ta can • tin
Latinoamérica ⓕ la·tee·no·a·*me*·ree·ka Latin America
latinoamericano/a ⓜ/ⓕ la·tee·no·a·me·ree·*ka*·no/a Latin American
lavadora ⓕ la·va·*do*·ra washing machine
lavandería ⓕ la·van·de·*ree*·a laundrette • laundry
lavar la·*var* wash (something)
lavarse la·*var*·se wash (oneself)
laxantes ⓜ pl lak·*san*·tes laxatives
leer le·*er* read
legal le·*gal* legal
legislación ⓕ le·khees·la·*syon* legislation
lejos *le*·khos far
leña ⓕ *le*·nya firewood
lentes ⓜ pl *len*·tes lenses
— de contacto de kon·*tak*·to contact lenses
lento/a ⓜ/ⓕ *len*·to/a slow
lesbiana ⓕ les·*bya*·na lesbian
levantar le·van·*tar* lift
levantarse le·van·*tar*·se get up
ley ⓕ lay law
libra ⓕ *lee*·bra pound (money)
libre *lee*·bre free (not bound)
librería ⓕ lee·bre·*ree*·a bookshop
libro ⓜ *lee*·bro book
— de frases de *fra*·ses phrasebook
— de viajes de *vya*·khes travel book
ligar lee·*gar* chat up
ligero/a ⓜ/ⓕ *lee*·khe·ro/a light (not heavy)
lila *lee*·la purple

limite ⓜ *lee*·mee·te limit
— de equipaje de e·kee·*pa*·khe baggage allowance
— de velocidad de ve·lo·see·*da* speed limit
limpio/a ⓜ/ⓕ *leem*·pyo/a clean
línea ⓕ *lee*·ne·a line
linterna ⓕ leen·*ter*·na flashlight • torch
listo/a ⓜ/ⓕ *lees*·to/a ready
literatura ⓕ lee·te·ra·*too*·ra literature
— de ficción de feek·*syon* fiction
— no novelesca no no·ve·*les*·ka nonfiction
llamada ⓕ ya·*ma*·da phone call
— a cobro revertido a *ko*·bro re·ver·*tee*·do collect call
llamar ya·*mar* call
— por telefono por te·*le*·fo·no ring (by phone)
llano/a ⓜ/ⓕ *ya*·no/a flat
llanta ⓕ *yan*·ta tyre
llave ⓕ *ya*·ve key
llegadas ⓕ pl ye·*ga*·das arrivals
llegar ye·*gar* arrive
lleno/a ⓜ/ⓕ *ye*·no/a booked out • full
llevar ye·*var* carry • wear
lluvia ⓕ *yoo*·vya rain
local ⓜ lo·*kal* venue
loción ⓕ lo·*syon* lotion
— para después del afeitado *pa*·ra des·*pwes* del a·fay·*ta*·do aftershave
loco/a ⓜ/ⓕ *lo*·ko/a crazy
lodo ⓜ *lo*·do mud
loro ⓜ *lo*·ro parrot
Los Estados ⓜ pl **Unidos** los es·*ta*·dos oo·*nee*·dos the USA
los/las dos ⓜ/ⓕ pl los/las dos both
lubricante ⓜ loo·bree·*kan*·te lubricant
lucha ⓕ *loo*·cha fight
lugar ⓜ loo·*gar* place
— de nacimiento de na·see·*myen*·to place of birth
luna ⓕ *loo*·na moon
— llena *ye*·na full moon
— de miel de myel honeymoon
luz ⓕ loos light

M

madera ⓕ ma·*de*·ra wood
madre ⓕ *ma*·dre mother
madrugada ⓕ ma·droo·*ga*·da dawn
mago/a ⓜ/ⓕ *ma*·go/a magician
maleta ⓕ ma·*le*·ta suitcase
maletín ⓜ ma·le·*teen* briefcase
— de primeros auxilios de pree·*me*·ros ow·*ksee*·yos first-aid kit
malla ⓕ *ma*·ya bathing suit
malo/a ⓜ/ⓕ *ma*·lo/a bad
mamá ⓕ ma·*ma* mum
mamograma ⓜ ma·mo·*gra*·ma mammogram
mañana ⓕ ma·*nya*·na morning • tomorrow
mandíbula ⓕ man·*dee*·boo·la jaw
mando ⓜ **a distancia** *man*·do a dees·*tan*·sya remote control
manifestación ⓕ ma·nee·fes·ta·*syon* demonstration (protest)
manillar ⓜ ma·nee·*yar* handlebar
mano ⓕ *ma*·no hand
mantel ⓜ man·*tel* tablecloth
mapa ⓜ *ma*·pa map
maquillaje ⓜ ma·kee·*ya*·khe make-up
máquina ⓕ *ma*·kee·na machine
— de boletos de bo·*le*·tos ticket machine
mar ⓜ mar sea
maravilloso/a ⓜ/ⓕ ma·ra·vee·*yo*·so/a wonderful
marcador ⓜ mar·ka·*dor* scoreboard
marcapasos ⓜ mar·ka·*pa*·sos pacemaker
marcar mar·*kar* score
marchas ⓕ pl *mar*·chas gears
marcos ⓜ pl *mar*·kos borders (photography)

marea ⓕ ma·*re*·a tide
mareado/a ⓜ/ⓕ ma·re·*a*·do/a dizzy
mareo ⓜ ma·*re*·o seasickness • travel sickness
mariposa ⓕ ma·ree·*po*·sa butterfly
marrón ma·*ron* brown
martillo ⓜ mar·*tee*·yo hammer
más mas more • most
más cercano/a ⓜ/ⓕ mas ser·*ka*·no nearest
masaje ⓜ ma·*sa*·khe massage
masajista ⓜ&ⓕ ma·sa·*khees*·ta masseur/masseuse
matar ma·*tar* kill
mate *ma*·te matte (photos)
matrícula ⓕ ma·*tree*·koo·la car registration • license plate number
matrimonio ⓜ ma·tree·*mo*·nyo marriage
mazo ⓜ *ma*·so mallet
mecánico/a ⓜ/ⓕ me·*ka*·nee·ko/a mechanic
mechero ⓜ me·*che*·ro cigarette lighter
medianoche ⓕ me·dya·*no*·che midnight
medias ⓕ pl *me*·dyas pantyhose • stockings
medicina ⓕ me·dee·*see*·na drug (medicinal) • medicine
medico/a ⓜ/ⓕ *me*·dee·ko/a doctor
medio ⓜ **ambiente** *me*·dyo am·*byen*·te environment
medio/a ⓜ/ⓕ *me*·dyo/a half
mediodía ⓜ me·dyo·*dee*·a noon
medios ⓜ pl *me*·dyos resources
— de comunicación de ko·moo·nee·ka·*syon* media
— de transporte de trans·*por*·te transport
meditación ⓕ me·dee·ta·*syon* meditation
mejor me·*khor* best • better
melodía ⓕ me·lo·*dee*·a tune
mendigo/a ⓜ/ⓕ men·*dee*·go/a beggar
mensaje ⓜ men·*sa*·khe message
menstruación ⓕ mens·trwa·*syon* menstruation
mentiroso/a ⓜ/ⓕ men·tee·*ro*·so/a liar
menú ⓜ me·*noo* menu
(a) menudo a me·*noo*·do often
mercado ⓜ mer·*ka*·do market
— de artesanía de ar·te·sa·*nee*·a craft market
mes ⓜ mes month
mesa ⓕ *me*·sa table
meseta ⓕ me·*se*·ta plateau
metal ⓜ me·*tal* metal
metro ⓜ *me*·tro metre (distance)
mezclar mes·*klar* mix
mezquita ⓕ mes·*kee*·ta mosque
microondas ⓜ mee·kro·*on*·das microwave oven
miembro ⓜ&ⓕ *myem*·bro member
migraña ⓕ mee·*gra*·nya migraine
milímetro ⓜ mee·*lee*·me·tro millimetre
militares ⓜ pl mee·lee·*ta*·res military
millón ⓜ mee·*yon* million
minusválido/a ⓜ/ⓕ mee·noos·*va*·lee·do/a disabled
minuto ⓜ mee·*noo*·to minute
mirador ⓜ mee·ra·*dor* lookout
mirar mee·*rar* look • watch
— las vidrieras las vee·*drye*·ras window-shopping
misa ⓕ *mee*·sa mass (Catholic)
mochila ⓕ mo·*chee*·la backpack
mojado/a ⓜ/ⓕ mo·*kha*·do/a wet
monasterio ⓜ mo·nas·*te*·ryo monastery
monedas ⓕ pl mo·*ne*·das coins
— sueltas *swel*·tas loose change
monitor(a) ⓜ/ⓕ mo·nee·*tor*/mo·nee·*to*·ra (skiing) instructor
monja ⓕ *mon*·kha nun
monopatinaje ⓜ mo·no·pa·tee·*na*·khe skateboarding
montaña ⓕ mon·*ta*·nya mountain

montar mon·*tar* ride
monumento ⓜ mo·noo·*men*·to monument
mordedura ⓕ mor·de·*doo*·ra bite
moretón ⓜ mo·re·*ton* bruise
morir mo·*reer* die
mosca ⓕ *mos*·ka fly
mosquitera ⓕ mos·kee·*te*·ra mosquito net
mosquito ⓜ mos·*kee*·to mosquito
mostrador ⓜ mos·tra·*dor* counter (shop)
mostrar mos·*trar* show
motocicleta ⓕ mo·to·see·*kle*·ta motorcycle
motor ⓜ mo·*tor* engine
motora ⓕ mo·*to*·ra motorboat
muchos/as ⓜ/ⓕ pl *moo*·chos/as many
mudo/a ⓜ/ⓕ *moo*·do/a mute
muebles ⓜ pl *mwe*·bles furniture
muela ⓕ *mwe*·la tooth (back)
muelle ⓜ *mwe*·ye spring
muerto/a ⓜ/ⓕ *mwer*·to/a dead
mujer ⓕ moo·*kher* woman
multa ⓕ *mool*·ta fine (payment)
mundo ⓜ *moon*·do world
muñeca ⓕ moo·*nye*·ka doll • wrist
músculo ⓜ *moos*·koo·lo muscle
museo ⓜ moo·*se*·o museum
— de arte de *ar*·te art gallery
música ⓕ *moo*·see·ka music
músico/a ⓜ/ⓕ *moo*·see·ko/a musician
musulmán/musulmana ⓜ/ⓕ moo·sool·*man*/moo·sool·*ma*·na Muslim
muy mooy very

N

nacional na·syo·*nal* national
nacionalidad ⓕ na·syo·na·lee·*da* nationality
nada *na*·da none • nothing
nadar na·*dar* swim
nariz ⓕ na·*rees* nose
naturaleza ⓕ na·too·ra·*le*·sa nature
naturopatia ⓕ na·too·ro·*pa*·tya naturopathy
náusea ⓕ *now*·se·a nausea
náuseas ⓕ pl **del embarazo** *now*·se·as del em·ba·*ra*·so morning sickness
navaja ⓕ na·*va*·kha penknife
necesario/a ⓜ/ⓕ ne·se·*sa*·ryo/a necessary
necesitar ne·se·see·*tar* need
negar(se) ne·*gar*·(se) refuse
negocio ⓜ ne·*go*·syo business
— de artículos básicos de ar·*tee*·koo·los *ba*·see·kos convenience store
negro/a ⓜ/ⓕ *ne*·gro/a black
nieto/a ⓜ/ⓕ *nye*·to/a grandchild
nieve ⓕ *nye*·ve snow
niño/a ⓜ/ⓕ *nee*·nyo/a child
no fumadores foo·ma·*do*·res nonsmoking
no incluido/a ⓜ/ⓕ een·kloo·*ee*·do/a excluded
noche ⓕ *no*·che evening • night
nombre ⓜ *nom*·bre name
norte ⓜ *nor*·te north
nosotros/as ⓜ/ⓕ no·*so*·tros/as we
noticias ⓕ pl no·*tee*·syas news
novela ⓕ no·*ve*·la novel
— negra *ne*·gra detective novel
— rosa *ro*·sa romance novel
novia ⓕ *no*·vya girlfriend
novio ⓜ *no*·vyo boyfriend
nube ⓕ *noo*·be cloud
nublado/a ⓜ/ⓕ noo·*bla*·do/a cloudy
nuestro/a ⓜ/ⓕ *nwes*·tro/a our
Nueva Zelandia ⓕ *nwe*·va se·*lan*·dya New Zealand
nuevo/a ⓜ/ⓕ *nwe*·vo/a new
número ⓜ *noo*·me·ro number
— de habitación de a·bee·ta·*syon* room number
— de pasaporte de pa·sa·*por*·te passport number
nunca *noon*·ka never

O

o o or
objetivo ⓜ ob·khe·*tee*·vo lens
obra ⓕ *o*·bra play (theatre) • work (of art)
obrero/a ⓜ/ⓕ o·*bre*·ro/a factory worker • labourer
océano ⓜ o·se·a·no ocean
ocupado/a ⓜ/ⓕ o·koo·*pa*·do/a busy
oeste ⓜ o·es·te west
oficina ⓕ o·fee·*see*·na office
— de objetos perdidos de ob·*khe*·tos per·*dee*·dos lost-property office
— de turismo de too·*rees*·mo tourist office
oficinista ⓜ&ⓕ o·fee·see·*nees*·ta office worker
oír o·*eer* hear
ojo ⓜ *o*·kho eye
ola ⓕ *o*·la saucepan • wave
olor ⓜ o·*lor* smell
olvidar ol·vee·*dar* forget
ómnibus ⓜ *om*·nee·boos bus (intercity)
ópera ⓕ *o*·pe·ra opera
operación ⓕ o·pe·ra·*syon* operation (medical)
operador(a) ⓜ/ⓕ o·pe·ra·*dor*/ o·pe·ra·*do*·ra operator
opinión ⓕ o·pee·*nyon* opinion
oportunidad ⓕ o·por·too·nee·*da* chance
oración ⓕ o·ra·*syon* prayer
orden ⓜ *or*·den order (placement)
orden ⓕ *or*·den order (command)
ordenar or·de·*nar* order (give command)
oreja ⓕ o·*re*·kha ear
orgasmo ⓜ or·*gas*·mo orgasm
original o·ree·khee·*nal* original
orilla ⓕ **del mar** o·*ree*·ya del mar seaside
oro ⓜ *o*·ro gold
orquesta ⓕ or·*kes*·ta orchestra
orquídea ⓕ or·*kee*·de·a orchid
oscuro/a ⓜ/ⓕ os·*koo*·ro/a dark
otoño ⓜ o·*to*·nyo autumn
otra vez o·tra ves again
otro/a ⓜ/ⓕ *o*·tro/a other
oxígeno ⓜ ok·*see*·khe·no oxygen

P

padre ⓜ *pa*·dre father
padres ⓜ pl *pa*·dres parents
pagar pa·*gar* pay
página ⓕ *pa*·khee·na page
pago ⓜ *pa*·go payment
país ⓜ pa·ees country (nation)
pájaro ⓜ *pa*·kha·ro bird
pala ⓕ *pa*·la spade
palabra ⓕ pa·*la*·bra word
palacio ⓜ pa·*la*·syo palace
palillo ⓜ pa·*lee*·yo toothpick
paloma ⓕ pa·*lo*·ma dove
palm ⓜ palm palm pilot
palma ⓕ **de coco** *pal*·ma de *ko*·ko coconut palm
panadería ⓕ pa·na·de·*ree*·a bakery
pañal ⓜ pa·*nyal* diaper • nappy
panorámico/a ⓜ/ⓕ pa·no·*ra*·mee·ko/a panoramic
pantalla ⓕ pan·*ta*·ya screen
pantalones ⓜ pl pan·ta·*lo*·nes pants • trousers
— cortos *kor*·tos shorts
pantera ⓕ pan·*te*·ra panther
pañuelo ⓜ pa·*nywe*·lo handkerchief
— de papel de pa·*pel* tissue
papá ⓜ pa·*pa* dad
papagayo ⓜ pa·pa·*ga*·yo macaw
papel ⓜ pa·*pel* paper
— higiénico ee·*khye*·nee·ko toilet paper
papeles ⓜ pl **del auto** pa·*pe*·les del *ow*·to car owner's title
paquete ⓜ pa·*ke*·te package • packet • parcel
para siempre *pa*·ra *syem*·pre forever

parabrisas ⓜ pa·ra·*bree*·sas windscreen
parada ⓕ pa·*ra*·da stop
— de autobús de ow·to·*boos* bus stop (city)
— de ómnibus de *om*·nee·boos bus stop (intercity)
— de subteráneo de soob·te·*ra*·ne·o metro stop
— de taxis de *tak*·sees taxi stand
paraguas ⓜ pa·*ra*·gwas umbrella
para *pa*·ra for
parar pa·*rar* stop
pared ⓕ pa·*re* wall (inside)
pareja ⓕ pa·*re*·kha pair (couple) • partner
parlamento ⓜ par·la·*men*·to parliament
parque ⓜ *par*·ke park
— nacional na·syo·*nal* national park
parte ⓕ *par*·te part
partida ⓕ **de nacimiento** par·*tee*·da de na·see·*myen*·to birth certificate
partido ⓜ par·*tee*·do match (sport) • party (politics)
partir par·*teer* leave
pasado ⓜ pa·*sa*·do past
— mañana ma·*nya*·na day after tomorrow
pasado/a ⓜ/ⓕ pa·*sa*·do/a off (spoiled)
pasajero/a ⓜ/ⓕ pa·sa·*khe*·ro/a passenger
pasaporte ⓜ pa·sa·*por*·te passport
pase ⓜ *pa*·se pass (permit)
paseo ⓜ pa·*se*·o ride • street
pasillo ⓜ pa·*see*·yo aisle (plane, train)
paso ⓜ *pa*·so pass (mountain) • step
pasta dentífrica *pas*·ta den·*tee*·free·ka toothpaste
pastelería ⓕ pas·te·le·*ree*·a cake shop
pastillas ⓕ pl pas·*tee*·yas pills
— antipalúdicas an·tee·pa·*loo*·dee·kas antimalarial tablets
— de menta de *men*·ta mints
— para dormir *pa*·ra dor·*meer* sleeping pills
patrón/patrona ⓜ/ⓕ pa·*tron*/ pa·*tro*·na employer
paz ⓕ pas peace
peatón ⓜ&ⓕ pe·a·*ton* pedestrian
pecho ⓜ *pe*·cho chest
pedal ⓜ pe·*dal* pedal
pedazo ⓜ pe·*da*·so piece
pedir pe·*deer* ask (for something) • borrow
peine ⓜ *pay*·ne comb
pelea ⓕ pe·*le*·a quarrel
película ⓕ pe·*lee*·koo·la film (for camera) • movie
peligroso/a ⓜ/ⓕ pe·lee·*gro*·so/a dangerous
pelo ⓜ *pe*·lo hair
pelota ⓕ pe·*lo*·ta ball
— de golf de golf golf ball
peluquero/a ⓜ/ⓕ pe·loo·*ke*·ro/a hairdresser
pene ⓜ *pe*·ne penis
penicilina ⓕ pe·nee·see·*lee*·na penicillin
pensar pen·*sar* think
pensión ⓕ pen·*syon* boarding house
pensionado/a ⓜ/ⓕ pen·syo·*na*·do/a pensioner
pequeñito/a ⓜ/ⓕ pe·ke·*nyee*·to/a tiny
pequeño/a ⓜ/ⓕ pe·*ke*·nyo/a small
perder per·*der* lose
perdido/a ⓜ/ⓕ per·*dee*·do/a lost
perdonar per·do·*nar* forgive
perezoso/a ⓜ/ⓕ pe·re·*so*·so/a lazy
perfume ⓜ per·*foo*·me perfume
periódico ⓜ pe·*ryo*·dee·ko newspaper
periodista ⓜ&ⓕ pe·ryo·*dees*·ta journalist

P

permiso ⓜ per·*mee*·so permission • permit
— de trabajo de tra·*ba*·kho work permit
permitir per·mee·*teer* allow
pero *pe*·ro but
perro/a ⓜ/ⓕ *pe*·ro/a dog
— guía *gee*·a guide dog
persona ⓕ per·*so*·na person
pesado/a ⓜ/ⓕ pe·*sa*·do/a heavy
pesca ⓕ *pes*·ka fishing
pescadería ⓕ pes·ka·de·*ree*·a fish shop
peso ⓜ *pe*·so weight
petición ⓕ pe·tee·*syon* petition
pez ⓜ pes fish
picadura ⓕ pee·ka·*doo*·ra bite (insect)
picazón ⓜ pee·ka·*son* itch
pie ⓜ pye foot
piedra ⓕ *pye*·dra stone
piel ⓕ pyel skin
pierna ⓕ *pyer*·na leg (body)
pila ⓕ *pee*·la battery (small)
píldora ⓕ *peel*·do·ra pill • the Pill
pinchar peen·*char* puncture
pintar peen·*tar* paint
pintor(a) ⓜ/ⓕ peen·*tor*/peen·*to*·ra painter
pintura ⓕ peen·*too*·ra painting (art)
pinzas ⓕ pl *peen*·sas tweezers
piojos ⓜ pl *pyo*·khos lice
piolet ⓜ pyo·*let* ice axe
piqueta ⓕ pee·*ke*·ta pickaxe
piscina ⓕ pee·*see*·na swimming pool
piso ⓜ *pee*·so floor (storey)
pista ⓕ *pees*·ta sports track • tennis court
pizarra ⓕ **blanca** pee·*sa*·ra *blan*·ka whiteboard
plancha ⓕ *plan*·cha iron (clothes)
planeta ⓜ pla·*ne*·ta planet
planta ⓕ *plan*·ta plant
plástico ⓜ *plas*·tee·ko plastic
plata ⓕ *pla*·ta silver
plataforma ⓕ pla·ta·*for*·ma platform
plato ⓜ *pla*·to plate
playa ⓕ *pla*·ya beach
plaza ⓕ *pla*·sa square
— de toros de *to*·ros bullring
pobre *po*·bre poor
pobreza ⓕ po·*bre*·sa poverty
pocos/as ⓜ/ⓕ pl *po*·kos/as few
poder ⓜ po·*der* power
poder po·*der* can (be able)
poesía ⓕ po·e·*see*·a poetry
polen ⓜ *po*·len pollen
policía ⓕ po·lee·*see*·a police
política ⓕ po·*lee*·tee·ka policy • politics
político/a ⓜ/ⓕ po·*lee*·tee·ko/a politician
póliza ⓕ *po*·lee·sa policy (insurance)
poner po·*ner* put
popular po·poo·*lar* popular
por por for
por (dia) por *(dee*·a) per (day)
por ciento por *syen*·to percent
por qué por ke why
por vía aérea por *vee*·a a·e·re·a by airmail
por vía terrestre por *vee*·a te·*res*·tre surface mail
porque *por*·ke because
posible po·*see*·ble possible
potable po·*ta*·ble drinkable
potro ⓜ *po*·tro pony
pozo ⓜ *po*·so well (water)
precio ⓜ *pre*·syo price
— de entrada de en·*tra*·da admission price
— del cubierto del koo·*byer*·to cover charge (restaurant)
preferir pre·fe·*reer* prefer
pregunta ⓕ pre·*goon*·ta question
preguntar pre·goon·*tar* ask (a question)
preocupado/a ⓜ/ⓕ pre·o·koo·*pa*·do/a worried
preocuparse por pre·o·koo·*par*·se por care (about something)

preparar pre·pa·*rar* prepare
presentación ⓕ pre·sen·ta·*syon* presentation
presidente/a ⓜ/ⓕ pre·see·*den*·te/a president
presión ⓕ pre·*syon* pressure
— arterial ar·te·*ryal* blood pressure
presupuesto ⓜ pre·soo·*pwes*·to budget
prevenir pre·ve·*neer* prevent
primavera ⓕ pree·ma·*ve*·ra spring (season)
primer ministro/a ⓜ/ⓕ pree·*mer* mee·*nees*·tro/a prime minister
primera clase ⓕ pree·*me*·ra *kla*·se first class
primero/a ⓜ/ⓕ pree·*me*·ro/a first
primo/a ⓜ/ⓕ *pree*·mo/a cousin
principal preen·see·*pal* main
prisionero/a ⓜ/ⓕ pree·syo·*ne*·ro/a prisoner
privado/a ⓜ/ⓕ pree·*va*·do/a private
probar pro·*bar* try (attempt)
producir pro·doo·*seer* produce
productos ⓜ pl **congelados** pro·*dook*·tos kon·khe·*la*·dos frozen foods
profesor(a) pro·fe·*sor*/pro·fe·*so*·ra lecturer • teacher
profundo/a ⓜ/ⓕ pro·*foon*·do/a deep • profound
programa ⓜ pro·*gra*·ma programme
prolongación ⓕ pro·lon·ga·*syon* extension (visa)
promesa ⓕ pro·*me*·sa promise
prometida ⓕ pro·me·*tee*·da fiancee
prometido ⓜ pro·me·*tee*·do fiance
pronto *pron*·to soon
propietaria ⓕ pro·pye·*ta*·rya landlady
propietario ⓜ pro·pye·*ta*·ryo landlord
propina ⓕ pro·*pee*·na tip (gratuity)
proteger pro·te·*kher* protect
propuesta ⓕ pro·*pwes*·ta proposal
protegido/a ⓜ/ⓕ pro·te·*khee*·do/a protected
protesta ⓕ pro·*tes*·ta protest
protestar pro·tes·*tar* protest
provisiones ⓕ pl pro·vee·*syo*·nes provisions
proximo/a ⓜ/ⓕ *prok*·see·mo/a next
proyector ⓜ pro·yek·*tor* projector
prueba ⓕ *prwe*·ba test
— del embarazo del em·ba·*ra*·so pregnancy test kit
pruebas ⓕ pl **nucleares** *prwe*·bas noo·kle·*a*·res nuclear testing
pueblo ⓜ *pwe*·blo village
puente ⓜ *pwen*·te bridge
puerta ⓕ *pwer*·ta door
puerto ⓜ *pwer*·to harbour • port
puesta ⓕ **del sol** *pwes*·ta del sol sunset
pulga ⓕ *pool*·ga flea
pulmones ⓜ pl pool·*mo*·nes lungs
puntero ⓜ **láser** poon·*te*·ro *la*·ser laser pointer
punto ⓜ *poon*·to dot • full stop • point
puro/a ⓜ/ⓕ *poo*·ro/a pure

Q

que ke what
quedar ke·*dar* stay (remain)
quedarse ke·*dar*·se stay (remain)
quejarse ke·*khar*·se complain
quemadura ⓕ ke·ma·*doo*·ra burn
— de sol de sol sunburn
quemar ke·*mar* burn
querer ke·*rer* love • want
quien kyen who
quincena ⓕ keen·*se*·na fortnight
quiosco ⓜ kee·*os*·ko newsagency
quiste ⓜ **ovárico** *kees*·te o·*va*·ree·ko ovarian cyst
quizás kee·*sas* maybe

R

R

rabo ⓜ *ra*·bo tail
radiador ⓜ ra·dya·*dor* radiator
rana ⓕ *ra*·na frog
rápido/a ⓜ/ⓕ *ra*·pee·do/a fast
raqueta ⓕ ra·*ke*·ta racquet
raro/a ⓜ/ⓕ *ra*·ro/a rare
rata ⓕ *ra*·ta rat
ratón ⓜ ra·*ton* mouse
ratonero ⓜ ra·to·*ne*·ro buzzard
razón ⓕ ra·*son* reason
realista re·a·*lees*·ta realistic
recibir re·see·*beer* receive
recibo ⓜ re·*see*·bo receipt
reciclable re·see·*kla*·ble recyclable
reciclar re·see·*klar* recycle
recientemente re·syen·te·*men*·te recently
recogida ⓕ **de equipajes** re·ko·*khee*·da de e·kee·*pa*·khes baggage claim
recolección ⓕ **de fruta** re·ko·lek·*syon* de *froo*·ta fruit picking
recomendar re·ko·men·*dar* recommend
reconocer re·ko·no·*ser* acknowledge • recognise
recorrido ⓜ **guiado** re·ko·*ree*·do gee·*a*·do guided tour
recto/a ⓜ/ⓕ *rek*·to/a straight
recuerdo ⓜ re·*kwer*·do souvenir
recuerdos ⓜ pl re·*kwer*·dos memories
red ⓕ re net
redondo/a ⓜ/ⓕ re·*don*·do/a round
reembolso ⓜ re·em·*bol*·so refund
referencias ⓕ pl re·fe·*ren*·syas references (work)
refrigeradora ⓕ re·free·khe·ra·*do*·ra refrigerator
refugiado/a ⓜ/ⓕ re·foo·*khya*·do/a refugee
regalo ⓜ re·*ga*·lo gift
— de bodas de *bo*·das wedding present
régimen ⓜ *re*·khee·men diet
registrar re·khees·*trar* check-in (hotel)
reglas ⓕ pl *re*·glas rules
reina ⓕ *ray*·na queen
reírse re·*eer*·se laugh
relación ⓕ re·la·*syon* relationship
relajarse re·la·*khar*·se relax
religión ⓕ re·lee·*khyon* religion
religioso/a ⓜ/ⓕ re·lee·*khyo*·so/a religious
reliquia ⓕ re·*lee*·kya relic
reloj ⓜ re·*lokh* clock
— de pulsera de pool·*se*·ra watch
remo ⓜ *re*·mo rowing
remoto/a ⓜ/ⓕ re·*mo*·to/a remote
reparar re·pa·*rar* repair
reproductor ⓜ **de mp3** re·pro·dook·*tor* de *e*·me pe tres mp3 player
república ⓕ re·*poo*·blee·ka republic
reserva ⓕ re·*ser*·va reservation
reservar re·ser·*var* book (reserve)
residencia ⓕ **de estudiantes** re·see·*den*·sya de es·too·*dyan*·tes college
residuos ⓜ pl **tóxicos** re·*see*·dwos *tok*·see·kos toxic waste
respirar res·pee·*rar* breathe
respuesta ⓕ res·*pwes*·ta answer
restaurante ⓜ res·tow·*ran*·te restaurant
revisar re·vee·*sar* check
revisor(a) ⓜ/ⓕ re·vee·*sor*/ re·vee·*so*·ra ticket collector
revista ⓕ re·*vees*·ta magazine
rey ⓜ ray king
rezar re·*sar* worship (pray)
rico/a ⓜ/ⓕ *ree*·ko/a rich
riesgo ⓜ *ryes*·go risk
río ⓜ *ree*·o river
ritmo ⓜ *reet*·mo rhythm
robar ro·*bar* rob
roca ⓕ *ro*·ka rock (stone)
rodilla ⓕ ro·*dee*·ya knee
rojo/a ⓜ/ⓕ *ro*·kho/a red

romántico/a ⓜ/ⓕ ro·*man*·tee·ko/a romantic
romper rom·*per* break
ropa ⓕ *ro*·pa clothing
— de cama de *ka*·ma bedding
— interior een·te·*ryor* underwear
rosa *ro*·sa pink
roto/a ⓜ/ⓕ *ro*·to/a broken
rueda ⓕ *rwe*·da wheel
ruidoso/a ⓜ/ⓕ rwee·*do*·so/a loud
ruinas ⓕ pl *rwee*·nas ruins
ruta ⓕ *roo*·ta route

S

sábana ⓕ *sa*·ba·na sheet (bed)
saber sa·*ber* know (how to)
sabroso/a ⓜ/ⓕ sa·*bro*·so/a tasty
sacacorchos ⓜ sa·ka·*kor*·chos corkscrew
sacerdote ⓜ sa·ser·*do*·te priest
saco ⓜ *sa*·ko coat
— de dormir de dor·*meer* sleeping bag
sala ⓕ *sa*·la room
— de espera de es·*pe*·ra waiting room
— de tránsito de *tran*·see·to transit lounge
salario ⓜ sa·*la*·ryo salary
saldo ⓜ *sal*·do balance (account)
salida ⓕ sa·*lee*·da departure • exit
salir sa·*leer* go out (exit)
salir con sa·*leer* kon date (a person)
salir de sa·*leer* de depart
salón ⓜ **de belleza** sa·*lon* de be·*ye*·sa beauty salon
saltar sal·*tar* jump
salud ⓕ sa·*loo* health
salvaeslips ⓜ pl *sal*·va·e·sleeps panty liners
sandalias ⓕ pl san·*da*·lyas sandals
sangre ⓕ *san*·gre blood
santo/a ⓜ/ⓕ *san*·to/a saint
sarampión ⓜ sa·ram·*pyon* measles
sartén ⓕ sar·*ten* frying pan
sastre ⓜ *sas*·tre tailor
secar se·*kar* dry
seco/a ⓜ/ⓕ *se*·ko/a dry
secretario/a ⓜ/ⓕ se·kre·*ta*·ryo/a secretary
seda ⓕ *se*·da silk
seguir se·*geer* follow
segundo ⓜ se·*goon*·do second (time)
segundo/a ⓜ/ⓕ se·*goon*·do/a second (place)
seguro ⓜ se·*goo*·ro insurance
seguro/a ⓜ/ⓕ se·*goo*·ro/a safe
sello ⓜ *se*·yo stamp
semáforos ⓜ pl se·*ma*·fo·ros traffic lights
semana ⓕ se·*ma*·na week
sembrar sem·*brar* plant
semidirecto/a se·mee·dee·*rek*·to/a nondirect
señal ⓕ se·*nyal* sign
sencillo/a ⓜ/ⓕ sen·*see*·yo/a simple
sendero ⓜ sen·*de*·ro path
senos ⓜ pl *se*·nos breasts
sensibilidad ⓕ sen·see·bee·lee·*da* film speed • sensitivity
sensual sen·*swal* sensual
sentarse sen·*tar*·se sit
sentimientos ⓜ pl sen·tee·*myen*·tos feelings
sentir sen·*teer* feel
separado/a ⓜ/ⓕ se·pa·*ra*·do/a separate
separar se·pa·*rar* separate
ser ser be
serie ⓕ *se*·rye series
serio/a ⓜ/ⓕ *se*·ryo/a serious
seropositivo/a ⓜ/ⓕ se·ro·po·see·*tee*·vo/a HIV positive
serpiente ⓕ ser·*pyen*·te snake
servicio ⓜ ser·*vee*·syo service • service charge
— militar mee·lee·*tar* military service
— telefónico automático te·le·*fo*·nee·ko ow·to·*ma*·tee·ko direct-dial

servilleta ⓕ ser·vee·*ye*·ta napkin
sexismo ⓜ sek·*sees*·mo sexism
sexo ⓜ *sek*·so sex
— **seguro** se·*goo*·ro safe sex
si see if
sí see yes
SIDA ⓜ *see*·da AIDS
siempre *syem*·pre always
silla ⓕ *see*·ya chair
— **de ruedas** de *rwe*·das wheelchair
sillín ⓜ see·*yeen* saddle
sillita ⓕ see·*yee*·ta child seat
similar see·mee·*lar* similar
simpático/a ⓜ/ⓕ seem·*pa*·tee·ko/a nice (person)
sin seen without
— **plomo** *plo*·mo unleaded
— **techo** *te*·cho homeless
sinagoga ⓕ see·na·*go*·ga synagogue
sintético/a ⓜ/ⓕ seen·*te*·tee·ko/a synthetic
sobre ⓜ *so*·bre envelope
sobre *so*·bre about • over (above)
sobredosis ⓕ so·bre·*do*·sees overdose
socialista ⓜ&ⓕ so·sya·*lees*·ta socialist
sol ⓜ sol sun
soldado ⓜ sol·*da*·do soldier
soleado/a ⓜ/ⓕ so·le·*a*·do/a sunny
sólo *so*·lo only
solo/a ⓜ/ⓕ *so*·lo/a alone
soltero/a ⓜ/ⓕ sol·*te*·ro/a single (unmarried)
sombra ⓕ *som*·bra shade • shadow
sombrero ⓜ som·*bre*·ro hat
soñar so·*nyar* dream
sondeos ⓜ pl son·*de*·os polls
sonreír son·re·*eer* smile
sordo/a ⓜ/ⓕ *sor*·do/a deaf
soroche ⓜ so·*ro*·che altitude sickness
sorpresa ⓕ sor·*pre*·sa surprise
su soo her • his • their
sostén ⓜ sos·*ten* bra
subir soo·*beer* climb
submarinismo ⓜ soob·ma·ree·*nees*·mo diving
subsidio ⓜ **de desempleo** soob·*see*·dyo de des·em·*ple*·o dole
subteráneo ⓜ soob·te·*ra*·ne·o metro • subway
subtítulos ⓜ pl soob·*tee*·too·los subtitles
sucio/a ⓜ/ⓕ *soo*·syo/a dirty
Sudamérica ⓕ sood·a·*me*·ree·ka South America
sudamericano/a ⓜ/ⓕ sood·a·me·ree·*ka*·no/a South American
sudar soo·*dar* perspire
suegra ⓕ *swe*·gra mother-in-law
suegro ⓜ *swe*·gro father-in-law
sueldo ⓜ *swel*·do wage
suelo ⓜ *swe*·lo floor (ground)
suerte ⓕ *swer*·te luck
suéter ⓜ *swe*·ter jumper • sweater
suficiente soo·fee·*syen*·te enough
supermercado ⓜ soo·per·mer·*ka*·do supermarket
superstición ⓕ soo·per·stee·*syon* superstition
sur ⓜ soor south
surf ⓜ soorf surfing
— **sobre la nieve** *so*·bre la *nye*·ve snowboarding

T

tabaco ⓜ ta·*ba*·ko tobacco
tabla ⓕ **de surf** *ta*·bla de soorf surfboard
tacaño/a ⓜ/ⓕ ta·*ka*·nyo/a stingy
tajo ⓜ *ta*·kho chopping board
talco ⓜ *tal*·ko baby powder
talla ⓕ *ta*·ya size (clothes)
taller ⓜ ta·*yer* garage (car repair) • workshop
tamaño ta·*ma*·nyo size (general)
también tam·*byen* also
tampoco tam·*po*·ko neither
tampones ⓜ pl tam·*po*·nes tampons

tapón ⓜ ta·*pon* plug (bath)
tapones ⓜ pl **para los oídos** ta·*po*·nes *pa*·ra los o·*ee*·dos earplugs
taquilla ⓕ ta·*kee*·ya ticket office (cinema, theatre)
tarde *tar*·de late
tarjeta ⓕ tar·*khe*·ta card
— de crédito de *kre*·dee·to credit card
— de embarque de em·*bar*·ke boarding pass
— de teléfono de te·*le*·fo·no phone card
— SIM seem SIM card
tarta ⓕ **nupcial** *tar*·ta noop·*syal* wedding cake
tasa ⓕ **del aeropuerto** *ta*·sa del a·e·ro·*pwer*·to airport tax
taza ⓕ *ta*·sa cup
teatro ⓜ te·*a*·tro theatre
— de la ópera de la *o*·pe·ra opera house
techo ⓜ *te*·cho roof
teclado ⓜ te·*kla*·do keyboard
tela ⓕ *te*·la fabric
tele ⓕ *te*·le TV
teleférico ⓜ te·le·*fe*·ree·ko cable car
teléfono ⓜ te·*le*·fo·no telephone
— móbil *mo*·bil mobile phone
— celular se·loo·*lar* cell phone
— público *poo*·blee·ko public telephone
telegrama ⓜ te·le·*gra*·ma telegram
telenovela ⓕ te·le·no·*ve*·la soap opera
teleobjetivo ⓜ te·le·ob·khe·*tee*·vo telephoto lens
telesquí ⓜ te·le·*skee* ski lift
televisión ⓕ te·le·vee·*syon* television
temperatura ⓕ tem·pe·ra·*too*·ra temperature
templado/a ⓜ/ⓕ tem·*pla*·do/a warm
templo ⓜ *tem*·plo temple
temprano tem·*pra*·no early
tenedor ⓜ te·ne·*dor* fork
tener te·*ner* have
— hambre *am*·bre be hungry
— prisa *pree*·sa be in a hurry
— resfriado res·*frya*·do have a cold
— sed se be thirsty
— sueño *swe*·nyo be sleepy
tensión ⓕ **premenstrual** ten·*syon* pre·mens·*trwal* premenstrual tension
tentempié ⓜ ten·tem·*pye* snack
tercio ⓜ *ter*·syo third
terible te·*ree*·ble terrible
terminar ter·mee·*nar* finish
terremoto ⓜ te·re·*mo*·to earthquake
testarudo/a ⓜ/ⓕ tes·ta·*roo*·do/a stubborn
tía ⓕ *tee*·a aunt
tiempo ⓜ *tyem*·po time • weather
tienda ⓕ *tyen*·da shop
— de fotografía de fo·to·gra·*fee*·a camera shop
— de provisiones de cámping de pro·vee·*syo*·nes de *kam*·peen camping store
— de recuerdos de re·*kwer*·dos souvenir shop
— de ropa de *ro*·pa clothing store
— deportiva de·por·*tee*·va sports store
Tierra ⓕ *tye*·ra Earth
tierra ⓕ *tye*·ra land
tijeras ⓕ pl tee·*khe*·ras scissors
tímido/a ⓜ/ⓕ *tee*·mee·do/a shy
tío ⓜ *tee*·o uncle
típico/a ⓜ/ⓕ *tee*·pee·ko/a typical
tipo ⓜ *tee*·po type
— de cambio de *kam*·byo exchange rate
toalla ⓕ to·*a*·ya towel
toallita ⓕ to·a·*yee*·ta flannel • wash cloth
tobillo ⓜ to·*bee*·yo ankle
tocar to·*kar* play (an instrument) • touch
— la guitarra la gee·*ta*·ra play the guitar

todavía (no) *to·da·vee·a (no)* (not) yet
todo *to·do* everything
todo/a ⓜ/ⓕ sg *to·do/a* all
todos/as ⓜ/ⓕ pl *to·dos/as* all
tomar *to·mar* drink • take
tono ⓜ *to·no* dial tone
torcedura ⓕ *tor·se·doo·ra* sprain
tormenta ⓕ *tor·men·ta* storm
toro ⓜ *to·ro* bull
torre ⓕ *to·re* tower
torta ⓕ *tor·ta* cake
tos ⓕ *tos* cough
tostadora ⓕ *tos·ta·do·ra* toaster
trabajar *tra·ba·khar* work
trabajo ⓜ *tra·ba·kho* work (occupation)
— a tiempo parcial *a tyem·po par·syal* part-time work
— a tiempo completo *a tyem·po kom·ple·to* full-time work
— administrativo *ad·mee·nees·tra·tee·vo* paperwork
— de limpieza *de leem·pye·sa* cleaning
— eventual *e·ven·twal* casual work
traducir *tra·doo·seer* translate
traer *tra·er* bring
traficante ⓜ **de drogas** *tra·fee·kan·te de dro·gas* drug dealer
tráfico ⓜ *tra·fee·ko* traffic
traje ⓜ *tra·khe* suit
— de baño *de ba·nyo* swimsuit
tramposo/a ⓜ/ⓕ *tram·po·so/a* cheat
tranquilo/a ⓜ/ⓕ *tran·kee·lo/a* quiet
tranvía ⓜ *tran·vee·a* tram
tratar de ligar *tra·tar de lee·gar* chat up
tren ⓜ *tren* train
trepar *tre·par* climb • scale
tribunal ⓜ *tree·boo·nal* court (legal)
triste *trees·te* sad
tú *too* you sg inf
tumba ⓕ *toom·ba* grave • tomb
tumbarse *toom·bar·se* lie (not stand)
turista ⓜ&ⓕ *too·rees·ta* tourist

U

uniforme ⓜ *oo·nee·for·me* uniform
universidad ⓕ *oo·nee·ver·see·da* university
universo ⓜ *oo·nee·ver·so* universe
urgente *oor·khen·te* urgent
Usted *oos·te* you sg pol
Ustedes *oo·ste·des* you pl
útil *oo·teel* useful

V

vaca ⓕ *va·ka* cow
vacaciones ⓕ pl *va·ka·syo·nes* holidays • vacation
vacante *va·kan·te* vacant
vacío/a ⓜ/ⓕ *va·see·o/a* empty
vacuna ⓕ *va·koo·na* vaccination
vagina ⓕ *va·khee·na* vagina
vagón ⓜ *va·gon* train carriage
— restaurante *res·tow·ran·te* dining car
validar *va·lee·dar* validate
valiente *va·lyen·te* brave
valioso/a ⓜ/ⓕ *va·lyo·so/a* valuable
valle ⓜ *va·ye* valley
valor ⓜ *va·lor* value
varios/as ⓜ/ⓕ pl *va·ryos/as* several
vaso ⓜ *va·so* glass (drinking)
vegetariano/a ⓜ/ⓕ *ve·khe·ta·rya·no/a* vegetarian
— estricto/a ⓜ/ⓕ *vs·treek·to/a* vegan
vela ⓕ *ve·la* candle • sail
velocidad ⓕ *ve·lo·see·da* speed
velocímetro ⓜ *ve·lo·see·me·tro* speedometer
vena ⓕ *ve·na* vein
vendaje ⓜ *ven·da·khe* bandage
vender *ven·der* sell
venenoso/a ⓜ/ⓕ *ve·ne·no·so/a* poisonous
venir *ve·neer* come
ventana ⓕ *ven·ta·na* window

ventilador ⓜ ven·tee·la·*dor* fan (machine)
ver ver see
verano ⓜ ve·*ra*·no summer
verde *ver*·de green
verdulero/a ⓜ/ⓕ ver·doo·*le*·ro/a greengrocer
verja ⓕ *ver*·kha gate
vestíbulo ⓜ ves·*tee*·boo·lo foyer
vestido ⓜ ves·*tee*·do dress
vestuario ⓜ ves·*twa*·ryo changing room • wardrobe
vez ⓕ ves time (occasion)
viajar vya·*khar* travel
viaje ⓜ *vya*·khe trip
vida ⓕ *vee*·da life
— nocturna nok·*toor*·na night life
vidrio ⓜ *vee*·dryo glass (material)
viejo/a ⓜ/ⓕ *vye*·kho/a old
viento ⓜ *vyen*·to wind
viñedo ⓜ vee·*nye*·do vineyard
violar vyo·*lar* rape
visado ⓜ *vee*·sa·do visa
visitar vee·see·*tar* visit
vista ⓕ *vees*·ta view
vitaminas ⓕ pl vee·ta·*mee*·nas vitamins
viuda ⓕ *vyoo*·da widow
viudo ⓜ *vyoo*·do widower
víveres ⓜ pl *vee*·ve·res food supplies
vivir vee·*veer* live
volado/a ⓜ/ⓕ vo·*la*·do/a stoned (drugged)
volar vo·*lar* fly
volver vol·*ver* return
votar vo·*tar* vote
voz ⓕ vos voice
vuelo ⓜ *vwe*·lo flight
— doméstico do·*mes*·tee·ko domestic flight

Y

y ee and
ya ya already
yip ⓜ yeep jeep
yo yo I

Z

zapatería ⓕ sa·pa·te·*ree*·a shoe shop
zapatos ⓜ pl sa·*pa*·tos shoes
zodíaco ⓜ so·*dee*·a·ko zodiac
zoológico ⓜ so·o·*lo*·khee·ko zoo

Index

For topics that are covered in several sections of this book, we've indicated the most relevant page number in bold.

D

E

F

G

H

10 Ways to Start a Sentence

When's (the next flight)?	¿Cuándo sale (el próximo vuelo)?	*kwan*·do *sa*·le (el *prok*·see·mo *vwe*·lo)
Where's the (station)?	¿Dónde está (la estación)?	*don*·de es·*ta* (la es·ta·*syon*)
How much is (a room)?	¿Cuánto cuesta (una habitación)?	*kwan*·to *kwes*·ta (*oo*·na a·bee·ta·*syon*)
I'm looking for (a hotel).	Estoy buscando (un hotel).	es·*toy* boos·*kan*·do (oon o·*tel*)
Do you have (a map)?	¿Tiene (un mapa)?	*tye*·ne (oon *ma*·pa)
Is there (a toilet)?	¿Hay (un baño)?	ai (oon *ba*·nyo)
I'd like (a coffee).	Quisiera (un café).	kee·*sye*·ra (oon ka·*fe*)
Can I (enter)?	¿Se puede (entrar)?	se *pwe*·de (en·*trar*)
Could you please (help me)?	¿Puede (ayudarme), por favor?	*pwe*·de (a·yoo·*dar*·me) por fa·*vor*
Do I have to (get a visa)?	¿Necesito (obtener un visado)?	ne·se·*see*·to (ob·te·*ner* oon vee·*sa*·do)